ENCYCLOPEDIA OF

ESTATE PLANNING

ROBERT S. HOLZMAN
JOHN J. TUOZZOLO

Bottom Line
Books

www.BottomLineSecrets.com

Bottom Line® Books publishes the advice of expert authorities in many fields. The use of a book is no substitute for legal, accounting, or other professional services. Consult competent professionals for answers to your specific questions.

Completely Revised Edition
10 9 8 7 6 5 4 3 2

Library of Congress Cataloging in Publication Data

Holzman, Robert S. & Tuozzolo, John J.
    Encyclopedia of Estate Planning

    Includes index.
    1. Estate planning—United States.
I. Title.
KF750.Z9H65 1985B   346.7305'2   86-31031
ISBN 0-88723-264-7   347.30652

Bottom Line® Books is a registered trademark of Boardroom® Inc.
281 Tresser Blvd., Stamford, CT 06901

Printed in the United States of America

About the Authors

Robert S. Holzman, BA, AM, PhD, spent his lifetime teaching and educating the American taxpayer and tax professionals. He is the author of no fewer than 20 scholarly works, most of which deal with the tax and accounting disciplines, although he also authored works on fire fighting, baseball and the Civil War. During his teaching career, he was often referred to as "the experts' expert" due not only to his publications but also to those professionals who were his students. Dr. Holzman received his BA from the University of Pennsylvania and both his Masters and PhD from New York University, where he became NYU's budget director and a professor of tax law at NYU's Graduate School of Business. He held a similar teaching post at the University of Connecticut. During his long and distinguished career, Dr. Holzman served as editor of the 15-volume *Tax Practitioners' Library* and several other publications. He also authored texts on estate planning, federal income taxation, tax-free reorganizations, *Dun and Bradstreet's Handbook of Executive Tax Management*, the *Accumulated Earnings Tax*, *Landmark Tax Cases* and *The Complete Book of Tax Deductions*. Dr. Holzman's breadth of knowledge in the tax arena provided the foundation upon which the *Encyclopedia of Estate Planning* rests. Combining a thorough understanding of the topic with understandable prose has made this text a "must have" research tool for all students who wish to be better prepared for the challenges of this field.

John J. Tuozzolo, BA, JD, MBA, MS Taxation, has spent over a quarter of a century assisting clients with their income, estate and business tax planning needs. He holds a BA from the University of Dayton, and a JD from the Marshall-Wythe School of Law of the College of William and Mary. He also earned a Masters of Business Administration from the University of Connecticut, where he studied under Dr. Holzman, and then earned a Masters of Science in taxation from the University of Hartford. He is a member of the Connecticut Bar Association and has served on its elite executive committees on taxation, as well as on its estates and probate executive committee. He has been the chair of the public education subcommittee of the estates and probate executive committee and helped produce not only educational brochures for the general public's use but also videotapes of general estate planning interest. Mr. Tuozzolo is also a long-time member of the National Academy of Elder Law Attorneys. In addition, Attorney Tuozzolo was an adjunct professor for many years in the accounting department at Western Connecticut State University. There he instructed courses for its Masters program in the areas of estate planning, corporate and shareholders tax, partnership and Sub-Chapter S taxation, as well as executive compensation. During his years as a principal in the Danbury, Connecticut, law firm of Collins, Hannafin, Garamella, Jaber & Tuozzolo, PC, he specialized in a variety of estate and business planning areas as well as the emerging area of elder law. The content of this *Encyclopedia of Estate Planning* is very much a history of Attorney Tuozzolo's practice and experience, as well as a documentation of Dr. Holzman's extensive knowledge and expertise.

Dedication

Our heartfelt words of appreciation:

To our readers, because you deserve to know what these pages offer. We hope that they help you and your family for years to come.

To the staff at Boardroom and Bottom Line Books, you always give of yourselves so willingly. What more could we ask?

To our colleagues and John's law partners, you have taught us more than just what is written in the law. We are eternally grateful.

To Dr. Jordon R. Dann and Judith Dann, RN, because you gave so much of yourselves so willingly without asking for anything in return.

To Mary Obre, probate paralegal extraordinaire, for your undying support in more ways than you'll ever know.

To our families and in particular our wives, for your encouragement, support, patience and good humor. They are our true partners in this endeavor and life.

To our Creator, we thank you for your blessings to allow us to produce this work and for the opportunity to help others.

The Authors

Table of Contents

INTRODUCTION

On June 7, 2001, President George W. Bush signed the Economic Growth and Tax Relief Reconciliation Act of 2001, H.R. 1836, which is widely regarded as one of the most sweeping pieces of tax legislation in 20 years. It contains more than 85 major provisions, 441 Internal Revenue Code changes and cuts $1.35 trillion in taxes over its implementation period.

Unfortunately, as far as estate and gift taxes are concerned, the rush to passage created many confusing areas. It has returned the much-maligned "carryover basis" rule that was once drummed out of the Tax Code by an unprecedented coalition of nonpartisan private sector tax professionals. The most disturbing aspect of the new tax law is the uncertainty inherent in its provision: In 2011, the estate tax will revert to its former provisions of 2001, unless Congress acts prior to 2011. This aspect of the new tax law is called a "sunset" provision because it terminates itself and reinstates the 2001 tax rate structure with all its problems and complexities.

One respected tax publication suggested that estate planning is therefore now more important than ever, due to the complexity of the new law and its uncertainty. Instead of outright repeal of the estate tax, the law phases it out between 2001 and 2010. However, it is only repealed for the 2010 tax year and many believe it will return. Sadly, the massive governmental expenditures occasioned by the tragic events of September 11, 2001, may force Congress to seek revenue sources from traditional places such as the estate tax.

This estate planning uncertainty coincides with the predicted historic wealth transfer from one generation to the next in the ensuing 15 years. Given this likelihood, it is essential that we learn to master the tools of effectively

1

transferring assets. The goal is very simple. Pass on as much as possible to those we wish to benefit, in the manner we wish for them to receive it, while maintaining as much use and control as allowed, without giving up excessive amounts to the government or to medical or long-term-care needs.

Since its first printing, the primary purpose of the *Encyclopedia of Estate Planning* has been to help the reader master the tools of effective estate planning. There have been many editions and revisions of this text. However, as the playing field and the rules of the game have dramatically changed, this edition brings with it major changes, including a summary of new tax laws. Yet the goal has and will remain constant. Master the tools and techniques outlined in this book and follow our suggestions and warnings, and you and your loved ones will reap the significant benefits of an effective estate plan.

The road ahead: A plan for the future

Experts claim that we do not plan to fail; rather, we fail to plan. If this is true, we must ask who should follow the path of planning for the future, as well as how and when? To answer this question, one key concept must be understood. Estate planning is not just for the wealthy or those over a given age or approaching retirement. It is for just about everyone. Somewhat elusively, as your life changes, so does your path, and your goals for a proper estate change as well. Therefore, the overwhelming majority of people should plan now, even though the future may call for readjustments. The "how" will be answered by our text.

Whether you are a young executive, a parent or near retirement, this text will help you determine your path. Whether you or your parents are in need of assistance or you wish to protect the family business, this text will assist you. Or, if you wish to protect your spouse or children from their own excesses, help is found in these pages.

Some ground rules

The goal of the *Encyclopedia of Estate Planning* is to explain, in plain language, the difficult concepts involved in forging an effective estate plan.

This revised text continues that effort and introduces important legal and societal changes into the discussion and into your planning process. One example is elder law. The advances of modern medicine have brought an increase in one's life expectancy. As a result of these advances, we are now concerned with the need for long-term care which can cost staggering amounts—up to $9,000 per month in one state alone. No estate plan can truly be considered complete without considering the possibility of long-term care.

Additionally, understand that the topic is not just for the wealthy. An abundance of information in this text will apply to most people. At different stages of life, it may be more important that you follow the techniques in some chapters than in others. We believe that there is, in fact, an estate planning life cycle. Depending on your age and family circumstances, your needs will vary, as will the need to concentrate on different areas of this text.

Regardless of what Congress does in the future to remedy the confusion associated with the new tax law, this text will have relevance for you. While many chapters are devoted to the federal estate and gift tax and an explanation of how this new law has changed the playing field of estate planning, many more are devoted to the protection and smooth transfer of one's assets, as well as the proper care of, and attention to, one's family. Too many times we have made tragic mistakes that could have been easily avoided with the proper advice. The result has often been to completely thwart the person's intent, many times to the extreme detriment of the family. Therefore, the relevancy of this text will remain regardless of the existence of the estate tax. In fact, if the tax were to remain repealed, we believe a new spirit of complacency would replace much of the urgency that currently exists in regard to proper estate planning, and people would begin to ignore basic concepts and protective measures, all to the detriment of their loved ones.

Do not be misled by those who would suggest that if you follow a few simple rules or purchase some boilerplate, one-size-fits-all document, you can master this field. This text is designed to present the areas of concern, and offer insight and suggestions to follow. But you must take the next step. You must seek professional advice to help formulate and implement your plan. Therefore, the text will highlight the key areas that you must address to better prepare you for the road ahead. It is not, however, a self-help or do-it-yourself text. It is not intended as legal advice, as there are too many state as well as federal rules that must be applied to each situation. This text presents an overview to better prepare you for your estate planning conference.

Finally, we urge you not to wait. The 2001 tax law should be impetus enough to commence your plan, yet too often tragic mistakes have occurred because individuals thought they had more time to plan or they did it themselves, without professional help. Somehow it never works out that way. If you fail to put your plan in place, you will fail those who are depending on you.

Text format

The *Encyclopedia of Estate Planning* has been designed using a building block approach following the general path many estate planning professionals follow. Generally, we find it helpful to lay the groundwork by discussing some preliminary topics so that the reader understands key terms, phrases and concepts. We do this in Chapters One through Four.

Chapters Five through Ten deal primarily with the last will and testament. For many people, and in many states, this is the single most important document involved in the transfer of assets. Chapter Eleven begins coverage of trusts, which have become an increasingly important element in estate planning. Trusts have so changed the field that this, as well as the new tax law, became the main reasons to revise this text. While the use of trusts presents many beneficial options, they are highly technical and have many varieties and uses. Chapters Eleven through Nineteen show the need to avoid "one-size-fits-all" canned documents.

Chapter Twenty begins our discussion of elder law. Today we hear statistics that as much as 40% of the population will need long-term care. Therefore, this has become an area of urgent concern. Chapters Twenty-One through Twenty-Nine deal with various facets of gifting. These topics are

4

fundamental to many of the discussions that follow throughout the text. The balance of the text deals with such topics as employment/employee benefits, family businesses, the proper use of insurance, how best to keep your executor informed, etc. All of these are used by estate planners on a regular basis. For example, we have always included the concept of writing a letter to your executor and doing a "dry run" to better prepare yourself. While we believe it is sound advice for our readers and clients, we never fully appreciated its true effect until receiving a heartwarming thank-you letter from a reader.

Appendices, general usage and key concepts

In the appendices, we have included a few forms and other helpful information. Appendix A is an Estate Planning Checklist and Questionnaire. It is a good starting point for your journey. Appendix B is a list of vital information which your executor, attorney, accountant and family will need. Appendix C is an asset and valuation sheet. As you may be the only one who knows key information about certain assets, this sheet could be most helpful to your fiduciary. Appendix D is the New Federal Estate and Gift Tax Unified Rate Schedule, along with some comparisons of changed provisions. This should give you an idea whether your estate is taxable at the federal level. We have also included, as Appendix E, the first three pages of the July 1999 federal estate tax return, Form 706. This will give you an idea of the questions asked by the IRS and whether or not your estate is taxable. If you take the time to fill it out, it may prove very enlightening.

In an effort to avoid the constant use of legal or neuter designations such as decedent, spouse, grantor, donor or donee, executor or executrix, etc., the authors have chosen to alternate the use of the designation "husband" or "wife" where appropriate and the singular male and female pronouns (he/his, she/her) instead of the neuter or legal designation. They are used interchangeably and alternately, and no negative gender connotation should be inferred. The intent is simply to make the text less cumbersome.

5

Finally, there are some basic terms and concepts which you should be familiar with before continuing with the planning process. The following is a limited glossary. The descriptions are designed to be a simple explanation of key terms.

Limited glossary

Accountant: Accountants offer a wide range of services aside from the traditional keeping of account records and preparation of tax returns, financial statements and the like. Many now offer valuable financial, income and estate planning services. As such, they can be an integral member of your estate planning team.

Administrator: A person/entity assuming the same responsibilities as an executor, but who is appointed by the court and not the decedent. They are representatives of limited authority charged to collect assets, pay debts and expenses and distribute assets to those entitled. They look to the courts for permission to act and generally must be bonded.

Administrator CTN: Where there is a will, but the executor refuses to serve, an administrator will be appointed *cum testamento annexo* or "with the will annexed."

Attorneys

  •**Attorney at law:** Generally referred to simply as your attorney or lawyer. As a member of the state bar, he is licensed to practice law in your particular state and before its courts. Many specialize in areas such as real estate, corporate and business law, trial law, criminal law and domestic law as well as estate planning, probate and elder law. Some are general practitioners and do a fine job in many of the areas in which they tend to specialize. You should be sure your attorney considers one of his specialties the area of estate planning. Note that elder law is a specialty in and of itself.

  •**Attorney in fact:** An individual authorized, by written instrument, to act in another's place to perform a particular act(s). The individual so authorized is called an attorney in fact, but he/she need not be, and usually is not, a licensed attorney. The empowering document is called a power of attorney which is a written instrument in which the attorney in fact is given specific rights and/or duties (i.e., power to sell 84 North Street, Litchfield, Connecticut).

  •**Power of attorney:** A written document wherein one person (the principal) grants the right to another (the agent) to act on behalf of the principal. Powers may be general (encompassing all actions), limited (some actions), springing (taking effect upon a specific event, i.e., your incapacity) and/or durable (surviving the incapacity of the principal). Generally, a durable power is preferable.

Beneficiary: One for whose benefit a trust is created or who is named as a recipient to benefit from the provisions of a trust, will or insurance policy. Generally, the designated beneficiary receives a benefit, profit, income, payout or the like by reason of being so named.

Community property: Property acquired by a husband and wife or either one of them during their marriage, not specifically acquired as separate property. After such acquisition, it is deemed to be acquired and held (regardless of whose name it is in) as a kind of marital partnership.

Disclaimer: A person's rejection or refusal to accept a property interest passing to him whether by reason of a gift or by reason of being beneficiary of an estate.

Donee: Person who receives a gift.

Donor: Person who makes a gift.

Estate: The word estate has many definitions in the legal sense. For most purposes in this text, it will refer to an individual's total assets which are available to him to use, plan for and gift away, and/or what will be left over upon death. At death, what is left over is usually referred to as one's estate (see below). Also, the assets of a trust are sometimes referred to as the trust estate, trust corpus or trust principal.

●**Probate estate:** Upon a person's demise, her estate may be made up of many different types of assets. Whether the probate court has jurisdiction over them is a question of the nature and form of ownership. For example, the decedent's home, if in her name alone, is said to be in her probate estate. Her life insurance or joint banking accounts which are payable on her death to someone named as the surviving beneficiary are said to be outside of the probate estate.

●**Taxable estate:** The decedent's taxable estate or gross taxable estate for IRS purposes takes into consideration all assets. This includes both the probate estate and those assets outside of the probate estate. Many clients miss this point and think, "Because it is payable to my daughter upon my death" it will not be taxed. This is a very common myth; do not fall into this trap.

●**Estate and gift tax:** At the federal level, under the new 2001 tax law, the estate tax will be phased out through 2009, repealed in 2010 and, unless Congress changes the law, reinstated in 2011 to the 2001 levels. The gift tax, however, is not repealed. Some states designate it as a death or succession tax. In practice, however, it is an excise tax levied upon the privilege of transferring property.

Executor: The individual or entity appointed in a will by the testator (see below) to carry out the directions and requests in the will. This includes distributing all of the estate's property after the testator's demise. The executor can be a person or a corporate fiduciary and usually receives his powers from the will as well as from the court and state law. Much like the administrator, the executor's duty is to collect the assets, pay debts and expenses, and finally to reclaim and distribute what is left over. However, the executor has much more guidance, as there is a will to direct him and powers to allow him to do his job without seeking court approval. For example, the will often gives him the power to continue a business.

Fiduciary: As a noun, this is a person holding a position analogous to the trustee. In fact, a trustee of a trust is called a fiduciary. She holds a position of faith and trust. Therefore, as an adjective it means "of the nature of a trust" or "relating to or founded upon a trust or confidence."

Fiduciary duty: Any person who qualifies as a fiduciary (i.e., executor, trustee, agent under a power of attorney) owes a fiduciary duty to act with good faith, candor and reasonableness toward all those who may be entitled to the fiduciary's fidelity.

Financial planner: An individual who will help you invest your assets in a portfolio that best suits your needs, goals and desires. There are various reputable groups that offer certification of financial planners. Sometimes your accountant, stockbroker and/or insurance agent are qualified in this area, but you should thoroughly research their qualifications and their fee arrangements. Some charge by the hour, others by a percentage of the portfolio managed and some simply on commission. Whenever your portfolio is not held in your name, it is best to research whether the planner is bonded and to what levels per account.

Gifts

●**Lifetime gifts:** A voluntary transfer to another of complete dominion and control over property. It is made gratuitously and without consideration during the donor's lifetime. The transfer must be complete so that the intended recipient actually receives what has been given.

•**Charitable gifts:** A gift made to a charity. Due to favorable tax treatment, there are types of charitable gifts where the donor and/or the donor's spouse may receive income generated by the gifted property for a specified period of time, but at the end of that period, the charity owns all rights to the property and the donor's rights end. The donor, therefore, may receive both income and possible estate tax deductions.

•**Uniform Gifts to Minors Act:** In order to facilitate gifts to minors, each state has adopted a version of this uniform law. It allows the donor to give property to a minor child's account, which is cared for by an adult custodian. Should the minor need the funds, the custodian may use them for the minor's benefit. The minor will receive the account balance outright upon her reaching majority or, in some states, at age 21.

Guardian: A person lawfully charged with the duty of taking care of another person and having the vested power to do so. If the person is charged with taking care of just the "person," he may be referred to as a "guardian of the person." If he is charged with taking care of just the "person's assets," he may be referred to as a "guardian of the estate." A child's father and mother are usually considered her "natural guardians." Your will should always name your choice of your children's guardian with an alternate guardian.

Heir at law: In the technical sense, this is the person who receives an estate from a decedent who left no will (who died intestate; see below). Often, in everyday parlance, people who are included in a will are referred to as a beneficiary or heir.

Insurance: A contract (policy) whereby, for an agreed fee (premium), one party (the insurance company) undertakes to compensate the other (the insured) for loss based on specified perils (risk). There are many types of insurance, including life, disability, fire and casualty, and many variations within each type. The estate planner will use several, and you should be familiar with the following:

•**Whole life:** Usually more costly, but offers a stable premium, guaranteed insurability and also builds a cash surrender value.

•**Term life:** Usually less expensive, but costs escalate as you age and you are not guaranteed insurability.

•**Group term:** Usually offered by your employer as a benefit.

•**Survivor life or second or last to die:** Usually a whole life product that insures a husband and wife and pays on the second death. It is designed to help pay estate or death taxes when they may become due, which is usually on the second death.

•**Split-dollar life:** An employer-sponsored plan whereby the employer and employee split the premium. It allows the employee to obtain larger amounts of insurance at lower initial cost.

•**Disability income insurance:** Designed to replace a certain portion of your income should you become disabled and no longer able to work.

•**Long-term-care insurance:** There are many versions of this, and you would be wise to discuss this with two or three recommended professionals. The products are designed to help pay not only for nursing home care (or a portion thereof), but also for in-home health care and a variety of other services needed by the elderly.

Intestate or to die intestate: A person is said to die intestate when she dies without having made or left a valid last will and testament. Each state provides for what happens or who will receive the probate estate in this event, and these laws are called the laws of intestate succession.

Last will and testament (will): The full term is a remnant of our roots in British common law. It refers to an estate where "lands and tenements are devised" and "chattels are bequeathed." Today, we shorten the complete phrase to simply a "will," signifying a written instrument, executed by an individual, which distributes the decedent's assets to her chosen beneficiaries upon her demise. Each state prescribes certain requirements for testing the validity of a will. Most notably, it usually must be in writing, signed by the testatrix and usually witnessed by as many as three disinterested individuals who saw the testatrix and the other witnesses sign, each in the presence of the other. The will is then offered to the court for admission and administration (probate).

Marital deduction: A deduction allowed on the federal estate and gift tax return (and most state returns as well where there is a similar tax) set up for amounts passing from the decedent to his spouse. Currently, at the federal level, the deduction is 100%, meaning a husband may give his wife (at death or during his life) an unlimited amount, provided she is a US citizen. This was not always the case, and as you will see, it may not always be best to use the maximum amount available.

Testator/testatrix: One who dies leaving a valid will.

Trusts: There are many different types of trusts. In simple terms, a trust is a right of property, real or personal, held by one party for the benefit of another. This text will discuss trusts in great detail. In the estate planning context, they are almost always written documents created by the "grantor/settlor/trustor," administered by a "trustee" who is a "fiduciary," under the terms of the trust for the benefit of the "beneficiaries." There can be discretion in the trustee to act under specified circumstances, or the trustee may have no discretion. The trust document will generally outline what is to be done and will prevail as long as it is not illegal or against public policy. As noted, there are several types, but it would be helpful to be familiar with the following categories:

- ***Inter vivos* trusts or living trusts:** Those created during a person's lifetime.
- **Testamentary trusts:** Those created in a person's last will and testament.
- **Funded living trusts:** Those where significant assets are added to the trust upon creation or thereafter.
- **Irrevocable trusts:** Living trusts that cannot be revoked. They are usually funded and are often used with a gifting plan.
- **Revocable trusts:** Living trusts that can be revoked. They can be funded or remain unfunded.
- **QTIP trusts:** Designed to preserve the marital deduction yet hold the property in a trust for the surviving spouse (wife) as a qualified terminal interest. Upon the wife's death, the assets go to the beneficiaries of the decedent's (husband's) choice and not those of the wife's choosing.
- **QDT trusts:** A trust for a noncitizen resident spouse designed to preserve the marital deduction.
- **Marital deduction trusts:** Those designed to preserve the marital deduction yet hold the property given to the surviving spouse under a trust umbrella.

Probate: Originally, relating to proof but, as time passed, to the proof of wills. Today, it is not only the judicial act or determination of a court having jurisdiction to establish the validity of a will, but also the court which oversees the entire administrative process. That is, the court supervises the process from the collection of assets, payment of bills, expenses and estate taxes to the final distribution of the assets to the beneficiaries.

Will substitute: A device or method of passing assets upon death without using a will. As you will see in this text, there are many ways to pass property upon your death. A simple joint savings account can act as a will substitute. This does not mean, however, that it is advisable to try to dispose of your entire estate by means of will substitutes.

Now that you have mastered some of the basic terminology, let us begin our journey.

Chapter Two

HIDDEN TRAPS
IN ESTATE PLANNING

The objective of estate planning, as discussed in Chapter One, is the transferral of as much of your wealth as possible to chosen parties in the most appropriate manner. This requires the avoidance of many traps and pitfalls. Otherwise, unnecessary taxes and other forms of diminution will erode what goes to the beneficiaries, and your intentions may be frustrated substantially or even entirely. It is crucial to realize that estate tax is just one of many possible eroding factors from which you must protect your assets and estate.

Major traps

Proper planning can avoid the traps lurking in the following areas:

1. Retention of some form of control over property so that it is deemed to be part of the transferor's gross estate when he dies, even though he has parted with the assets and is not exercising any control over them. (See Chapter Fifty-Three, "The Dry Run.") Avoidance of "strings" may have to be part of one's planning. For example, a father may have transferred assets to a trust for the benefit of his minor children, reserving the right to allocate trust property to each child until the youngest reached age 21, when the father expected to know enough about the financial and other strengths of each child to make a final decision. If the father became mentally incompetent before that date, he could not release the retained power, and the property would be taxed as part of his estate when he died. Nothing could be done about it.

2. Making gifts or other transfers in good faith and in compliance with state laws. For example, transfers of real estate, to be valid under state law, generally have to be in writing, in proper format and recorded in a designated

county office. Many deeds have been executed and left in the client's attorney's office "until further notice," which may never come.

3. Holding property in joint ownership. This can be disastrous if the parties become estranged and hostile. In addition, the Internal Revenue Service includes half the value of the property in the gross estate of the first co-owner to die if the co-owners are husband and wife. For others (i.e., mother/daughter), unless the executor can prove otherwise, the IRS will include the full value of the property in the estate of the first co-owner to die. (See Chapter Twenty-Two, "Choice of Forms of Ownership.")

4. Unwitting possession of "incidents of ownership" of insurance on the decedent's life. A young man may take out insurance on his life, naming his mother as beneficiary. He plans to change the name of the beneficiary when he marries, so the policy reserves for the insured the right to make such changes. After marriage, he gives the policy to his bride but does not release the right. Since he retained his right to change the beneficiary, even after his wife has become the owner, the proceeds will be included in his federal gross estate and may be taxable. If she dies before or with him, this could have drastic tax ramifications. "Incidents of ownership" causes inclusion in the estate.

5. Reliance upon the wrong "experts." The seller of an insurance policy may claim that the transaction can be arranged so that the proceeds will be exempt from federal estate tax. That statement doesn't satisfy the Internal Revenue Service or the courts. Another common trap occurs when an insurance agent, as part of an estate plan, recommends that his client exchange certain policies or contracts for others. True, some policies may be exchanged on a tax-free basis. But not all types of insurance, endowment or annuity contracts may be exchanged tax free. A tax specialist should check the Internal Revenue Code requirements in order to ascertain whether ordinary income tax is payable upon the exchange.

6. Failure of an attorney to follow instructions. One woman told her son, a practicing lawyer, that she wanted to make a gift to her six children, to be apportioned equally. She gave him a substantial sum and told him to invest the

money in a mutual fund setting up trust funds for the children. Fearful that his mother would not have sufficient income, he deviated from her instructions and had the mutual fund company draw up a trust in which she would retain the right to take trust income and principal if she needed the funds. The remaining principal was to be apportioned among the surviving children when she died. She learned of his deviation only when she began getting money from the trustee, which at its own discretion sent her checks. She ordered her son to conform to her original intention that the trust be irrevocable with no reservation to herself. But he had not done this by the time she died, so the principal was included in her gross estate, although she had no intention of retaining any strings on her gift.

7. Reliance on the IRS. If the testator, his executor or attorney asks the IRS about the tax treatment of an item and faithfully follows the reply, tax and interest will still be imposed if this advice was incorrect. In the words of a famous judge, "Harsh as it may be, one accepts the advice of a revenue official at his peril." But under the so-called Taxpayer Bill of Rights of 1988, there is no penalty where a taxpayer can show that he had relied upon *written* information furnished by IRS personnel acting in their official capacity.

The Revenue Reconciliation Act of 1989 expanded the list of authorities upon which taxpayers may rely (previously contained in Treasury regulations) to include proposed regulations, private letter rulings, technical advice memoranda, actions on decisions, general counsel memoranda, information or press releases, notices and any other similar documents published by the IRS in the *Internal Revenue Bulletin* and the *General Explanation of Tax Legislation* prepared by the Joint Committee on Taxation. The IRS is required to publish not less frequently than annually a list of positions for which the Service believes there is no substantial authority and which affect a significant number of taxpayers.

8. An inexperienced executor or executrix. Errors and omissions made by the fiduciary can be very costly to the estate and to the beneficiaries, although, under certain circumstances, it is the executor who is held personally liable for his mistakes. Frequently, for sentimental reasons or as a gesture of confi-

dence, a husband names his wife or adult child to serve as executor or executrix. This could be a very costly mistake, both from the viewpoints of the estate and of the fiduciary. A person may seek to save an inexperienced relative who is unfamiliar with the subject by providing in the will that the executor won't be required to make good from his own pocket for his failure to exercise reasonable care, diligence and prudence. Some state laws, however, hold that such a provision in a will is void.

9. The terms of a will may be contradictory, thereby undermining some of the testator's wishes. For example, the marital deduction is available only where property passes to the surviving spouse. But not infrequently, a will contains a basic contradiction providing (a) that all remaining property will go to the surviving spouse, and (b) that any property remaining (what she did not use, implying some form of trust) after her death will go to the children or other designated parties. The marital deduction may be lost because the property did not go to the surviving spouse either outright or as qualified terminable interest property (QTIP). Even if (a) states that the property is to go to her outright with all rights, referred to as "fee simple," (b) could contradict that. Sometimes the percentages just don't add up. We've seen cases of both less than and greater than 100% of an estate being bequeathed.

10. An estate plan may have been devised solely on the basis of tax considerations. Taxes are an important element of estate planning. But taxes should not be the only matter considered. For example, to qualify for the maximum marital deduction, a husband may leave his entire estate to his surviving spouse. If she has no need or desire for more wealth, there's an opportunity to use and integrate the unified credit effective exemption amount, a bypass trust or an outright gift to their children or to his children from a previous marriage, or other persons he would like to provide for.

11. A decedent's instructions or acts may result in excessive estate tax valuations. One individual instructed his executor to retain a certain stock despite its ups and downs in the stock market. The IRS claimed that these

shares should be valued at more than the market price, asserting that the decedent had probably known more about the company than anyone else, and hence his estimate of its worth was more reliable than that of outsiders. Sometimes a person lists real estate for sale with a broker so that he can deduct insurance and maintenance charges in connection with property held primarily for sale. Actually, he doesn't really want or intend to sell, but only to claim some deductions, so he lists the property at such a high figure that there will be no buyers. The IRS is likely to value the property at the inflated figure that he himself had set to discourage buyers.

12. Use of an unqualified appraiser. A competent appraiser can save considerably on estate taxes; an incompetent one is a liability. In one case, the values set by the executor's appraiser were far lower than those set by the IRS's appraisers. The court accepted the latter because cross-examination revealed that the executor's appraiser had once failed the American Institute of Real Estate Appraisers' examination.

13. Despite their advantages, buy-sell agreements may contain many traps for the unwary. (See Chapter Forty-Two, "Buy-Sell Agreements.") If a shareholder owns enough stock to name a corporation's president and directors, it is dangerous for the corporation to own insurance on his life to fund such an agreement. Here the proceeds might be included in his gross estate. (See Chapter Thirty-One, "Planning with Life Insurance.") Implementation of such a buy-sell plan may concentrate stock ownership of a corporation with nonoperating income in so few hands that undistributed income may be subject to a special personal-holding-company tax. In a buy-sell agreement, also beware of a formula clause so complicated that the survivor of a deceased shareholder can demand an accounting or otherwise put the corporation to great trouble.

14. Acceptance of a general power of appointment can be very costly. (See Chapter Forty-Seven, "Powers of Appointment.") Often the existence of such a power isn't recognized by the parties. When he was 10 years old, one individual's parents set up a trust for his benefit to last 21 years. At any time, he or his legally appointed guardian could terminate the trust or withdraw any of

its principal or accumulated income. Although not so labeled, this amounted to a general power of appointment. So when this person died at age 28, the value of the trust property was included in his gross estate. The fact that he never knew he had a general power of appointment was irrelevant.

15. Throwing out records relevant to the establishment of tax liability. Destruction of records (by the surviving spouse, for example, when he wants to straighten out the house) can result in higher taxes because proper claims and deductions on income and estate tax returns can't be substantiated. Incidentally, an individual who prematurely destroys evidence needed in a tax audit is subject to personal penalties. (See Chapter Fifty-Four, "A Letter to Your Executor.") Also, as individuals age, it is not uncommon for them to "clean house," especially after one spouse dies. On more than one occasion we have seen elderly clients unwittingly destroy original wills and trusts.

16. Gifts of income-producing properties to children under age 14 may no longer save federal income taxes. A child's unearned income in excess of $1,500 in 2001 (indexed for inflation) is taxed at the parents' top marginal rates. The child's minimum tax will not exceed the amount by which the parents' tax would be increased if the parents' income included this unearned income of the child. These gifts, however, still have estate planning value, as will be discussed in succeeding chapters. Note also, under the 2001 tax law—with its reduction in the lowest tax brackets—additional savings in this area may be gained.

17. Beneficiaries who become nonbeneficiaries because of death prior to the testator's or refusal to accept what had been left to them. Provide for contingent or residual beneficiaries so that your property will go to persons of your own choice even though it may be a second choice.

18. Waiting too long. Gifts not made on an annual basis can mean loss of annual gift tax exclusions. (See Chapter Twenty-Three, "Taking Advantage of the Annual Exclusion.") Transfers within three years of death can now remove most property from the gross federal estate, but the requirement of acting more than three years before death still applies to transfers of life

insurance and transactions such as the release of a retained power. Also, if an individual waits too long to take out needed life insurance to implement an estate plan, he may have become uninsurable.

19. Inflation can make your planned disposition unrealistic. When you give property away, you also give away its future appreciation, which may be substantial.

20. The Uniform Gifts to Minors Act is often used by parents to lower their income tax after the child attains age 14. Many parents, however, have been found explaining themselves to either the IRS or the courts for not turning over the assets when the child reached the appropriate age (in most states, age 21). Never be the custodian of your children's accounts if you want this asset out of your estate. Many parents have been caught in this trap.

21. Many parents have used these same children's accounts to pay for what the IRS considers support obligations (e.g., private school tuition). In these cases, the IRS taxed the parents as having been relieved of a support obligation (which relief is taxable income to them). This is money they had already paid tax on and given to their children—a very harsh result. You should not use your child's funds to relieve yourself of a support obligation, but you can use them for items you are not required to provide.

22. Your gifting plan could be thwarted if you were to become incompetent. The IRS will allow a person to grant the right to continue the gifting program through a properly drafted power of attorney. The legal requirements are quite specific. Also, it would be prudent to execute other documents allowed in your state, such as living wills or advance directives indicating your health-care preferences, and also to appoint a health-care agent or proxy.

23. Planning for the uncertainties of life. Health problems, disabilities, business setbacks and divorce are all uncertainties of life. Consider prominent athletes or actors who have become disabled and/or divorced in recent years. It could happen to any of us. Therefore, while planning and considering irrevocable trusts, consider the possibility that your life circumstances may change. Consider an escape hatch. For example, consider disability insurance.

16

Also, when considering funding your trusts, note that life insurance may very well answer both the funding dilemma and allow you to reverse an irrevocable plan in a divorce situation by stopping the premium payments.

24. The quickness of the aging process. If we don't see our parents regularly, we may be amazed that one day all seemed fine and the next they are looking into long-term care. The aging process or the need for elder planning comes upon your loved one(s) with the suddenness and speed of a midsummer tornado. Don't take for granted that anyone will last forever. Start now.

25. Well-intended advice may be the most costly. Estate planning has as many makes, models and variations as there are automobiles. What is right for your neighbor may not be right for you. But your friends at the senior center and other well-intentioned acquaintances want to offer advice. The best advice: Just don't listen. The advice is usually not well founded and is often wrong. This "free" advice might cost you more than the advice you seek out. Get advice from a professional and pay a reasonable and fair fee.

26. Beware of the salesperson. Estate planners generally are paid by the number of hours they spend with you. Usually, they are attorneys or accountants, and most work with reliable and trusted life insurance salespeople and certified financial planners. In formulating your plan, work with those who are not commissioned salespeople. For insurance products your planner recommends, he will usually give you the names of trustworthy (ask for a couple) agents, who can help you find the products you need. Always deal with top-rated companies and get several competing quotes. These products need to be in place many years into the future and the companies behind them must match earnings projections to remain in business.

27. The human element. Of all the traps you face, the most distressing can be the "human element." Unfortunately, after your death, even the most sacred of promises may wane with the passage of time and estrangement. Therefore, when we say, "Leave nothing to chance," we mean put your requirements in writing if you expect these promises to be kept. Don't expect

your loving daughter, with a greedy husband, to treat her sisters the way you want just because she says she will. Put it in writing.

28. The greatest trap of all is *complacency*, the belief that all of the pieces will automatically and satisfactorily fall into place. This rarely happens unless you make it happen.

Conclusions and advice

• There are many traps for the unwary.

• When dealing with retained rights versus a completed gift involving such things as life insurance incidents and/or buy-sell agreements, you need expert advice. The key is to give it "all" away (see Chapter Fifty-Two, "Let Go of All Retained Strings.")

• Be sure your directives and documents are clear, concise and properly drafted. Don't wait. It can have everlasting consequences.

• Life situations change; therefore, systematically schedule and follow through on updates and reviews.

• Estate taxes are just one of several possible ways your estate can be subjected to needless depletion.

• The 2001 tax law is very complex and filled with traps and pitfalls for the unwary. This has heightened the need to seek expert advice to assist you throughout your planning process.

Chapter Three

THE FEDERAL ESTATE AND GIFT TAX

Historical perspective

Many people believe the federal unified transfer tax on estates and gifts is one of the most unfair confiscations of property since that famous evening "tea party," when several Bostonians decided to show their displeasure with the British imposition of taxation on the colonies.

Taxpayers feel that the wealth they have accumulated over their lifetime is the product of after-tax income.

Therefore, they reason, levying an additional death tax not only seems to be a double tax, but a penalty against preserving assets for one's future needs. Additionally, it is a penalty on the passage or transfer of these after-tax assets to one's heirs upon death. Likewise, to prohibit a person's right to give away assets that she already had paid income taxes on as they were being earned during her lifetime is equally disturbing. Unlike our forefathers, however, some support the theory that the purpose of this tax is not primarily to generate revenue, but rather to redistribute wealth. In either case, the result seems inescapable: The tax should be minimized to the greatest extent legally possible. Hopefully Congress will aid us in that endeavor and rectify the further dilemma it has created with the 2011 sunset provision, by taking swift action. However, no one is predicting that this will occur soon.

Interestingly, for married couples, the situation used to be even worse. Before the unlimited marital deduction came into being under President Reagan in 1981, if a wife left her husband the entire amount of her estate, which exceeded certain levels, a tax was levied on this transfer. Again, this was a very harsh and unfair result. The couple had worked long and hard for these assets and paid income taxes to generate them. Yet the survivor, after his wife's demise, was forced to pay an estate tax on assets he may very well have helped generate and/or paid income taxes on in order to help accumulate.

The current system and the new 2001 tax law

Today, the situation has improved somewhat. Were it not for a few very complex and confusing provisions (i.e., carryover basis) and the now famous sunset or reinstatement provision in 2011 (reinstating the 2001 law), the new law would be deemed a success. However, due to these complexities and uncertainties, many argue that the ills of the estate tax system may make it a candidate for substantial reform. Under President Reagan, the concept of the unlimited marital deduction was enacted. It remains a cornerstone today, yet may lull individuals into a false sense of security. A wealthy wife, knowing that if she predeceases her husband with a simple will in place that leaves everything to him, can sleep soundly knowing that her husband will be safe from the tax collector.

Unfortunately, when he dies, the situation changes. Her failure to plan and use the tools available to her could leave all of her assets at risk. Additionally, this does not even begin to consider events such as a second marriage or his illness or incapacity. Traditionally, an estate planner might have suggested utilizing the wife's unified credit effective exemption amount (see page 22), as well as such protective devices as qualified terminal interest property (QTIP), by-pass and/or credit-shelter trusts.

There are several new ideas that your planning advisers will discuss with you. Note, however, that the foundation of the estate tax has remained the same; it is a tax on the transfer of assets from one party to another. While there used to be a distinction between lifetime and death transfers, the tax rate has been unified on all transferred assets, except in 2010 when the estate tax is repealed for one year while the gift tax remains unchanged. The key seems to be examining the following crucial factors at the time of the transfer—each must be meticulously planned for, as soon as possible. They are:

(1) the determination of completeness of ownership at the time of the intended transfer (i.e., Do I own this asset and can I dispose of it?); (2) inclusion of assets actually transferred (Will it still be part of my estate after an attempted gift?); (3) a transfer's completeness versus retention of rights or dominion and control (Have I given away all that is required to qualify?); (4) timing (When is the best time [lifetime or death] and what is the best manner for disposing of this asset?); (5) valuation (Are there special factors that can be taken advantage of that only I know about?); (6) availability of deductions and credits (plan for these); (7) the tax itself (How large will it be? Where will my executor find the funds to pay for the tax?); and, finally, (8) retention of some assets for the executor's use (If the tax is large, should some of my gifts be set up in such a manner that my executor can gain access to funds to help settle the estate?).

If you realize that you have some degree of control over items 1 through 4 and, to a lesser extent, 5 and 6, you will understand the essential elements of mastering the ability to minimize the tax. As always, you will need help, but your vigilant effort will pay off. Additionally, if you reduce the size of your estate, you will reduce the assets available for depletion in the event of long-term medical care. In doing so, you may be able to maximize, through gifting, what is outside your estate to either pass on to others (i.e., via a trust) or help pay some of the estate taxes.

We will mention here that some states also have their own versions of an estate tax. These may have different names, rate structures and procedures, and some are even designed to avoid increasing an estate's overall tax liability by using what is commonly referred to as a "sponge tax" (your state simply takes the amount of the state credit given on the federal return). Note, that as of July 1, 2001, 37 states and the District of Columbia had this type of tax. However, the new tax law reduces the credit by 25% beginning in 2002 until it is finally repealed entirely in 2005. It will change to a "deduction" until the repeal of the estate tax in 2010. Note, also, that even a smaller group of states have a gift tax.

Key concepts

- Unified tax rate (see Appendix D): Under the 2001 tax law, the top rate is reduced to 50% in 2002 with a $1 million exemption. Currently (2002), there is one unified rate on transfers, whether they are made by gift or upon death. The rate quickly reaches the top bracket of 55%, although a unified credit is available to reduce the size of the tax to some extent (also shown in Appendix D).

- Generation-skipping tax (GST): Under the 2001 tax law, the GST remains an additional tax on the transfer of amounts over $1,100,000. This amount was recently adjusted by an inflation index and is assessed on transfers (indexed for inflation) to certain designated generations below that of the transferor. The effective GST tax rate on direct skips at death was 33.48% (see Appendix D). Yet as the estate tax rate was lowered in 2002, so was the GST tax. As the exemptions increases, the GST tax will be lowered. However, when added to a potential estate tax of any significance, it is obvious that the government is attempting to discourage distribution of family wealth to generations beyond one generation below the transferor. Note, the GST is also slated for the one-year repeal in 2010.

- Unlimited marital deduction: Currently, a spouse can receive, by lifetime gift or upon death, unlimited tax-free amounts from her spouse as long as certain standards are met. Note that there are restrictions for noncitizens.

- Unified estate and gift tax credit (referred to as unified credit exemption equivalent under the new law) (see Appendix D): Between 2002 and 2009, each person/estate will possess the ability to transfer either during his lifetime or at death the sum of $1,000,000 (in 2002), increasing to $3.5 million in 2009. From 2002, when the credit is $1 million, to 2008, when it is $2 million, the increase is slowly phased in. Note that this is the amount that can be passed free of taxation although it has been referred to as a credit. Appendix D refers to the amount as an exemption equivalent. This text has maintained the use of unified credit for ease of identification purpose.

• Annual gift tax exclusion: Each person (donor) may give to any number of persons (donees) the sum of $11,000 per year (indexed for inflation) as an annual exclusion without depletion of the donor's unified credit. The gift must be a present interest, and complete dominion and control must pass from the donor. All gifts for that year are added together, and in some contentious cases, holiday and birthday presents were included to determine if the level had been exceeded. If the amount is exceeded, a gift tax return (Form 709) must be filed.

• Gift splitting: A married donor may increase her annual exclusion to $22,000 per year per donee if her husband will agree to gift split. This means that he agrees or consents, on the gift tax return (Form 709), that his wife may use his $11,000 annual per-donee exclusion to increase her annual per-donee exclusion to as much as the full $22,000. The husband need not contribute any funds to the gift, but must sign the gift tax return consenting to the gift split.

• Qualified terminal interest property (QTIP): Under prior law, in order to qualify for the marital deduction, property passing to the decedent's spouse had to pass outright, free of any restrictions. Generally, the survivor had to have the unlimited right to access all principal and income, or the marital deduction was lost. With the advent of several social and economic changes, Congress enacted the QTIP concept, and QTIP trusts have become commonplace. Generally, as long as the surviving spouse is guaranteed the unqualified right to receive all of the annual income from the corpus or principal of a bequest from the decedent spouse, this will qualify for the marital deduction. There will, of course, be a tax upon the remaining balance in the trust on the death of the surviving spouse.

• Federal gross taxable estate: Life insurance, regardless of cash value, is included if the decedent held what is known as "incidents of ownership." Joint accounts are included, even if the decedent never contributed to the account. The same applies to jointly held stock, or accounts held in your children's names under the Uniform Gifts to Minors Act, if you are the custodian. This can be a very costly error. The government will also include IRAs, 401(k)s and similar accounts, as well as final wages, vacation pay, commissions and bonuses in your federal gross taxable estate. It's up to you to try to see that there is as little there as possible for it to tax.

- IRAs—a double tax of staggering proportions: Due to several converging social and economic factors—a healthy economy and stock market as well as the proliferation of employee benefits—many taxpayers find themselves with sizable tax-free retirement accounts such as IRAs, rollovers, 401(k)s or similar accounts and correspondingly sizable federal taxable estates. This does not mean that we are seeing overwhelming numbers of multimillionaires, but rather that when you combine a good work ethic, a healthy economy and stock market, employee retirement plans that have done well and governmental encouragement of retirement accounts, we see more and more clients with significant portions of their estates so invested. These accounts have also been allowed to build tax free, and for many taxpayers there is an almost "sacred cow" approach to drawing them down. Yet most accountants will advise that if your estate is taxable at the federal level, there will be severe depletion of your tax-free retirement account. In the wrong scenario, we have seen a combined income tax, estate tax (state and federal) and probate or administrative expenses of well over 70% and these were not overwhelmingly large estates. An extreme penalty to pay for the right to build assets tax free. We strongly encourage you to discuss this with your accountant.

Conclusions and advice

- On June 7, 2001, President Bush signed into law the Economic Growth and Tax Relief Reconciliation Act of 2001 (throughout this text referred to as the "2001 tax law"). Most estate planners look not five or 10 years forward, but 10, 20 and sometimes multiple generations forward to produce sound estate plans. Yet, depending on the political winds that are blowing in Congress, we may see a return of the estate and gift tax as we knew it prior to

2001. To complicate matters, the 2001 tax law resurrected "carryover basis." This concept first appeared in the Tax Code in 1976, causing so many problems that it was repealed before it became effective. This will be discussed in greater detail in the chapters that follow.

• Use both Appendices D-2 and E to determine the size of your estate, including all of your assets, life insurance, pensions, IRAs and the like. Review the rate schedules in Appendix D, and if your assets or those of you and your spouse approach taxable levels, you would be well advised to consider some tax planning methods in your estate plan. Simple wills or simple trusts send needless dollars to the tax collector.

• Some of the trusts that estate planners often use for surviving spouses, children and/or charities will be applicable regardless of the size of your estate or the status of the tax law.

• Beware of the double taxation of your retirement accounts. This problem alone could cost your family hundreds of thousands of dollars.

• Ask your accountant about taking more than the minimum from your retirement account. If you are considering a gifting program, you will pay income tax, but will avoid estate tax, resulting in substantial savings for your family and heirs.

Chapter Four

THE MARITAL DEDUCTION: MAXIMIZING THE OPPORTUNITY

As we said in Chapter Three, the marital deduction is a most significant factor in reducing the size of an estate for federal estate tax purposes. The deduction permits an individual to pass on to his surviving spouse 100% of his adjusted gross estate free of estate tax. But because very substantial portions of each estate may pass free of estate tax under the expanded unified credit, estate planners must consider the overall impact of taxes on both estates in deciding how much marital deduction to claim in the estate of the first spouse to die. This is one of the most crucial decisions that you face and the 2001 tax law has made it more critical by increasing the size of the unified credit effective exemption amount.

Each spouse can currently leave up to $1 million (in 2002) free of federal estate tax, and under the 2001 tax law this will gradually increase to $3.5 million in 2009. If all property passes to the surviving spouse, the credit applicable to the estate of the first spouse to die could be completely lost. The credit amount that may pass tax free includes both lifetime and upon-death transfers that would otherwise be taxable. (See also "Disclaimers" in this chapter.)

Note that money and other property passing from a decedent to a surviving spouse may qualify for the marital deduction even if it passes in the form of a terminable interest, provided the interest is a qualified terminable interest. Executors now have added responsibility, as well as flexibility, in deciding whether or not to take the marital deduction for all or a portion of the qualified terminable interest.

What is meant by property passing to a surviving spouse

Property passing to a surviving spouse qualifies for the marital deduction. The definition of "passing" includes:

1. Property left by will.

2. Property acquired under state laws of intestacy when the decedent has not left a valid will. For example, state law might provide that a decedent's property go to her next of kin, but at least a portion of it would go to the surviving spouse.

3. Property going to the surviving spouse despite the language of a valid will, because the widow "took against the will" by claiming the part of her husband's estate to which she was entitled as dower. In most states, the husband may have a comparable right.

4. Property which the widow co-owned with right of survivorship.

5. Insurance proceeds received by the surviving spouse under a policy on the life of the decedent.

6. Completed lifetime gifts to the spouse.

7. Property that the decedent had the right to transfer under the authorization of a third party, if the decedent named the spouse as recipient.

8. Property in which the surviving spouse has a qualifying income interest, if the donor or the executor irrevocably elects to claim the marital deduction for the underlying qualified terminable interest property. (For the rules, see Chapter Eighteen, "Where the Surviving Spouse Can't Touch Anything but Income.")

The property passing to the surviving spouse means only what she actually receives, not what the will states she should receive.

Sometimes a disappointed heir threatens to contest a decedent's will. If the surviving spouse agrees to pay the claimant directly from the amount of property slated to pass to her from the decedent, it is then reduced according to the settlement. The marital deduction is correspondingly reduced. As a teaching point, very often people attempt to be creative to solve a problem or attain a goal or simply provide for alternative results in the event of the unexpected. When planning your estate and utilizing the marital deduction, do not run afoul of the rules prohibiting restrictions on gifts to your spouse. Here are some unfortunate examples of this.

Nonqualified terminable interests are not deductible

A common form of nonqualifying terminable interest is a residence owned by the husband. His will provides his wife with the right to reside in the house for as long as she lives, then the property is to pass to the children. The marital deduction will be lost because her interest in the property is a nonqualifying terminable interest because she can't leave the house to anyone of her choice and she has no right to income payable at least annually.

If property is left to a spouse subject to a contingency, there is a nonqualifying terminable interest, even if that contingency doesn't occur. One man's will left his property to his wife "to have and to hold absolutely." But the will also stated that if she remarried, the property was to go to their children. Because the property was subject to this condition, it was not eligible for the marital deduction. And because the property was not certain to be included in the wife's estate, it could not be a qualified terminable interest.

The right to sell—but not to give

Another man left all his real estate to his wife for life, giving her the right to sell any or all of it as she saw fit. The will provided that any of the real estate that the wife still owned at the time of her death was to go to the children. The realty interest left to her obviously couldn't qualify for the marital deduction, as she did not have a complete interest in the property. Although she could sell it, the will did not empower her to give it away. Perhaps the power to give the property away was omitted from the will through carelessness. At any rate, the deduction was lost.

But if the decedent's will merely contains words like "it is my wish and desire" that any of the property his widow holds at the time of her death go to the children, the property passing to her will qualify for the marital deduction. She receives the property unconditionally. It is likely that she would honor her husband's request, but the choice is hers alone.

Cases like these led the United States Supreme Court to declare, "The achievement of the purpose of the marital deduction is dependent to a great degree upon the careful drafting of wills." The language of the will, not the good intentions of the testator or the lawyers, determines the qualification for the marital deduction.

Disclaimers

If the surviving spouse makes a disclaimer of any property interest that would otherwise be considered as having passed to her from the decedent, the disclaimed interest is considered as having passed directly to the person entitled to receive the interest as a result of this disclaimer. Thus, the disclaimed interest is not entitled to the benefit of the marital deduction. (See Chapter Forty-Nine, "Disclaimers and Renunciations.")

Effects of state law

The question of the marital deduction for federal estate tax purposes may be subject to state law. If a marriage has not been recognized by the state in which the spouses resided at the time of death of one of them, there can be no marital deduction. Further, any interest passing to the surviving spouse must be valid under the property laws of the state in which it was created.

Bequests to a noncitizen spouse

The estate tax marital deduction is allowed for property passing to a noncitizen spouse if the spouse becomes a US citizen before the estate tax return is filed. Further, the spouse must have been a US resident at all times from the date of the marriage to the date of death. In addition, all property, probate and nonprobate, passing to a noncitizen qualifies for the marital deduction if the property is transferred or irrevocably assigned to a qualifying domestic trust (QDT) before the estate tax return is filed. There is no requirement that this trust be created by the decedent. It may be created by the executor or the surviving spouse. However, the trust instrument should be properly drafted and part of the estate plan for fear of losing this favorable treatment. Property passing from a nonresident noncitizen to a noncitizen spouse qualifies for the estate tax marital deduction if it passes in a QDT.

Maximizing the marital deduction

The decision to maximize the marital deduction should be made with counsel from your estate planning adviser. Under many circumstances, it is wise to forgo at least a portion of the marital deduction and instead use up the decedent's unified credit. In this event, a couple could pass, tax free, two unified credits (in 2002 $1 million each or $2 million total under the new tax law). Otherwise, if the marital deduction is maximized on the death of the first spouse, then unless a disclaimer is used, the first credit will be lost.

Consider how or in what format to utilize the marital deduction or how much of a bequest to make to your spouse. While outright bequests have the advantage of simplicity, they also allow all assets to be commingled with the survivor's assets. Thereafter, the survivor's total assets are subject to creditors, medical bills, nursing homes, remarriages and the like. If the survivor has children by a previous marriage, this could be a rather thorny problem.

An additional question is whether or not to place these assets into a trust. As we will show in Chapter Eighteen, a trust can be as restrictive as a QTIP (income only) trust or more liberal, requiring or allowing distributions of principal. There are many variations to these types of trusts. Also, if you are not maximizing the marital deduction, your trust may be more restrictive, as credit-shelter or by-pass trusts often are. Yet, they can give all concerned a sense of security, knowing that, in the event of a death, their estate will reap the benefit of two unified credits.

Second-to-die (or survivorship) insurance

When an estate plan calls for the maximum use of the unlimited marital deduction, no federal estate tax is paid upon the value of property passing to the surviving spouse under the conditions mentioned in this chapter. However, when the survivor dies, there is usually an increased amount of property to be taxed: The widow's own property plus what she had received, courtesy of the unlimited marital deduction, from her husband's estate. The result is a larger estate tax than would have been levied if her husband's estate had paid tax on the value of the property passing to her upon his death. This is partially due to the progressive rate schedules, as well as to inflation. However, had there been a tax on the first death, there would have been an opportunity cost for the taxes, which we do not have if the deduction was maximized.

One solution: Survivorship life insurance. Under this policy, the insurance company pays out nothing when the husband dies, as there is no tax or need. When the wife subsequently dies, the insurance company pays the executor or heirs an amount that had been calculated to pay the estate tax estimated to be levied upon the value of her own estate, plus what she had received under the unlimited marital deduction and presumably some reasonable appreciation.

The cost of such a policy is far less than the cost of insuring each spouse separately, because the insurance company will eventually pay out only one amount. If one spouse has health problems or there are substantial age differences, we have found that insuring one spouse to the same level is a reasonable, albeit more expensive, approach. It may be less expensive than a survivor policy where one person is "rated." In such a case, should the insured die first, the policy, held in trust, will be paid off, and the funds also held in trust are used to pay the tax when the second spouse dies.

Inasmuch as the estate of the second spouse to die must pay the tax nine months after her death, this arrangement can supply needed funds and avoid an unnecessarily early sale of estate assets. Often, the policy is owned by a trust. (See Chapter Thirty-One, "Planning with Life Insurance.")

With the advent of the 2001 tax law, the unified credit effective exemption amount is increased (see Appendix D-2) to $3.5 million in 2009. In theory, if your planner could guarantee your survival until 2009, then the combination of two unified credit effective exemption amounts would be $7 million. Or if both spouses passed away in 2010, there would be no tax at all. The reality, however, may be that in 2011, when the estate tax is reinstated, you would receive only a $1 million unified credit or, if both you and your spouse die in 2011, a total of only $2 million of unified credit.

Your estate planner should suggest a contingency plan with this in mind. For example, if you consider the alternatives of paying a tax or making an investment in an insurance product which benefits your heirs, the choice of insurance would seem prudent.

Sometimes the marital deduction is not desired

There are occasions when an individual doesn't want to leave a surviving spouse any amount that would qualify for the marital deduction. If, for example, a spouse has ample wealth of her own, the testator might elect to provide for other people or for institutions. Or the survivor might be very ill or elderly.

Conclusions and advice

• In cases of prior marriage and divorce, be sure your present marriage is recognized as valid under state law.

• Consider leaving a surviving spouse qualified terminable interest property to provide the executor with flexibility in reducing taxes in both spouses' estates.

• Do not use conflicting language in the will that might forfeit the marital deduction. The language should be reviewed by someone who is familiar with federal estate tax law.

• In some cases, you may better serve your objectives by deliberately by-passing part or all of the marital deduction.

• The marital deduction is not available for property passing to a non-citizen resident spouse. However, the estate tax marital deduction is allowed for property passing to a noncitizen resident spouse in a qualified domestic trust. Property passing outside the probate estate is treated as passing in a qualified domestic trust if it is transferred to the trust before the estate tax return is due. A qualified domestic trust must meet certain specified conditions. Annual gifts also qualify, but must be less than $110,000 per year recently adjusted for inflation.

• There are many choices on your estate planning menu. It is important that you and your counselors thoroughly consider them all. The marital deduction can be coupled with both a credit-shelter trust and/or survivorship insurance. In some situations, i.e., a second marriage, you may wish to use the concept of qualified terminal interest property or QTIP trusts to accomplish your goals. (See Chapter Eighteen, "Where the Surviving Spouse Can't Touch Anything but Income.")

• Couples should not forsake two credits simply to maximize the marital deduction. However, under the 2001 tax law, as the credit grows (i.e., in 2006 it is $2,000,000) you may not need two full credits and this is where careful and experienced planning is needed.

• Don't forsake tried-and-true remedies, such as second-to-die insurance coverage, just because the estate tax will be purportedly repealed in 2010. Remember, in 2011, if the estate tax is reinstated at the former 2001 level, the insurance may not be available to you in 2011 at any price.

LEAVE NOTHING TO CHANCE— MAKE A WILL

Your will is a statement that directs the disposition of your property when you die. Not only does a will ensure that your assets go to recipients of your choice, but it specifies how and when they are to receive them. If, for example, a beneficiary is young or financially unsophisticated, the will might provide that the property go to a trustee or a guardian for a specified period of time, with the income of the trust being paid to or on behalf of the beneficiary.

If you die without leaving a valid will, however, the disposition of your property will be in accordance with the intestacy laws of the state in which you reside. The property will go to your next of kin (heirs at law) in proportions and in a sequence mandated by the state. Although it is very rare, if there is no will, and there is no known next of kin within the definition of state law, your property may revert to the state.

What the will should do: Executors and guardians

Your most important task is to dispose of your assets in the manner you desire. To do this, you will need a trustworthy well-informed agent, known as an executor or executrix.

Your will should name the executor who will administer your estate. This means locating all assets, pursuing claims and collecting what is owed. The executor will dispose of assets in the most favorable manner and follow your specific gifting instructions or exercise such discretion as you have decided on and included in your will. Most important is the executor's job to ensure that what you desired as an end result actually occurs. To ensure that your estate is managed by people with ability, interest and loyalty, name contingent or successor executors. Keep your prospective executor(s) informed on the latest information concerning your assets and your desires or directives.

After you have selected a reliable executor and successor executor, don't let the matter rest. If they become unable or unwilling to serve, adjust your will and name new executors. And if you have minor children, the will should certainly name a guardian for them. Your choice of guardian might be the most important decision you can make, as he and/or she will raise your children.

Further, if you die without leaving a valid will, or if your executor is unable or unwilling to serve, a state court will choose an administrator who is paid out of estate assets. He may be interested only in collecting a fee, which could be far greater than what his services are worth. (See Chapter Ten, "Avoiding Appointment of an Administrator.")

Your words and intentions may have to be interpreted

Bear in mind that your will is a legal document. It should be prepared by a lawyer—but not just any lawyer. The law is highly specialized. The attorney who handles your business affairs may be competent with contracts, claims and other commercial matters, but unless he has specialized knowledge in the field of estate planning, he may overlook various traps. Standards must be met if the will is to serve your purposes. In commenting on one suit where a decedent's will had been prepared by his brother-in-law, who was an insurance agent, not an attorney, the court observed sadly, "This tax litigation is the consequence." Do not think that merely any written attempt to pass on property will accomplish your desired dispositions.

In this age of the Internet, do-it-yourself will kits and fill-in-the-blank documents are very accessible. It is often difficult to convince people to seek competent legal and/or accounting advice. We are always troubled knowing clients would spare no expense for their children's health or well-being, but would place the children's financial and guardian care in the hands of the unschooled, or be ruled by a cookie-cutter document. A few years back, a reputable magazine showed a picture of a young couple sitting on their porch overlooking a beautiful Maine beach. The caption told the story that to save $50, Grandpa wrote his own will. It cost the couple more than $50,000 to finally obtain the house he wanted them to have. Don't make this mistake. There is too much to lose, whether it's money, taxes or your family's well-being. It's just not worth it.

Also, be certain that the will expresses your wishes without ambiguity. Beneficiaries should be identified by name—"my son" means little if another boy is born after the will was drawn. Review the will when children are born, marry or die, and when Congress enacts substantial changes in the tax law, as happened with the 2001 tax law.

The will should always provide for residual or contingent beneficiaries in case a named beneficiary dies before you do, or the beneficiary, for whatever reason, refuses the bequest. This precaution prevents assets from being dissipated by being divided among next of kin or lost outright through escheat, meaning reversion to the state.

What a will cannot do

Even with a well-drawn will, you do not have full discretion as to the disposition of your property. State law dictates varying percentages of the estate that a surviving spouse is entitled to receive. The state in which you are domiciled may require that a surviving wife receive a certain percent of your property as a widow's or surviving spouse's share. If you leave her a lesser amount, she can "take against the will," receiving her required percent at the expense of your other beneficiaries. Some states still use the old legal designation for this right, known as *dower*. The corresponding right that may be claimed by a surviving husband is called *curtesy*, as well as a surviving spouse's share. In some states, children are entitled to specified percentages of the estate regardless of whether the parent provided for them in his will.

A decedent's right to dispose of property is further limited in a few states —for example, state law may hold that bequests to charitable organizations are not valid unless made more than 30 days before death.

A will may not carry out a testator's wishes if he hasn't anticipated various problems. It may not be possible on the basis of existing records for the executor to prove that the decedent had clear title to, or full ownership of, the property he wished to convey. The executor may not be able to identify or locate certain assets. Or the will may make certain bequests, but the estate lacks the money or property to implement them.

Conclusions and advice

• Make sure that your will is a clear and concise expression of all your wishes and desires. Leave nothing to chance and always provide a residuary clause so that if your intended beneficiaries are not around, someone of your choosing will inherit.

• Make certain that your executor will know where your assets are and what your exact intentions are.

• Have your will reviewed when there are changes in the tax law, in the needs of your beneficiaries, in your income or in theirs. If you move to a different state, check whether formal requirements are different, such as the minimum number of witnesses needed.

• Do not assume that you can leave your property to anyone you select, in whatever amounts you see fit.

• Do not assume that once you have made a will, everything will be taken care of according to your directions.

• Do not assume that your excellent family or business lawyer will also be competent in the entirely different field of estate planning.

• It is likely that additional changes will occur due to the 2011 sunset provision. Therefore, you must stay up to date with the estate tax provisions in the 2001 tax law or ask your attorney or accountant to notify you when there is a need to review your estate plan.

Chapter Six

THE WILL—
A MULTI-PROVISIONAL
DOCUMENT

A word of caution

Before the advent of the use of trusts as will substitutes, most estate planners used the will as the tried-and-true instrument. However, the current trend is avoidance of the use of wills and the jurisdiction of the probate court by the use of will substitutes. To fully understand the process and why the will has lost some of its luster, it should be understood that the probate court and its associated delays and expenses are at the core of the controversy (See Chapter Nineteen, "The Great Debate.")

Assets owned by the decedent in her name alone at the time of her death are generally said to be in her probate estate. They are, therefore, subject to probate court rules, jurisdiction and thus its expenses and delays.

The will distributes probate assets. The exception to this would be assets payable on death such as life insurance, accounts held jointly or accounts payable to a named beneficiary. Living trusts (as opposed to testamentary trusts), on the other hand, generally distribute assets which are not subject to the jurisdiction of the probate court—hence, the inclination of many to use the living trust instead of the will. We will discuss this topic at length, but understand, especially with all of the hype over trusts and probate, that this text presents all of the alternatives in a logical framework. The will is described first as it is the most familiar, but also because it is a most essential document even if trusts are your main estate planning documents. For even if you choose the trust approach, you will have what is commonly referred to as a "pour over" will. Therefore, the discussion at hand is both a useful and a necessary one.

Common provisions

The experienced estate planner can produce many different wills and/or will provisions for diverse clients. This is why we stress the need to avoid kits or fill-in-the-blank documents.

However, there is often no common ground nor provisions essential in every will. The key is to know what is necessary. For example, if your estate is less than $300,000 and you receive a 15 to 20 page document, chances are you're being taken advantage of. Unfortunately, things like this do occur.

What provisions will you want to include? Here's a reminder list with brief explanations. Some are covered in greater detail elsewhere. If you don't see a given example in your document, it may not apply to your situation, but ask your planner to be sure.

• Statement of marital status: Spouse's name and the name(s) of your children, if any, and their ages. *Note:* Include children by prior marriages or out of wedlock, even if embarrassing; otherwise this could have devastating effects.

• Appointment of executor, guardians, trustee(s) and their alternates: Always give full name and, if there are two by the same name, signify by status, i.e., my brother or Sr./Jr., etc. Always name alternates. Consider corporate fiduciaries as possible choices if need be.

• Granting of fiduciary powers: Your executor needs certain powers to deal with the probate assets, the estate in general and the trustee(s) after the trust is funded; the trustee(s) themselves need certain powers to deal with the trust assets. This includes the power to invest. You must grant your fiduciaries the powers to so act. Most states have adopted a form of the Uniform Fiduciary Powers Act, which may be incorporated into the will simply by referring to the appropriate state statute. It is advisable to do so.

• Debt, expense and tax clause: A common trap is to push off these charges to the residuary beneficiary. Many a plan has failed because these charges totally depleted the residuary. This clause can be as simple as a few lines and as complicated as many pages. Debts, expenses and taxes, as well as the funeral bills and the expenses of the last illness, by law must be paid before the beneficiaries begin to receive their entitlement. Talk to your adviser about the proper sharing of this burden, especially if you are considering large specific bequests and a smaller residuary.

• Personal property clauses: Very often wills provide a simple mechanism to dispose of personal property. For example, personal property can be left to the executor to dispose of as he sees fit, but you would have cleared with him what you really wanted done and trust that he will carry out those wishes. *Caution:* We have seen many arguments over personal property (of great or little value). Make preparations beforehand. In one example, the children of the decedent's prior marriage and his widow insisted we supervise the opening of the decedent's home safe, which contained about $138,000 in cash. After income tax on alleged unreported income, interest and penalties, as well as estate tax, approximately $40,000 was left. Certainly, the decedent could have planned better.

• Anatomical requests: We strongly recommend informing all concerned before and after executing your will. Do not leave these requests solely for publication in your will.

• Burial requests: As with anatomical requests, these instructions should be in your letter to your executor and also discussed with family and friends beforehand.

• Specific bequests:

  • Always state that if the person does not survive you, the gift lapses (is not paid).

  • If it is an asset, real or personal, and not cash or a percent of the estate, always state that if it is sold or disposed of, the gift lapses.

  • For real property that you wish to remain in the family, consider a restriction against sale or lease to outsiders or a reversion to either another family member with a similar restriction or to a charity.

  • Specific bequests may be to any person or entity and may be in any form. They may be, for example, to a charity, a favored niece or goddaughter. They can be for a specific amount or a specific asset or a set percentage of your estate. If a person has set up trusts during her lifetime, she can bequeath amounts to those trusts. We will discuss the credit-shelter trust below. As the credit is a specific amount, this, too, can be considered a specific bequest.

- The marital deduction clauses often used in wills can also be a specific bequest: "I bequeath to my husband the maximum amount which can pass free of federal taxation."

- While there is no limit to the number of specific bequests a will may have, always include a residuary clause.

- Bequests to children are common, and if your children lack the maturity to handle the bequest, consider putting the property into a trust with a "spendthrift provision."

- Credit-shelter trusts: See section below, "Trusts and Tax Provisions."

- Marital deduction: See section below, "Trusts and Tax Provisions."

- Qualified domestic trust (QDT) clause: See section below, "Trusts and Tax Provisions."

- Children's trusts: Generally parents do not wish their children to inherit their hard-earned assets (and retained funds) until they have reached a certain level of maturity and sophistication. For each child, that age may be different, and, when they are young, it is impossible to predict. Most planners recommend that if both parents were to die prematurely, trusts be established for the children until they at least reach age 21. Typically, the trusts are held longer and provide for discretionary payments of income and principal by the trustee during the child's formative years. Usually, a standard is set out, such as for health, maintenance, support and education. Thereafter, the trust provides for an incremental mandatory principal distribution at given ages, such as one-third of the principal balance at age 25, one-half of the balance at age 30 and the remaining balance at age 35. These trusts also often incorporate spendthrift provisions, which will be discussed in Chapter Fourteen.

- Residuary clause: A residuary clause is an absolute must. Once, after an excruciatingly long conference where a wealthy client had provided for literally dozens of specific bequests without a residuary, she asked, "Why do I need that?" The reply: "For the lottery ticket in your purse." She exclaimed, "I never thought of that!" Many things happen after the will is executed, from personal injury cases to the deaths of beneficiaries. Also, if you use a pour-over will (see Chapter Eleven), your residuary clause will send all of your remaining assets to the residuary trust.

- Simultaneous deaths clause (see Chapter Eight): You should anticipate that you and your spouse may die in a common accident. Your children will need guardians, which your will should provide for. It may be prudent to repay family members for loans given or gifts made to purchase assets if, in a joint death, others may end up with this asset.

- Disinheritance death clauses: Many clients prefer to state why they chose not to include a child, spouse or another person who may feel for some reason that they should be entitled to a bequest. Other clients think that if they leave the person $1, she cannot contest the will. Some believe if they make a bequest, but indicate that "...if he contests this will in any way, then he shall receive nothing," the limited bequest will be effective. Spouses generally may not be totally disinherited, as state law provides them with a statutory share. Some states have a similar rule for children. Such disinheritance provisions or clauses, however, have received mixed results. The best defense is competent advice, preparation and, in this case, a record of what has transpired.

Creative provisions

Estate planners over the years have developed a variety of creative provisions, based upon their experiences or unfortunate previous circumstances. Only the most qualified estate planning advisers will be up to date with most of these tools:

• The spendthrift provision to prevent creditors from attaching a beneficiary's interest in a trust.

• Prohibiting a trustee from using trust income to eliminate an obligation of support the trustee has toward a beneficiary (i.e., trustee mother using daughter's trust income for her private school education). Otherwise, this would cause taxable income to the trustee mother.

• Educational trust funds, made as a specific bequest for younger children, when older children have already been educated.

• Granting the power to the executor to seek permission of the appropriate court to hold a beneficiary's share in a special trust, even though not originally set out as such, due to changed circumstances such as drug or alcohol problems or severe mental health reasons.

• Reversions if charities do not honor your wishes with the use of real estate. Note, however, the possible loss of deductions. Sometimes the charities will not agree to the restrictions and will refuse the gift if it is so encumbered.

• A charitable remainder trust (see Chapter Seventeen) can be incorporated in your will and benefit family members for a term of years with the remainder going to charity.

• Many charitable bequests, scholarships, foundations and other good deeds.

• For those families with special children, a "special needs trust." (See Chapter Twenty.)

• For a spouse whose partner is suffering from a potentially long-term illness requiring extensive nursing home care, such as Alzheimer's, many planners consider a gift of only the minimum required by statute to a trust for that spouse. Usually, this will also include a gift of the balance of the estate to the children instead of the spouse in the event the healthy spouse dies prematurely. The intention is for the children to take care of their infirm parent with the excess funds that would otherwise be lost to his medical care, if he were the heir of all his wife's estate.

• For parents with estranged children or children being raised by a former spouse, your estate planner can inform you about a host of provisions.

Trusts and tax provisions

Generally, your will can achieve all of the tax benefits that are available to any decedent by either an outright bequest to your spouse or by incorporating in the will what is known as a *testamentary trust*. A testamentary trust is a trust established in your last will and testament.

The credit-shelter trust can be set up as an *inter vivos trust* (a trust established during your lifetime) or one within your last will and testament. Typically, a spouse with an estate over the credit amount in her own name (e.g., $2 million in 2002) will set up a credit-shelter trust (also known as a by-pass or credit-equivalent trust) for her spouse for his lifetime. The amount of the trust, assuming the will was executed in 2002, would be the amount of the credit determined in the year of her death ($1 million in 2002 and increasing to $3.5 million in 2009) with incremental increases between these years. No specific dollar amount is mentioned; rather, the bequest provides that it will be funded to the amount of that year's unified credit (see Appendix D).

Should the wife die, the husband beneficiary would have whatever rights the trust might grant. Because this trust is technically being taxed and the wife's unified credit being used to eliminate the tax, there is no need to pass the tests required of the marital deduction. If, for example, her husband was a spendthrift or was not the father of her children, the wife may wish to be very restrictive. On the other hand, if there were no concerns, she could be more liberal, always keeping in mind the effects of depletion from long-term health-care needs, remarriages and the unpredictable nature of life.

Upon the husband's death, the principal balance left in this by-pass trust would neither be taxed in his estate nor be subjected to his creditors, assuming he did not have a general power of appointment. The remaining principal would then pass to the remainder beneficiaries the wife had chosen. If her death occurred in 2002, the original corpus would have been $1 million. Assuming no depletion and reasonable growth, a sizable sum could pass tax free to her chosen heirs.

Using the above example, the balance of the decedent's estate could pass through her will. Assuming she wished to pay no tax, she must bequeath the balance to her husband outright or, more appropriately, to a marital deduction trust. Again, the client has some flexibility in her decision making. She can be as restrictive as limiting her husband's rights to a QTIP trust. In this case, he will and must receive all of the annual income. The trustee might also have the right to invade principal on the husband's behalf, which is usually limited to an ascertainable standard such as health, reasonable support, comfort, maintenance and education.

As noted before, upon the husband's death, the balance remaining in this QTIP or marital trust will be considered as having been in his estate and taxed accordingly. Although the trust provisions state that the balance will go to the heirs chosen by the wife in her will, it is customary that the trust's assets pay the tax bill and not the husband's estate on which the tax is levied. Note that in order for a non-US citizen to attain favorable tax treatment through his spouse's will, a qualified domestic trust should be set up.

All of these trusts can attain the same tax treatment whether set up through your last will and testament or by means of separate *inter vivos* trusts with pour-over wills.

Elder law and testamentary trusts

A trust created in your last will and testament is called a testamentary trust, while trusts created during one's lifetime are called living or *inter vivos* trusts. Under current federal law (Title XIX), testamentary trusts for the benefit of an individual are not considered to be an "available asset" of that individual. This means that the trust will not disqualify the beneficiary under Title XIX rules from programs and benefits. (See Chapter Twenty.)

This is a substantial concern in planning for the elderly and the disabled, as outright gifts from the estate usually cause the individual to lose some eligibility. While in some states and in some cases this rule has been challenged, it has logic. An individual certainly would not leave a disabled nephew a bequest that might disqualify him from current eligibility. Yet the individual may very well leave his nephew a trust to make the quality of his life better.

Conclusions and advice

• There is no right or wrong decision about using a will or a living trust with a pour-over will. In some states, one form is more prevalent than the other, and depending on the size of your estate, one may be less expensive and more appropriate. As always, consult your estate planner.

• Don't forget the key elements, especially relative to your age and family needs. For example, if you have minor children, you must appoint guardians, executors and where appropriate trustees, as well as alternates.

• Take the first step and put a plan in place. You are far better off having something you are 75% comfortable with than nothing at all. Clients with no will are happy to realize that the state won't end up with their money, but not when they hear their ne'er-do-well brother-in-law may end up as guardian of the children and "control" over their money, their smile disappears.

• A will can attain all of the tax savings that a trust offers. The pros and cons of wills vs. trusts will be discussed in Chapter Nineteen.

• Many clients start but never complete the process of estate planning for many reasons, including facing one's mortality, expense, fear or procrastination. None of these excuses can justify the unfortunate results of incomplete estate planning that we have observed.

Chapter Seven

JOINT AND MUTUAL WILLS

A husband may desire to leave all of his property, or a substantial portion of it, to his wife. But he fears that if he dies first, then upon her death, his remaining property will go to his wife's own relatives, friends and favorite charitable organizations. For her part, the wife may have comparable concerns. Even if the wills did make proper provisions, they can be revised after the first death. A common solution to this problem is a revocable trust which contains their respective assets and becomes irrevocable on the first death. This solution retains the marital deduction and, if there is anything remaining, assures the designated survivors will benefit. Another solution which has some proponents is the use of joint (or mutual) wills. Not all states allow and/or favor these concepts which, to some extent, establish a "contract" between spouses. Discuss these respective methods with your attorney, if these are your goals.

Joint (or mutual) wills

A solution to this common situation may take either of two related forms: the joint will or mutual wills.

A joint will, which is signed by both spouses, customarily provides that, on the death of one, all of the deceased spouse's property, or a designated substantial portion of it, will go to the survivor. On the death of the second spouse, that party's property (including what remains of the first spouse's wealth) will pass to specified relatives, friends and chosen charitable organizations of each spouse in amounts or in proportions that were agreed to when the will was prepared.

The main advantage of the joint will is that in it both spouses can make generous, perhaps total, provision for the survivor, with the assurance that their own relatives, friends and charities will not be by-passed upon the death of the second spouse. The main disadvantage is usually loss of the marital deduction, which is available only in the case of property that goes unencumbered to the surviving spouse. The marital deduction isn't available in joint wills because what the surviving spouse receives is not an outright transfer of property to do with as she sees fit. This is a requirement of the marital deduction, and because the surviving spouse does not have the right to dispose of this property according to her own wishes when she dies, the deduction is lost. The survivor receives the property subject to a preexisting formula of disposition. (See Chapter Four, "The Marital Deduction.") In one case, however, a husband and wife jointly signed a will providing that if they died simultaneously or so closely together that the survivor did not have time to probate the will, properties would go to beneficiaries designated in the document. Any property not so disposed of would go to the children in equal amounts. The marital deduction applied to this situation, according to the Internal Revenue Service (Technical Advice Memoranda 8523004, February 22, 1985).

Approved wording for use in a joint will

Here is an example of language used in a very simple form of joint will, quoted by the court in one case:

> "After the death of either of us, and after the payment of our funeral expenses and just debts, we give, devise and bequeath all the balance of our estate...of whatsoever kind and nature and wheresoever situated that either shall die seized and possessed of, to whomsoever shall be the survivor of us....At the time of the death of the survivor of us, or if we should both die at the same time, if there be anything left, then we give, devise and bequeath to our children, Raymond D. Dekker and Lillian Laughlin, all of our property...share and share alike."

A joint will can be very complex where detailed provision is made for ultimate specific bequests or proportions of the estate to various relatives, friends and the favorite charitable organizations of each spouse.

Approved wording for use in mutual wills

Mutual wills are separate testaments by each spouse, prepared after they agreed on how property dispositions at death will be made. One spouse, in effect, is agreeing to leave certain amounts or proportions of his property in a specified manner in return for the other spouse's agreement as to how she will leave her property. It becomes an enforceable contract.

Here is the language of a wife's mutual will quoted by a court in one decision:

"In consideration of the mutual will on this date executed by my husband, W.D. Newman, I give, devise and bequeath to my husband, W.D. Newman, all of my property, both real and personal, and all effects of every kind and nature whatsoever and wheresoever situated, of which I may die seized and possessed, or to which I may be entitled at the time of my decease, to have and to hold same as an absolute estate forever. This will is a mutual will executed contemporaneously with the aforesaid mutual will of my husband, W.D. Newman, and each is consideration for the other, and the provisions of same are reciprocal, and it is the express intention and desire, based upon said consideration, that each of our respective wills be irrevocable....

"In the event my husband shall be deceased at the time of my decease, then I give, devise and bequeath all of my property ...to my children, Arthur Newman, Mildred Jones and William D. Newman, Jr., in equal shares, share and share alike; and in the event that any of my said children predecease me leaving a child or children surviving, I direct that such child or children of my deceased child shall take per stirpes the parent's share, and in the event any of my said children shall be deceased at the time of my death leaving no child or children surviving, then I direct that the share of my said deceased child shall be divided among my children surviving me or their child or children surviving, who shall take per stirpes the parent's share."

The husband's will was similar in all of its provisions, except that where the wife's will left everything to the husband, his will left everything to her.

Mutual wills, too, can be very complex, especially in cases where only a specified amount or proportion of each spouse's property will go to the survivor, or where there is a detailed scenario as to how property remaining at the death of the second spouse is to be apportioned among various beneficiaries.

Approved wording for use in consent to other spouse's will

One spouse may, by a separate document, consent to be bound by the terms of the other's will in the case of property dispositions and other arrangements. Here is an example of the language of one such agreement quoted in court:

"I, EMMA BRESSANI, wife of RICHARD V. BRESSANI, also known as RICHARD VALENTINE BRESSANI, the maker of the foregoing Will, having read it in its entirety, and clearly understanding that my said husband by his said Will disposes not only of his separate estate, in case there be any such, but also all of our community property, including the share thereof which I would be entitled to take and receive by law upon his death, as well as his own share or interest therein, and being fully convinced in my own mind of the reasonableness and equity of said Will and the wisdom of its provisions, and in consideration of the provisions made for me therein, hereby elect to and do accept, acquiesce in and consent to said Will and all of its provisions, including disposition at the death of my said husband and [sic] all of our community property. I hereby accept such of the said provisions of said Will as apply to or concern me."

Danger of mutual wills

The possible weakness of mutual wills is that after property dispositions are agreed to by both spouses and the wills are reviewed by lawyers of both, one spouse subsequently may write a new will. Usually there is always a paragraph which specifically cancels any previous will. The consequence is that the wife, let us assume, has made dispositions in return for reciprocal commitments by her husband which he, without her knowledge, has later canceled. State laws and court decisions vary as to whether a mutual will creates a legal obligation or merely a moral one.

Under the laws of some states, the child of a party to mutual wills cannot be deprived of his rights if one spouse's will is replaced by a later version.

Common disasters

Joint and mutual wills should provide for the property dispositions to be made if both parties die simultaneously or when it is not possible to determine the order of dying in a common disaster. (See Chapter Eight, "Simultaneous Deaths of Spouses.")

What's right for you

Living in the Northeastern snowbelt, we usually can count on a mid-February phone call, at a time when the temperature is well below freezing with snow knee deep, from a client wintering in 80-degree weather. We call these phone inquiries "sun strokes."

The conversation normally goes something like this: "My good friend and neighbor here at 'Peaceful Palms' has been telling me that his financial adviser has put him into this great program and investment vehicle. It's fully insured and fully guaranteed with no probate, no attorney's fees, no death taxes and, best of all, nursing homes can't touch it. What do you think?"

These calls are very exasperating for the professional estate planner, but we understand the lure and tremendous sway people have over those who "want to believe."

Our usual response is to tell the client to think about what a person has to gain when they are selling you something, and get a second or even a third opinion. At least one opinion should be from an adviser whose job it is to counsel them about their estate planning choices, not merely to sell them a "stock off the shelf" product. In the case of a one-size-fits-all trust package, a canned joint will package or possibly long-term health-care coverage, they should consult a professional in the field. Recently, a nationally televised program aired a segment on the sale of promissory notes, allegedly "insured and guaranteed," being sold by trusted commissioned insurance agents. But the operative words here were "commissioned agents." A simple conference with an accountant who could have looked into the matter might have saved these small investors millions of dollars.

The foregoing paragraphs are simply to explain that mutual wills are only for a few, and joint wills, for even fewer. Yet some, to make a quick buck, will prepackage a form and suggest it's the new elixir of choice. Don't be fooled; be skeptical. Don't listen to your friends, neighbors or commissioned salespeople. They may all be truthful, honorable and quite possibly even knowledgeable. But be cautious and have everything verified by an objective professional (one who charges for his time and only that) whose only interest is to establish a long and continuing relationship with you. It is well worth the cost. In our opinion, the cost of peace of mind is cheap. Don't be tempted by those schemes brought on by your well-intentioned neighbors or those less honorable. And, if you are tempted, you can always call your trusted adviser, even if it is mid-February.

Conclusions and advice

• Realize that the use of joint or mutual wills may forfeit the marital deduction. Balance the consequences before making your choice.

• Inasmuch as state laws vary as to the effect of making joint and mutual wills, and simultaneous deaths of spouses, have the wills checked by an attorney who is familiar with the particular laws of your state. In some states, a beneficiary is not an acceptable witness. In others, the will must be handwritten. Competent advice is always the key.

• Provide for what is to happen if both spouses die simultaneously. If state law made disposition of a husband's property where his wife survived him by fewer than a specified number of hours/days, a detailed survivorship clause in the husband's will would have precedence over the state law.

• Do not use joint or mutual wills if divorce is likely.

• Do not take it for granted that a mutual will would not be repudiated.

• The parties should make living wills which state their wishes about life-sustaining treatment. Specific statements can be made about desired medical procedures such as cardiopulmonary resuscitation, artificial measures of nutrition, kidney dialysis, artificial respiration, surgery and medicines. These have nothing to do with wills *per se*, but are generally discussed with you by any skilled estate planner.

• If you think your situation may call for a joint or mutual will, consider the use of the revocable living trust. It may be a more desirable solution. Here, those assets that the parties wish to be retained for the surviving spouse, yet later passed on to specific beneficiaries (i.e., husband or specific children), can be placed in the trust during the spouses' lifetime. The trust can provide that it becomes irrevocable when one spouse dies. It can also provide that the desired assets flow to a specific child on the death of the second spouse. It is important to remember that tax savings devices such as the marital deduction and the credit shelter provisions can be utilized in connection with such a revocable living trust.

Chapter Eight

SIMULTANEOUS DEATHS OF SPOUSES

There is a tendency to assume that one spouse will die before the other does. However, it is wise to have contingency plans in case both spouses die in a common disaster, where it isn't possible to determine the sequence of their deaths. The order of their deaths is significant in many areas, such as the distribution of jointly owned property, life insurance, the marital deduction, powers of appointment and obtaining two unified credits.

Uniform simultaneous death legislation

State, not federal law, covers the sequence of deaths in a common disaster where there is not sufficient evidence that the parties died otherwise than simultaneously. Most states have adopted some version of the Uniform Simultaneous Deaths Act, to solve the problem of the passage of property when distribution depends upon the order of death when the circumstances are not ascertainable.

Reason for a will

The sequence of death can be an important planning issue. For the wealthy, it may impact on the use of the couple's two unified credits or the marital deduction. For the elderly, or where one spouse is in debt, it may mean keeping assets out of the reach of long-term-care facilities or creditors.

Young couples often receive family assistance in buying their first home. If they die simultaneously, without a proper repayment provision in their wills, one set of relatives might end up with all of the assets. Consider, also, the couple who cannot agree on guardians or remainder beneficiaries. Their wishes will have a much better chance of being carried out if they are properly articulated in your will.

Joint ownership of property

In a state that has adopted the Uniform Simultaneous Deaths Act, where there isn't sufficient evidence that two joint owners of property or "tenants by the entirety" have died other than simultaneously, the property so held is to be distributed one-half as if one had survived and one-half as if the other had survived. Ordinarily, in a joint tenancy, upon the death of one owner, all of the property goes to the survivor(s). In the case of a tenancy by the entirety, which can be used only by legally married couples, the entire property goes to the survivor. (See Chapter Twenty-Two, "Choice of Forms of Ownership.")

For federal estate tax purposes, where property is held in a tenancy by the entirety at the time of, say, the wife's death, one-half the value of the property will be included in the wife's gross estate. The other one-half will be part of the husband's estate. This is in accord with the Uniform Simultaneous Deaths Act.

Life insurance

Where there is a policy of insurance upon the life of one person, payable upon her death to a named beneficiary, the insured will be presumed to have survived the beneficiary under the Uniform Simultaneous Deaths Act. It is therefore advisable for a contingent beneficiary to be named so that the proceeds go to a specifically selected person should both the insured and the beneficiary die in a common disaster.

In one situation, a wife owned insurance policies on her husband's life. They were killed simultaneously in an airplane crash, and the Internal Revenue Service sought to include the policy proceeds in her gross estate. But under the Uniform Simultaneous Deaths Act, at the moment of her death the proceeds of the policies on his life had not yet matured by reason of his death, so only the value of the policies at that moment, and not the death benefit, was included in her estate.

The marital deduction

In states where the Uniform Simultaneous Deaths Act is in force, and it is impossible to determine the sequence of death of husband and wife, the estate is not entitled to the marital deduction since no property could have passed from one spouse to the other.

Except for qualified terminable interest property, no marital deduction is available in cases where the interest passing to a surviving spouse is a terminable one. (See Chapter Four, "The Marital Deduction.") The will often specifies that the only conditions under which passage of property to the survivor would be ineffectual are (1) a common disaster in which both spouses die, or (2) death of the surviving spouse within six months of the testator's death. If neither of these conditions occurs, then the marital deduction is preserved.

Reverse simultaneous death clause

A will may provide that, in the case of a common disaster, the person who wrote the will shall be deemed to have died first. The wills of both husband and wife can contain such a provision. The property going to the spouse surviving under this created presumption will qualify for the marital deduction. Also, in larger estates, a couple may wish to use this concept so both can qualify for their unified credits. It is possible to have a spouse presumed to outlive the other in order to fund a credit-equivalent trust, thereby taking advantage of two unified credits. This is an extremely important point and should not be missed.

Power of appointment

The gross estate may include a power of appointment created by will where the party to whom the power was granted, the holder, died prior to the probating of the will that created the power. This may come about where the creator of the power and the holder die in a simultaneous accident. If, under state law, the holder's power of appointment becomes effective immediately and is not postponed until probate or until any other time later than the death of the creator of the power, then the holder possessed the power at the time of death. Therefore the property subject to the power is included in the gross estate of the holder, even though there never was an opportunity to exercise the power.

Will provisions

Consider providing that if the spouses die in a common disaster, each spouse will leave their now-orphaned children the assets which would otherwise have gone to the surviving spouse.

A will or other instrument or form of property disposition may provide for two or more beneficiaries in a designated manner of succession. For example, property may be bequeathed to an individual's son and daughter, with the provision that if these beneficiaries should not survive the testator, their shares will pass to the testator's grandchildren; the amount each grandchild receives would be a proportion of what the original beneficiaries would have received. The Uniform Simultaneous Deaths Act provides that where two or more beneficiaries are named to inherit successively by reason of survivorship under another person's disposition of property, and there is not sufficient evidence that these beneficiaries died otherwise than simultaneously, the property thus disposed of will be divided into as many equal portions as there are successive beneficiaries. These portions would then be distributed respectively to those who would have inherited in the event that each designated beneficiary had survived.

Conclusions and advice

• Have local counsel check the simultaneous deaths law of the particular state in which you live, as state law may govern federal tax treatment.

• Name contingent beneficiaries on all dispositive documents in the event of simultaneous deaths.

• Check carefully to see whether you are willing to have the Uniform Simultaneous Deaths Act apply in light of the unified credit. If you are not willing, adopt a reverse simultaneous death clause in your will. Review periodically.

• Do not assume that spouses will die at different times, despite major differences in age or state of health.

• Do not assume that the Uniform Simultaneous Deaths Act is confined to spouses. For example, it also applies to unrelated joint owners of property.

• Even if spouses die in a common disaster, the simultaneous deaths law may not apply. There may be evidence that one died before the other.

• This is another case where the new 2001 tax law presents us with some interesting planning dilemmas. As noted, the unified credit will increase from $1 million in 2002 and 2003 to $1.5 million in 2004 and 2005, and then up to $2 million in 2006, 2007 and 2008, and finally up to $3.5 million in 2009. At these levels you may not need two full unified credits. Therefore, when drafting your wills, the Simultaneous Death Clause could be ignored for some time, with smaller estates. However, if the estate tax is allowed to return in 2011, the unified credit may drop back to the 2001 level, causing your estate plan to be potentially flawed because it may be necessary to have a reverse assumption made, in order to save unnecessary taxation from occurring. You could postpone addressing the problem until 2011, but our advice is to take care of this now.

• Be sure to ask your estate planner to help in this area. The planner will understand and explain to you the choices and pitfalls involved. Remember also the potential for appreciation and/or increase in the size of your estate by 2011. Also consider providing for relatives who may have "loaned or given" you assets. It may be appropriate that they receive a bequest to "repay" them for their generosity before others share in your estate.

Chapter Nine

BEQUESTS IN PERCENTAGES

A will often makes bequests in the form of specific dollar amounts, such as, "To my beloved daughter Mabel, if she survives me, the sum of $25,000." But this standard practice assumes:

1. That the dollar value of the estate to be distributed is known with some reasonable degree of accuracy.

2. That there will be enough wealth available to implement the designated dollar bequests.

Dollar amount available for beneficiaries is unpredictable

Making such assumptions, especially in times of economic uncertainties, can create problems. Specific-dollar bequests do not guarantee that the decedent's estate will be distributed in accordance with his wishes, although this is one of the principal objectives of estate planning. These factors make specific-dollar bequests unadvisable:

• The actual size of an estate may depend largely on matters that can't be determined without extensive appraisals by specialists, efforts to make arm's-length sales or actual litigation. For example, stock in a closely held corporation may never have been sold in a truly arm's-length transaction. In that case, the value of the stock is questionable. Establishment of value for federal estate tax purposes may have to await negotiations with the Internal Revenue Service, or lawsuits that could take years. Even after a settlement is made with the IRS, the executor may have to wait some time for a buyer who will pay an acceptable price.

• Substantial assets may not be susceptible to valuation at the time a will is written. There might be unknown wealth, an inheritance, a winning lottery ticket, a long-forgotten interest in a uranium mine, an unspectacular franchise in what unexpectedly becomes a choice location, a personal injury or wrongful-death claim resulting in a large award. The very event that took the decedent's life may have made his estate wealthy.

- You may not suspect the true value of jewelry, works of art, old stock certificates and other property. Or a nuisance value claim might unexpectedly produce a large payout.

- Between the time of the writing of the will and the testator's death, inflation may have swollen the dollar amount of the assets mightily.

Who really benefits from dollar bequests

If the estate's assets are worth more than the testator had believed, the real beneficiaries are the remaindermen (residuary beneficiaries), who will receive whatever is left after specific-dollar bequests are made to the other beneficiaries. In this situation the remainderman may not be the person(s) for whom you would wish to provide most generously.

An individual might have the specific-dollar bequests in his will reviewed frequently to ensure that each beneficiary's portion is realistic in light of the testator's wealth at that time. But the certainty of a dollar bequest is just what makes it uncertain. What is the dollar itself going to be worth?

Solution: Make your bequests in the form of percentages of your estate rather than predetermined dollar amounts. If inflation or assets of unsuspectedly high value make the estate worth more than you had anticipated, the originally conceived allocations of your dollar worth will be self-adjusting. On the other hand, if the estate should prove to be smaller than you had anticipated, the beneficiaries you named continue to be the recipients of your bounty, but bequests will automatically be scaled down proportionately.

How to make percentage bequests

The percentages you apportion to the beneficiaries may be made applicable to what remains after certain specific bequests are made: A certain piece of jewelry for your sister, stock in your business for your son and daughter, dollar

60

amounts for your favorite charities. Some specific-dollar bequests could also be made to individuals, with percentages then being designated for the residue of your estate.

The percentages should take into account certain minimum provisions required by state law. For example, most states provide a decedent's widow with a dower or elective right to a specified percentage of her late husband's wealth that she is entitled to claim at the expense of other beneficiaries if the will has left her a lesser amount. A surviving husband may have a comparable elective right, sometimes referred to as curtesy, against his wife's assets. In a few states, children are entitled to a minimum percentage of a parent's estate under specified circumstances.

Conclusions and advice

- Check with local counsel for the minimum percentages that your state requires you to leave a spouse or children in light of dower, curtesy and child-entitlement laws.

- Make contingency or alternative revisions of the percentages to provide for the possibility that a named beneficiary may die before you do or may renounce her inheritance. Consider that you and your named beneficiary may die simultaneously.

- Do not assume that your dispositions must be on an "all or none" basis—that is, all in the form of dollar bequests or all in the form of percentages of your estate.

- Do not assume that percentage bequests will automatically make all the adjustments required by changing circumstances. For example, this procedure will make adjustments attributed to inflation in the value of your assets. But you need to pay special attention to deal with the varying effects of inflation upon the incomes and requirements of each beneficiary. For instance, one beneficiary may be living on a fixed income, while another is a business person whose salary or profits may pretty well follow inflation.

Chapter Ten

AVOIDING APPOINTMENT OF AN ADMINISTRATOR

An individual's greatest responsibilities to her estate and beneficiaries is to make realistic plans for the selection of the proper executor or executrix. But the person or persons painstakingly designated may not actually serve in this capacity due to their death, lack of interest or incompetence, or "unavailability" when the time arrives. Another possible problem occurs when the decedent's will cannot be accepted for administration (probate) because of technical shortcomings, such as lack of the minimum number of witnesses stipulated by state law.

In any of these cases, the local court with jurisdiction over decedents' estates will name an administrator or administratrix. Such a person would have powers similar to those of the nonexistent or nonqualified executor, but sometimes with severe limitations.

Dying intestate

A dying person with a valid last will and testament that is located and admitted for administration, commonly called probate settlement, has her estate administered by an executor. Should the executor fail or be unable to serve, and no successor is named in the will, then the court will usually appoint an administrator CTN ("with the will annexed").

If a person dies without a will, she is said to have died intestate, and an administrator is named to settle her estate. In brief, his job is to (1) locate and amass all assets, (2) liquidate assets for ultimate distribution to avoid waste, (3) pay funeral expenses as well as bills incurred during the decedent's last illness, (4) pay other creditors and federal and state estate and death taxes, (5) pay administrative costs and (6) distribute the balance to the heirs.

It is important to note that an administrator receives his powers from the probate court and not the decedent's will, as there is none. Therefore, there is usually no power to continue a business under most state laws; this right must be approved by the courts, and yet the appointed administrator may not be capable, both by lack of education and inexperience, of running the business. While a will generally grants the executor several powers to avoid needless depletion of the estate through a forced sale of assets in other than optimum times, an administrator has no such powers. For this reason alone, all business owners should consider a will as a mandatory business document. Obviously, it is in everyone's interest to pass his property through valid testamentary documents. The alternative, dying intestate, allows state law to take over and dictate which heirs will receive your assets. The additional problem is that the estate is administered by an administrator unfamiliar with the business.

Shortcomings of administrators

A court-appointed administrator is unlikely to have any concern for your beneficiaries and their interests. He may not have the knowledge or ability to implement your plans. He may be a relative of the judge or a political crony with no interest in the administration of your estate beyond collecting his fee, which he is unlikely to discount. He may not even be competent.

Obviously, not all administrators fall into this dismal classification. The administrator may be even more suitable than the person you named. But you can't afford to take a chance on which administrator will be named because of your failure to make proper plans to see that your choice, who feels a sense of responsibility to you, will serve. It is, most assuredly, in the best interest of your estate plan and your beneficiaries that you name an executor. At the very least, an administrator is unlikely to have known you or your plans for your heirs and/or beneficiaries. Nor will he know your preferences or any special directives you may want fulfilled.

How an administrator can be counterproductive

An administrator's performance can hurt your estate in the following ways:

1. He may fail to collect all of the estate's assets by neglecting to make a diligent and careful search for every property. The discovery and gathering in of the decedent's properties may require a great deal of hard work and imagination, as will be explained in future chapters.

2. The estate may be subjected to unnecessary penalties and interest payments because of sloppy or tardy filing of estate and other tax returns. In some instances, the beneficiaries can compel an administrator to bear the consequences of his mistakes out of his own pocket. But few beneficiaries know this.

3. Amounts may be paid to otherwise valid claimants whose rights are unenforceable under state law because of late submission or technical reasons.

4. The administrator may devote too little time and vision to the task of seeking out the best markets for estate assets that must be sold to raise funds.

5. He may be indifferent to the pleas of beneficiaries for prompt honoring of bequests. This may be the result of the administrator's inexperience, that is, he may be so fearful of making a mistake that could penalize him personally that he pays out nothing until the federal tax liability is finally determined. For example, if an executor or administrator has any knowledge or reason to believe that the distribution of estate assets would jeopardize the ability of the Internal Revenue Service to collect its taxes, he can be held personally responsible for distributions that leave the IRS without payment. This rule does not apply, however, if the administrator has no reason to believe that IRS claims would be imperiled by implementing a bequest made in the will.

6. To avoid difficult or time-consuming problems, the administrator may dump estate assets too quickly to obtain the best possible price. For example, he may not wish to run the decedent's business, which could be a very

important estate asset. In consequence, the business may be liquidated or otherwise disposed of in excessive, expensive haste. Actually, the decedent may have wished to have the business continued so that her children could take over the operation. The administrator here, instead of seeking to implement the decedent's objectives, has frustrated them.

7. The estate may be kept open too long so that the administrator can "earn" more fees, and these fees will come out of the pockets of those who may have a better right to the money.

8. The administration may fail to obtain insurance on estate-owned assets. Perhaps the type of insurance required couldn't have been obtained without extensive shopping around.

9. The administrator may not be honest. This might apply to an executor, of course. But presumably the testator took great care to select someone whose probity was substantially demonstrated many times.

10. Under the 2001 tax law and the complicated carryover basis rules, the administrator must not only research and determine the cost basis of your assets, but also must allocate the step-up amongst your heirs. These are very important tasks to leave to someone who might be unsophisticated financially.

How to avoid the naming of an administrator

To ensure that the executor you choose will serve, you should:

1. Ask your designated executrix whether she will actually serve if named in your will. Do this periodically. Is this person's health still satisfactory? Has she taken on full-time responsibilities elsewhere? Is she still interested in you and your beneficiaries? If not, replace her.

2. Ensure your designated executrix's agreement to serve by recommending knowledgeable and able attorneys, accountants and (where appropriate) appraisers and brokers who can help her carry out her responsibilities comfortably and with expert guidance.

3. Name one or more successors or contingent executors so that, if the person of your choice doesn't serve, your second or third choice will settle your estate rather than an administrator whom you never would have engaged.

4. Name a bank or trust company as coexecutor. This virtually assures the permanence and continuity of an executor you have seen fit to name.

5. Make certain that your will is valid so that the executor chosen by you will qualify. Have an attorney who is familiar with state law check such requirements as the minimum number of witnesses necessary. State laws vary on the technicalities to be met.

6. Be sure that your will can be found when the time comes to have it probated. A perfectly executed and technically correct will is useless if nobody knows where it is. Leave your will in your attorney's office, or with your federal income tax work papers.

Conclusions and advice

• Make available to your executor-to-be the names of your attorney, accountant, broker, insurance agent and other persons knowledgeable about aspects of your affairs so that he can do the best possible job. Otherwise, the executor you have named may be removed by the court as incompetent, to be replaced by an administrator. (See Chapter Fifty-Four, "A Letter to Your Executor.")

• Make plans to keep your business out of the hands of an administrator. (See Chapter Forty-Three, "Business-Continuation Arrangements.")

• Advise your attorney, spouse or any other interested person to take action if for any reason your named executor isn't able to serve. For example, if the will is technically flawed and therefore inadmissible to probate, have the court petitioned to name as administrators the individuals you have chosen as executors. (Unfortunately, you can't be sure the court will agree.)

• Do not assume that the executors named in your will are going to outlive you, or will be perpetually willing and/or competent to serve.

• Do not name as executor a spouse, adult child or friend whose inexperience might result in performance so poor that a court will replace him with an administrator.

• Do not choose as an executor an unimaginative person who will resign in frustration after he discovers that certain information is not available. Actually, a resourceful person may be able to discover everything that is needed with a little hard work, time and attention. For example, if there were any insurance policies on the decedent's life, although the policies themselves or even premium notices cannot be found, he could call the National Consumers Insurance Helpline, which operates a missing policy service at 800-942-4242 and ask for a missing-policy questionnaire. The name, address, etc., of the decedent is forwarded by this group to all companies that participate in the Helpline (unfortunately, all insurers are not participants in the program). Also, an executor may trace heirs or others who may know where the decedent had assets. A thorough and energetic executor can find just about anybody or anything today. With the use of several helpful references and the Web, your executor can unearth accounts and people that letters to local banks or tax returns don't surface. Just keeping a watchful eye on the decedent's mail during the probate process is likely to uncover most assets. But your fiduciary must be willing to take the time to do this and not be primarily concerned with the speedy closure of the estate and/or collecting a fee.

• The 2001 tax law returns the carryover basis law. Therefore you must provide your executor with as much information as possible about the cost basis of each asset you own. This is crucial and your executor or administrator must find out what, if anything, is missing. Also they have important allocation duties when it comes to the partial free "step-up" in basis. (See Chapter Twenty-Two, "Choice of Forms of Ownership.")

TRUSTS: AN OVERVIEW

Understanding the field of trusts is as difficult as learning the nuances of your first computer. However, the stakes are quite different as is the potential effect on your estate—upon your demise.

To set the stage, we generally speak about two types of trusts—testamentary and *inter vivos*.

Testamentary trusts are those created in a person's last will and testament. As wills do not take effect until the person dies, these trusts have no viability until death. They cannot be funded, as they do not exist until the person dies. Hence, a testamentary trust is unfunded with only an expectation of receiving assets upon the testator's death.

The other major category of trusts is the *inter vivos* trust. *Inter vivos* or living trusts are executed and funded, albeit with possibly the most modest of donations, during the lifetime of the person creating the trust (settlor, grantor, trustor, etc.).

For the most part, Chapters Eleven through Nineteen will deal with living or *inter vivos* trusts which have experienced significant change and revitalization over the past few decades. These changes involve tax law and estate planning in general. These advances also include protective measures for family members who are seriously ill, the recently divorced or widowed, and young children or those with special needs.

As you will see, there is something for just about everyone. Caution: Not every trust is right for every person; nor do every person's needs justify the cost of drawing up sometimes expensive documents. There may be other ways to efficiently handle a situation. In truth, like most issues you face, there are always alternatives. Again, we caution you to first seek competent counsel and remember that if the person is selling a product instead of charging you for his time and advice, you would be wise to seek a second and confirming opinion.

Types of *inter vivos* trusts

The major subset of *inter vivos* trusts is the distinction between ones that are revocable and ones that are irrevocable. In a revocable trust, someone, usually the settlor, retains the power to change, amend, modify or completely revoke the trust. In some cases, beneficiaries, trustees, courts or disinterested third parties might also be given some or all of these rights.

The irrevocable trust simply cannot be revoked by the settlor and generally cannot be changed or modified. Some irrevocable trusts do have provisions allowing a trustee to modify the instrument prospectively to conform to changes in the law. Generally, however, once they are set up, they cannot be changed. Many states presume, unless the document provides to the contrary, that a trust is irrevocable. Therefore, be sure your instrument clearly identifies which type of trust you intend.

Funded vs. unfunded or dry trusts

Another subset of *inter vivos* trusts deals with the status of its assets. In order to create the trust, an element of consideration must pass between the grantor and the trustee. Yet, $1 is sufficient to pass this hurdle, and therefore the question of funding can best be explained by the following situational uses or examples:

• A funded irrevocable Crummey trust (see page 73) might be set up by a parent or grandparent for his children or grandchildren using his annual gift tax exclusion for each beneficiary.

• A funded irrevocable Crummey trust might be used by a couple to buy survivor life insurance to help pay the death taxes when both have died.

• A funded charitable remainder trust might be used to provide for the sale of appreciated, yet low-income-earning, assets, to be reinvested into higher-yielding assets. No tax will be paid on the sale, and the grantor receives higher annual income.

- An unfunded revocable trust with a pour-over will may be your choice of documents to distribute your estate. Upon your death, this simple will pours everything from your estate into the previously unfunded trust. This trust contains all of the tax and other planning provisions you have designed.

- A funded revocable trust with a pour-over will is the same as the above, except that during your lifetime, assets have already been placed under the protection of the trust. This offers some asset protection and trustee involvement in the event of your incapacity. Many estate planners recommend these over unfunded trusts, even though it requires the transfer of current assets.

- Life insurance trusts are commonly referred to (as such) and may be revocable or irrevocable as established by the grantor. Unless there is a cash surrender value, the policies themselves may have no value, and therefore the trusts were often called "dry trusts." They are, however, funded.

- A qualified personal residence trust is a funded irrevocable trust designed to eliminate a personal residence from the grantor's gross estate.

The next chapter offers more examples of different uses for trusts in the estate planning arena. The above examples show that there are several funding options for revocable or irrevocable trusts. Generally, the options are limited only by one's goals, desires, imagination and, of course, available assets.

Common misconceptions

A common misconception among the general public is that trusts are only for wealthy individuals. This may be the result of high-profile, newsworthy trusts, such as that of Jacqueline Kennedy Onassis or the trust involving *The New York Times*. Or because trusts are usually more costly to set up than wills, or because of the stereotype of "trust fund" heirs as "rich people."

However, trusts are not only for the wealthy. They are for almost anyone, or for anyone prepared to venture into the field of estate planning, willing to have an open mind on the best way to approach the attainment of his goals. This is true whether the goal is preservation of assets, protection of loved ones, saving on taxes (both income and estate taxes), enhanced privacy, reducing fees on death or on what passes to your heirs.

As far as expenses, try to keep things in perspective; this is also true of your estate planning documents. Your average new car may cost between $20,000 and $30,000. If you have bought or leased a car for your family for transportation, you can afford to pay the equivalent of a monthly loan payment to protect your family's future. That car won't run forever, but your estate plan will remain as solid as Gibraltar. Another word of caution. This is your family. Just as you would not put them in an unsafe vehicle, do not forsake the estate planning professional for the Internet or similar schemes or do-it-yourself kits.

A second misconception is equally pervasive, but not as serious. Many people believe that if they have a trust, presumably funded, there is no need for a will. But, even with a funded trust, it is likely that there will be assets left over. Unfortunately, that "something" may be a substantial asset or, in some cases, an important element of one's estate plan.

For example, the decedent's death may be a cause of action that could produce a large accidental settlement. Without a will to pour that asset into the previously created trust, the settlement would pass under the laws of intestate succession. Possibly you have young children; without a will, the courts will be forced to guess your choice of guardian. Although the pour-over will may be somewhat simple, it is a necessary component of your estate plan. Your family's welfare is at stake.

Probably the most dangerous of all myths about trusts is that you can "avoid probate," all taxes, maintain complete privacy, pay less administrative costs and expenses and attain a level of successful estate planning that wills cannot provide. The relative merits of many of these arguments will be discussed in Chapter Nineteen. However, it is important to understand that extremely competent estate planners have different opinions about the relative merits of trusts and wills.

Given the difference in state laws, procedures and taxation, as well as your individual situation, it takes qualified estate planning advice to help you choose what is best for you. Do not lose sight of the fact that there are many different types of trusts for many different types of situations. Proper planning can help you pick from the potpourri of provisions, and from the many vehicles and funding mechanisms available.

Trusts, therefore, are not for just the wealthy, or for the faint of heart. They can be a multifaceted tool. Yet, there are no guaranteed, foolproof instruments to accomplish everyone's goals and/or meet their every need.

Common estate planning trusts

It is not possible for us to include every possible trust variation or fully explore each one. Your adviser will help you in this area. Here are the most common trusts and trust provisions. Our goal is to give you sufficient knowledge to discuss trusts and their applicability to your estate, and pique your interest to explore other possibilities.

Commonly used trusts:

Marital deduction trusts: Designed to provide for the surviving spouse amounts meant to qualify for the marital deduction.

QTIP trusts: Designed for the surviving spouse and to qualify for the marital deduction as qualified terminable interest property.

QDT trusts: Designed for the noncitizen resident spouse and to qualify for the marital deduction.

Credit-shelter trusts (or by-pass or credit-equivalent trusts): Designed to use the decedent's unified credit. Trust may be for the benefit of the surviving spouse or any person.

Life insurance trusts: Trusts that own life insurance as part of their assets.

Irrevocable trusts with Crummey powers: Trusts where the Crummey power (see below) is used to preserve the annual gift tax exclusion.

Generation-skipping trusts: Trusts that skip a generation and take advantage of the amount that may be passed tax free to the second generation below that of the grantor. The 2001 tax law has significantly affected these.

Dynasty trust: A trust designed to remain in operation through many generations. By recent state law, it has been sanctioned, but not by all states.

Qualified personal residence trusts: A split-interest trust that allows the grantor to remove his residence from his estate.

Charitable remainder trusts: A split-interest trust allows the grantor to have income, yet gives the principal to charity upon the demise of both the grantor and his spouse.

Grantor trusts: Trusts, usually family related, where the grantor is taxed on the income, although the benefits may be designated for other family members.

Income tax defective trusts: A type of grantor trust designed purposely to be income taxed to the grantor, although the assets remain out of the grantor's estate.

Short-term trusts: No longer an effective estate planning tool, but can grant use of property for a short time to another and then return it to the grantor.

Voting trusts: Used in the business context to allow an owner to put his shares in trust to be voted by the trustee.

Qualified subchapter S trusts (QSST): One of the trusts sanctioned by the IRS to own an S corporation's shares.

Electing small-business trust: The other trust sanctioned by the IRS to own S corporation shares.

Grantor retained interest trusts (GRIT): Split-interest trusts in which the grantor retains rights and the remaindermen own the residual rights in the asset.

Special needs trust: Designed for persons with disabilities.

Income-only trust: Designed for people entitled to government benefits.

Common provisions:

Spendthrift: Protects trust assets against creditors and prohibits beneficiaries from squandering or assigning (discounting) their benefits.

Income sprinkle clause: Income can be dispensed disproportionately among beneficiaries.

Ascertainable standards: Such as health, maintenance, support and education, by which a trustee decides to make a distribution.

Crummey power: Allows donee limited access to a gift to a trust in order for the gift to qualify for the annual gift tax exclusion.

Power to disburse income and principal (mandatory and discretionary): Trustee's power, usually discretionary if beneficiary is a minor, mandatory for income in a QTIP trust.

5 + 5 power: Annual power of the beneficiary to withdraw principal. Anything exceeding this 5 + 5 limit ($5,000 or 5% of corpus) would cause trust corpus to be in the beneficiary's federal gross taxable estate.

Inflation/recession-proofing your trust: Grant trustee powers to increase payments as inflation causes living needs to change.

Staggered principal distributions: For minor children upon attaining ages 25/30/35, as an example.

General powers of appointment: Beneficiary can appoint principal to anyone he chooses (including himself).

Special or limited powers of appointment: Power to appoint is limited to a specific class, i.e., children of grantor (see Chapter Forty-Seven).

Alternate trustee selection process: Trustee replacement clause.

Fiduciary Powers Act and other powers: Incorporate them into your document; include right to retain current assets and to continue to operate decedent's business.

Submission of trust to court jurisdiction: Gives trustee/beneficiaries right to go to court and ask it to begin supervision; often prevents impasses between trustee and beneficiaries.

Business, home and other advancement of loans to the beneficiary: Often a useful provision to help beneficiary access his share.

Purchase of life insurance on grantor: Vital in life insurance trust.

Business continuation: Needed provision where businesses are involved.

Charitable bequests: Attains charitable deductions.

Escape clauses and exit strategies: Allows for termination if trust size is too small or for other reasons, i.e., divorce.

Trustee removal clauses: Often useful if you have disputes. Beneficiaries should not have the right to remove a trustee, but they may submit question to the courts.

Minimizing trust fees: Set forth language negating common presumptions, i.e., scheduled fees.

Holding trust property for liquidation at the proper time: Granting the rights to retain property.

Powers to amend, revoke and modify: For revocable trusts.

Retained interests: For revocable trusts only.

Old law meets new generation

Much of the American legal system concerned with wills, estates and trusts is based upon what occurred many centuries ago in Great Britain. In most states, British common law still has an effect on our statutes and court-made rules. Additionally, the laws dealing with trusts have, to a large extent, been somewhat developmentally lacking as far as both legal precedent (court cases interpreting trust law), and passage of new state statutes.

To some extent, this is because trusts were not widely used. Until recently, abuses were not that common, and very few high-profile cases made it to the court system. At the same time, many state legislators did not see trust law as a pressing area of reform.

However, in our opinion, this does not mean that reform is not needed. Consider a hypothetical multimillion-dollar lottery winner. Assume he is married, with three adult children and six grandchildren, and that he takes $20 million as a lump sum, after taxes, and that he and his wife will never even use the income from his winnings.

Aside from income, estate and generation-skipping taxes, a logical estate planning goal would be to provide for the family for generations to come. What a legacy he and his wife could leave if they could set up a trust that would essentially last forever!

However, many states still follow the old British law known as the "rule against perpetuities." Without delving into legal technicalities, suffice it to say that this law was designed to stop trusts from passing through several successive generations without ever distributing the principal to a beneficiary outright. When the rule was designed, British knights wanted to keep their properties out of the hands of their female descendants and drafted trusts that never ended. The rule prevented trusts from lasting beyond a certain date.

Today, in the United States, the law has little or no value, except to ensure that at some point a trust will cease, regardless of its utility. In many states, that "point" is still 21 years after the death of the last trust beneficiary who is alive on the day the instrument was created (in legal terms, "a life in being plus 21 years").

Many states are considering revoking this law; many have already done so. Therefore, if you win such a lottery prize or if you simply wish to so provide for your family, you are well advised to ask if your state still follows this antiquated rule. If it does, seek out a state which allows such a dynasty trust and hire counsel that can assist you in forming one.

The Uniform Laws Committee of the American Bar Association has done important recent work on trusts. It has prepared and suggested a Uniform Trust Act which will help clarify the law in many areas that sorely need explanation. Ask your estate planning adviser if a version of the law has been passed in your state and how it affects what you are planning to do.

Conclusions and advice

• Trusts are not only for the wealthy. The key to success is to match your needs with the trusts and provisions available.

• Do not assume that you have nothing with which to fund a trust. Life insurance often allows you to provide for your family using the protective measures of a trust.

• Beware of well-intentioned advice or commissioned salespeople. Your qualified estate planning adviser can usually recommend several professionals known for their integrity and who do business with companies of equal integrity.

• Each state has different laws dealing with wills, trusts, estates, probate and/or creditors' rights. Be sure you are dealing with an attorney who knows the law in your state.

• If you would like to pass assets on to successive generations (a dynasty trust), determine if your state still follows a version of the "rule against perpetuities." If it does, and substantial assets are involved, shop around. Find a state that allows trusts to extend to successive generations and find a qualified attorney in that state. Remember, such trusts must be integrated with both the generation-skipping tax and the normal estate and gift tax rules.

• If Congress repeals the estate tax in its entirety without a sunset provision or establishes a high unified credit effective equivalent amount, the use of trusts will be even more popular than it is today. Be wary of abuses. We encourage you to discuss the debate cited in Chapter Nineteen, its logical extensions for your particular situation and state with your advisers.

Chapter Twelve

PRACTICAL EXAMPLES OF THE TRUST USED AS A FINANCIAL UMBRELLA

One of the primary functions of an estate plan is to give the estate owner peace of mind. A successful estate plan can ensure that one's wealth or its income will be safeguarded against inexperience, diminishing abilities in advancing years or unpredictable life events. A trust is one of the most effective vehicles for establishing this peace of mind.

The trust is a separate and distinct entity from its creator. A trust holds property and performs acts in its own name for the benefit of one or more other parties (i.e., its beneficiaries). The creator of a trust abandons dominion over property in the trust. If the settlor fails to abandon her incidents of control over the trust sufficiently, the trust may fail in its purpose. That is, it may not be insulated from estate and income taxation nor from creditors. If a trust is properly set up and operated, a person's former property or its income will be used to carry out her wishes, while she is protected from tax and certain other consequences of property ownership. Usually, it is the retention of powers over the trust or its property that determines taxability.

The person who forms a trust is known as the grantor, the trustor or the settlor, among other names. The trust itself is created under the law of a particular state, and this can provide the opportunity for shopping around. The laws of some states allow greater freedom for the investment of trust assets.

The trustee is named to administer the property and to distribute it to the beneficiaries in accordance with the directions of the grantor. Neither the grantor nor her spouse should serve as a trustee of the trust, unless it is a revocable trust (see Chapter Eleven) or the powers of the trustee are purely administrative and permit no exercise of discretion.

In a simple trust, all of the trust's income must be distributed each year to named beneficiaries, with no discretion lodged in the trustee. Otherwise, it is a complex trust for federal income tax purposes.

Practical uses of trusts in estate planning

Here are some samples of common types of estate plans using trusts:

1. An individual wants to give property to persons who are too young or too financially unsophisticated to own property. The property can be transferred to a trust with a knowledgeable trustee who will safeguard the principal and provide the beneficiaries with the income to the extent called for in the trust agreement. Variations on this plan can be used to turn the principal over to the beneficiaries under certain conditions, if desired, or to increase payments to beneficiaries when there are special needs for money. This may be done in the form of a testamentary or an *inter vivos* (revocable or irrevocable) trust. It depends upon the goals and desires of the owner of the asset.

2. An individual wishes to transfer property to relatives or other people or organizations without actually giving them the property at this time. By transferring the property irrevocably to a trust, he has gotten the value of this property out of what will be his gross estate when he dies. Death within three years of setting up the trust will trigger inclusion only if the grantor has retained powers in himself, or his death triggers distributions under the trust. Meanwhile, the property will be held by the trust, the trustee having been given powers to determine who will eventually get the property or certain portions of it. For example, the trustee (but not the grantor) may be given discretion to transfer property or income to named persons or classes of people (such as the grantor's children or grandchildren, unidentified by name) according to their personal needs (i.e., support or education) or business objectives.

3. A person may have more income than she needs. Interest, dividends, rents and the like from income-producing properties are being taxed at her

maximum tax rate because of her high business earnings. She can irrevocably transfer whatever portion of these income-producing properties she chooses to a trust for the benefit of relatives, friends or charitable organizations. She may use her annual exclusion or even some of her unified credit. The beneficiaries, not the grantor, will be taxed on the income (charitable organizations escape this). Further, the grantor might have thought that a limited life trust would be appropriate by the end of that period of time, as the income beneficiaries will have established their own substantial earnings pattern or will have been relieved of the financial burden of raising children. When the trust is terminated, the remaining principal will pass to the designated income beneficiary. Generally, the grantor or her spouse should not receive the property back upon the death of the income beneficiary. (See Chapter Sixteen, "The Short-Term Trust and Its Relatives vs. the IRS.")

4. A mother may wish to give property to her son but she fears that his gambling or extravagances will result in the property ending up in the hands of creditors. (See Chapter Fourteen, "Spendthrift Trust Provisions.")

5. An individual agrees to transfer property for the benefit of someone else but wishes to get this property back again under certain circumstances. For example, an alimony trust permits an ex-spouse to transfer property for the former spouse, but upon the former spouse's death or remarriage, the use of the trust income will cease and another party will become the beneficiary. The trust agreement should designate the contingent party, which might typically be a named hospital or university (not the grantor or his new spouse).

6. An individual may wish to provide for the care of a handicapped child, who is not receiving other benefits, by transferring assets to a trust to provide for the lifetime maintenance and comfort of the child. The child is assured of care despite the parent's possible business reverses.

7. An individual wants to make certain that her business will be operated after her death for the benefit of her family. Her executor, if not familiar with business problems or anxious to be rid of his responsibilities as quickly as possible, might sell the enterprise as soon as he could, possibly for an

inadequate price. To prevent this, a trust, *inter vivos* or testamentary, can be set up so that trustees chosen for their commercial experience and reliability will continue the business instead of disposing of it. (See Chapter Forty-Three, "Business-Continuation Arrangements.")

8. A wife would like to provide a suitable annual income for her husband for as long as he lives. He doesn't want the problems of administering properties. Therefore, she sets up a trust to which she supplies income-producing assets that will provide the desired amount, with the principal to go to named charities when he dies. But she is concerned that this income may prove insufficient due to extraordinary medical expenses or the failure of other investments. So the trustee is given the right to use the principal for the husband's benefit under certain defined circumstances.

9. A person has named several beneficiaries in her will, but much of her property is in a form that can't satisfactorily be divided into a number of parts: a closely held business, a collection of first editions, a producing oil well, a partnership in a fast-food franchise. Fractional interests, if they could be sold at all, would bring a much lower price. Beneficiaries will predictably have different ideas as to when to sell and the price to ask. So the property owner transfers her properties to a trust, in which the beneficiaries receive fractional interests in the trust. The trustee, in her sole discretion, will either sell the entire property as a unit or sell items separately at the best time, price and benefit for all the beneficiaries.

10. A wife wants to leave property to her husband, with the children to receive whatever is left when he dies, without paying two estate taxes on substantially the same property. She sets up a trust for the benefit of her husband. It will terminate and distribute its properties to the children when he dies. Now there is only one estate tax, because what he will own when he dies is merely a life interest, with no value as of the moment of his death. (See Chapter Eighteen, "Where the Surviving Spouse Can't Touch Anything but Income.")

11. An individual would like to part with some property so that it won't be part of her estate when she dies and at the same time create an annual income

80

tax deduction for herself. For example, a physician owns the building in which she practices. She transfers this property to a trust for the benefit of her children. But she needs the building for her practice, so she leases it back from the trust, the rent being a business deduction for her. (See Chapter Twenty-Seven, "Sale-and-Leaseback; Gift-and-Leaseback.")

12. An individual wants her widowed daughter-in-law to have an income for as long as she doesn't remarry. She transfers income-producing securities to a trust for the daughter-in-law's benefit, the trust to terminate and transfer the principal according to the settlor's instruction if the daughter-in-law remarries or if she cohabits with another unmarried adult. There could be several such disqualifying events the settlor might be well advised to add.

13. A mother wishes to set up a trust for the benefit of her several children or grandchildren. The trustee is given instructions or discretionary power to apportion trust principal for the beneficiaries—typically, when one of the children marries, has a child, undergoes surgery, needs to maintain her standard of living, remains with the family business that the other children have abandoned, wishes to go into business or seeks to go to medical school. But the mother doesn't want any child to know the other's share. She sets up individual trusts, each with a separate trustee and instructions or discretionary powers. On requisition by each trustee, funds are provided by a pour-over trust established by the mother. None of the beneficiaries can find out what the others are getting.

14. A person wants to ensure that her pet animals are well provided for when she dies, but she can't be certain that her executor (an individual or a bank) will be cooperative. She sets up a trust for the benefit of her pets, choosing a sympathetic trustee.

15. When an individual gets older, she may fear that she will lose her business or investment judgment without realizing it. She is concerned that her failing abilities may deprive her of the property or income that she needs. She transfers this property to a trust with a competent trustee for her own benefit. Because the trust property is being used for her own benefit, she will

be taxed on its income. But she has made certain that she won't dissipate the principal.

16. Someone has been making contributions to her favorite church, charity, college, hospital, etc., for many years. She would like to have the contributions continue in her name for all time, or for a period of years—for example, until the new library building is completely financed. Income-producing properties are transferred to a trust for this purpose.

17. A wife wants to leave her husband the largest amount that will take full advantage of the marital deduction (see Chapter Four, "The Marital Deduction: Maximizing the Opportunity," and Chapter Eighteen, "Where the Surviving Spouse Can't Touch Anything but Income") and yet minimize taxes in both their estates. By living trust or will, she can leave amounts to one trust that qualifies for her unified credit and another amount to another trust qualifying for the marital deduction as qualified terminable interest property. Her fiduciary can decide which assets pass, estate tax free, to the trust using the marital deduction, and which assets pass to the trust using the unified estate and gift tax credit. In effect, there is no tax on her death and each spouse utilizes their own unified credit. Note that both of these trusts are often placed in the same document and can be funded by the pour-over will.

18. A financially successful immigrant wishes to leave money to the town where she was born. No deduction is allowed for a charitable bequest to a foreign political subdivision. But a bequest is deductible when made to a United States trust for purely charitable purposes, such as doing charitable works in areas that can include her place of birth.

19. Someone is distressed by the many demands made on her by charitable organizations, so she transfers properties to a trust that she establishes for benevolent purposes. Now she can refer requests to the trustees.

20. Trusts may be a vehicle for providing a life income to a designated person, with the principal going to a charitable organization subject to this life interest. (See Chapter Seventeen, "Charitable Remainder Trusts.")

Conclusions and advice

• Generally, if you wish to attain estate or income tax benefits, you must let go of any meaningful incident of ownership of trust properties. That includes the right to say how much each beneficiary receives annually, even though you don't exercise this right and nothing can come back to you personally in any event. Renunciation of incidents of ownership made within three years of death will not keep the value of the property out of your estate. However, absolute gifts within that period are generally no longer included in your estate.

• A grantor is treated as holding any power or interest that was held by an individual who either (1) was the grantor's spouse at the time the power or interest was created or (2) became the grantor's spouse subsequent to the creation of that power or interest.

• Remember that a trust may be used for your own benefit as well as that of other beneficiaries. However, you will be taxed on benefits.

• There are separate income tax brackets for trusts that retain income. For example, if income is retained for ultimate distribution to the children of the grantor, the trust will file a Form 1041. The trust will pay a tax on the income based upon tax brackets for trusts and estates (as amended by the 2001 tax law) which generally reach the maximum rates faster than the individual tax brackets, often resulting in a higher overall tax being paid.

• Trusts are created under state law. Therefore, have your trust set up by a lawyer who is familiar with the laws of the state in which it is created. For example, will a spendthrift trust be recognized in your state? This may be a crucial point for you, your beneficiary and his creditors.

• The primary grantor and the primary beneficiary are the key to all IRS tax determinations.

• Two or more trusts are treated as one if (1) they have substantially the same grantor(s) or primary beneficiary(ies) and (2) the trusts' principal purpose is to avoid federal income tax.

• In the case of married persons, the unified credit may not be fully available to each spouse upon the first death if the decedent's assets are not large enough. For example, if the credit is $1 million (for 2002), and a spouse dies with assets of less than that amount, the difference will be lost. However, if the other spouse has assets valued at more than the applicable credit, he/she will be limited to whatever is applicable. A solution: Interspousal transfers to equalize their holdings, which can be done tax free. Thereafter, each spouse should transfer upon death the amount of his/her credit to a credit-shelter trust for the benefit of the other. This amount will be equal to the excess of the largest sum which may pass tax free after application of all available credits to his/her gross estate. This is called the credit-equivalent trust and should be labeled as a pecuniary bequest and not a fractional part of the estate. Provision may also be made for payments by the trustee of whatever trust income or principal is required during the spouse's lifetime or, alternately, of amounts of trust income or principal within stipulated limits on income and/or principal. Usually, there is some kind of ascertainable standard, such as health, maintenance, support and education, that is used. This concept is also often called a by-pass or credit-shelter trust.

• Inasmuch as the timing of death is usually unpredictable, a living trust may be used so that there is no interruption in the individual's business affairs or of a plan to distribute assets. We have often said that the time of one's death can be known so as to implement estate planning only where his birth certification contains an expiration date. Therefore, many estate planners advocate the use of funded revocable trusts for precisely this reason. When the unexpected occurs, the successor trustee takes over without loss of continuity. This methodology, however, requires the transfer of assets to the trust during one's lifetime.

Chapter Thirteen

MAXIMIZING BENEFITS: A PRACTICAL EXAMPLE

Assume a married couple has a combined federal gross estate of more than $2 million (in 2002). What would their estate planner recommend in the form of a living trust? To some extent, this situation has been answered in other chapters. However, we offer you a realistic example and its solution.

This chapter will present the twofold approach that your planning process will actually follow. First, we will identify the basic provisions you may want and/or need. Then, we will refine these provisions and identify other areas where you must make decisions.

Situation

In order to make this example more meaningful, we base it on the Weaver Family.

Husband:	Steve, Sr.	Age 47
Wife:	Beth	Age 39
Children:	Steve, Jr.	Age 16 (by first wife)
	Amy	Age 12 (by Beth)
	Bill	Age 8 (by Beth)

Net joint gross estate without life insurance*	$2,400,000
Life insurance on Steve	$750,000
Life insurance on Beth	$250,000

*Assume assets are split equally between Steve and Beth at $1,200,000 each

Before discussing any solution, understand that in the wrong set of circumstances—a simple "I love you" will and close proximity of deaths (with Steve's death first, in 2002)—Beth could die with a $3.2 million estate (including life insurance) and only a $1 million credit. If she chose not to include Steve, Jr., in her will, he would be unprovided for. Worse yet, Beth's estate would have paid hundreds of thousands of needless dollars in estate tax.

Your choices/solutions

#1a. Your estate planner will likely recommend that your assets remain equally split (separately owned) so that each owns in his/her own name alone (or in a living trust) approximately one-half of the family assets. This would help position the Weavers to receive two unified credits. Then he will suggest that each creates in his/her will or living trust a credit-shelter or by-pass trust provision for the surviving spouse.

This would guarantee that upon the death of the first spouse (in this case, Steve, Sr.), his estate would not lose the unified credit. Rather, the full credit amount would be placed in the by-pass trust. At the later death of Beth, her estate would also receive her unified credit. If her death also occurred in 2002, both estates would receive the full credit of $1 million and $2 million would have passed tax free.

#1b. Steve, Sr., and Beth will have to decide who will be the beneficiary of his by-pass trust. The usual choice is Beth and/or Beth and the children. In Steve's instrument, it is likely that on Beth's death the remainder beneficiaries would include all three children. Possibly he may treat Steve, Jr., preferentially, depending on what Beth does in her documents. Beth would have to make similar decisions, as it is always possible that she could pass away before her husband.

#1c. What rights do you give the beneficiaries of the by-pass or credit-shelter trust? Remember, this trust need not qualify for the marital deduction; therefore, you can be as liberal or as restrictive as you want. Here are a few choices:

(i) Income (mandatory or discretionary with a standard).

(ii) Income (discretionary only with a standard such as health, maintenance, support and education).

(iii) Principal (mandatory or discretionary with a standard).

(iv) Principal (discretionary only with a standard such as health, maintenance, support and education).

(v) Draw-down rights (usually limited to just the spouse and, for tax purposes, limited to the greater of $5,000 or 5% of principal per year. Sometimes this is known as the 5 + 5 right).

(vi) Many other provisions (see page 73 and 74, and you can be as creative as you wish without fear of losing the marital deduction).

#2a. Next, the Weaver's estate planner will point out that each estate is over the unified credit amount by $200,000. Rather than subject each estate to a potential tax, it would be best to consider utilizing the marital deduction. Although we usually speak in generalities about the tax rate, we estimated that the amount would be taxed in the neighborhood of 40% under the 2001 tax law. Therefore, it is easy to explain that failing to take advantage of the marital deduction would cost $80,000 in estate tax and fees on this balance.

#2b. Because the marital trust must qualify for the marital deduction, the surviving spouse can be the only lifetime beneficiary (see Chapter Four, "The Marital Deduction: Maximizing the Opportunity"). The surviving spouse must therefore receive, at a minimum, all of the annual income.

#2c. The trustee's rights to distribute principal, as well as other spousal rights such as general powers of appointment, are not required in order to qualify for the marital deduction, but are often given. As suggested, a QTIP trust was allowed for the specific reason of limiting the spouse's rights to income only, and yet qualified for the marital deduction. Note that, while the spouse is alive, no other person may have current rights in this trust. Rights may only be designated to a remainderperson(s), who takes over upon the spouse's demise. Yet Steve may choose to give Beth a whole range of rights similar to those set forth in #1c above.

#2d. As with the by-pass or credit-shelter trust, depending upon what Steve, Sr., and Beth have discussed, their respective marital trust provisions may provide differently upon the death of the surviving spouse. In other words, Steve, Jr., may benefit as a remainderman from one or both trusts, if the parties agree. However, Beth could change her documents after Steve, Sr., died, but his trusts and the distributions called for therein would remain intact, as they cannot be changed after his death unless Beth had a general power of appointment.

#3. Whether the Weavers execute separate wills or an individual or joint trust, it is likely they will provide for a continuation of the trust should they both die before their children are above certain levels of maturity. Their estate planner will likely recommend that the trust principal be held for, and income and principal be distributed to, the children as follows:

Income: Discretionary for their education, health, maintenance and support until the respective child reaches a certain age.

Principal: Same as above

Principal: Mandatory distributions of a child's share at given ages
             Example:

             One-third of the trust balance at age 25.

             One-half of the trust balance at age 30.

             Remainder balance at age 35.

#4. In some instances, estate planners will recommend generation-skipping trust provisions. (See Chapter Fifteen, "Generation-Skipping Trusts.")

#5. In all likelihood, the Weavers' estate planner would also recommend that, at a minimum, Steve's life insurance policy should be transferred to an irrevocable life insurance trust for the benefit of Beth and the children. For transfers of existing policies to an irrevocable trust, there is still a three-year throwback rule. This could potentially thwart the plan to keep the proceeds from estate taxes. A new policy could be purchased. If a current policy were used, the Weavers would be gambling that Steve, Sr., would live three years after the transfer. However, if he so survived or used a new policy, then the insurance amount would also pass tax free on both Steve's and Beth's deaths and be held in trust for the children, thereby saving substantial amounts in estate taxes.

This is a very important point. Many clients have substantial amounts of life insurance for very valid reasons, but fail to consider the estate tax implications. Here, with Beth's early demise after Steve's death, his life insurance was paid and ended up in Beth's estate, and would then be taxed at the same 40% rate or more upon her death. Instead, by use of the trust, there would be no tax, and the entire amount would remain available for the benefit of the children. Many planners would also recommend a similar trust for Beth's life insurance.

#6. The Weavers would obviously have several other provisions to consider. Certainly, their choices of guardians and trustees would be most important at this time. Note that the choice of trustees is an interesting planning point. If Beth survives, trusts will exist primarily for her benefit. She will therefore want substantial input into whomever Steve names as trustees for trusts that will benefit her if she survives. He will want input into her document. In other words, your choices of trustees are not just for the children.

The 2001 tax law and the future

Recently a respected accountant asked how we were advising clients such as the Weavers, in light of the 2001 tax law. The implication was the likelihood of the estate rates being lower with a possible full repeal and its effect on life insurance. The question itself was alarming as it suggested that situations like the Weavers' were a thing of the past.

Taxes are just one consideration for a family unit. Granted, they are an important element, but other family concerns cannot be overlooked. Several congressional and two presidential elections plus possible economic shifts will seal the fate of the estate tax in 2011 or before. We may see its return, in an all too familiar form, albeit adjusted for inflation, or with assistance for small or family businesses and farms.

You cannot predict what law will be in effect at the time of your demise. We believe it wise to stay the course and assume the estate tax will return in 2011 in one version or another. Thus, the Weaver's plan would not change to any great extent. Depending on your age, if the size of your estate warrants the purchase of life insurance, do so. In the worst case, you simply have added protection, and a larger inheritance for your loved ones. The difficulty will be in determining the amount due to the uncertainty of events. Also remember, the insurance available to you today may not be available tomorrow nor at the same price.

Conclusions and advice

• By combining the use of two credit-shelter trusts, a couple can pass $2 million tax free in 2002. This will not increase until 2004. If your joint estate exceeds one credit, split the estate, if possible, and hold the assets, as best as possible, one-half in each spouse's name. Then use this amount to fund the credit-shelter trust on the death of the first spouse. This way you will not lose the first credit.

• With a credit-shelter trust, you can be creative in your provision selection. Remember, your spouse may not honor your wishes and can change his/ her documents. Your documents, if you die first, cannot be changed unless you give your spouse a general power of appointment, which is generally not done in a by-pass trust.

• Life insurance retains one of the vestiges of the old tax law. If you donate it to a trust and die within three years of the gift, it is taxed as if it were in your estate. If possible, use new policies.

• Approach your estate planning conference with your questions prepared. Fill out the information called for in Appendices A, B and C, but do not make any snap decisions. Quiz your estate planner for the best ways of handling different situations. For example, for Steve, Jr., a separate trust funded with a new 15-year, fixed-premium term policy might be just the thing to keep harmony in the Weaver family.

Chapter Fourteen

SPENDTHRIFT TRUST PROVISIONS

You wish to provide for your daughter during her lifetime, but you also want her to be the actual beneficiary of assets upon your death. If, however, you have reason to suspect that she will run up huge debts or otherwise waste her inheritance, you can set up a spendthrift trust for her. Courts have held that the grantor of property to a trust has the right to protect the beneficiary against her own voluntary improvidence or financial misfortune. The property that is to produce the beneficiary's income is never hers; therefore, neither she nor her creditors can squander it.

As we noted in the preceding chapters, the concept of a spendthrift trust is simply a group of provisions added to your trust document that gives or establishes the protective measures you desire. To qualify as a spendthrift trust, only a few simple phrases and concepts need be included in your multipage and multipurpose document. However, as an effective estate planning tool, it is an essential element of a first-rate plan.

How it works

A trust is set up and furnished with income-producing assets. Often, it is an irrevocable trust as you do not want the asset back. The trustee, a bank or other independent fiduciary, is given discretion as to when, under what circumstances and in what amounts to pay out the income. The trust can provide that if the trustee isn't satisfied that the beneficiary will be using the money for what the trust agreement and correlative instructions have defined as normal living expenses and pleasures, no money will be paid out at that time. Usually, the undistributed income is simply accumulated and the trust will pay the income taxes at its tax bracket. If the trust instrument provides that income is to be paid out for support, the beneficiary daughter may argue in court that she is not getting enough to meet that test, especially if she is still of the age where her parents are legally obliged to support her. If the arrangement was created by will and the parents are dead, their obligation of support is nebulous, and in any case, most spendthrift trusts are created for persons of legal age. Ordinarily, the trustee can't be compelled to pay out anything more than he feels is appropriate and this is in the trustee's sole discretion. A line of persistent creditors cannot change the trustee's mind if discretionary powers have been bestowed. Nor can trust principal be touched by the daughter or her creditors, for the principal is held by the trustee, not only for the daughter's benefit, but for a (group of) specified remainderperson(s), should she die or should certain specified events occur which divest her of her interest. However, if the daughter's estate has been named a remainderperson(s), creditors may seek to attach the daughter's remainder interest. Income that is not paid out by the watchful trustee under the discretionary powers may, if so provided and in accordance with the trust agreement, be paid out at such future time, if ever, as the trustee deems appropriate. Undistributed income may be made part of the trust principal if that is the way the trust instrument was written.

Actual language used in trust instruments

One spendthrift trust recognized by the court as having accomplished its intended purpose read as follows:

> "The Trustees shall pay or apply for the benefit of my son...so much of the net income of said trust, up to the whole thereof, as the Trustees may from time to time deem necessary or advisable for his proper care, maintenance and support. The balance of said net income, if any, shall be accumulated by the Trustees, and from time to time added to the principal of the trust estate."

Here, the trustees had the discretionary authority, and perhaps some further guidelines, to determine what was "necessary" for the beneficiary's proper care, maintenance and support.

In some instances, a grantor seeks to prevent the beneficiary's creditors from attaching amounts otherwise payable to the beneficiary by such language as "that said Trustee shall pay the net income therefrom in monthly installments...during his life, and not into the hands of any other person, whether claiming by his authority or otherwise."

In one case, the trust agreement declared:

> "Each and every beneficiary under this trust is hereby restrained from and shall be without right, power or authority to sell, transfer, pledge, mortgage, hypothecate, alienate, anticipate or in any other manner affect or impair his, her or their beneficial and legal rights, titles, interests and estates in and to the income and/or principal of this trust during the entire term thereof; nor shall the rights, titles, interests and estates of any beneficiary hereunder be subject to the rights or claims of creditors of any beneficiary, and all the income and/or principal of this trust shall be transferrable, payable and deliverable solely to the beneficiaries as herein provided, and the Trustees may require the personal receipt of any beneficiary as a condition precedent to the payment of any money or other property to such beneficiary."

This provision was held to be legal under the laws of the state in which it was drawn. Under another section of this same law, ordinary creditors were permitted to reach all income of a beneficiary of such a provision except for the amount necessary for his support and education.

Some trust instruments contain an outright forfeiture provision of the beneficiary's rights if she takes any steps that are contrary to the grantor's instructions that the money not be available to other parties. One agreement provided for the forfeiture of a beneficiary's rights "if from any cause whatsoever the said income or principal, or any part thereof, shall or, but for this proviso, would at any time become payable to or for the benefit of any person, firm, association, corporation, political subdivision, state or federal government, other than such beneficiary."

Effect of state law

Counsel should check the state law to determine whether spendthrift trusts will be recognized in the face of creditors' claims. Some states regard spendthrift trusts as a fraud against the creditors. Usually, a gambling debt is not regarded as a valid and enforceable claim under state law.

The language of a trust instrument or of a state law does not apply to the Internal Revenue Service. So, even if trust income can be withheld by the trustee under the trustee's discretionary powers, and neither the beneficiary nor her creditors can reach this money, that most persistent of all creditors, the IRS, is not bound by the wording of private agreements or of the law of a particular state.

Federal gift tax

A spendthrift trust agreement usually provides that the trustee has discretion to decide whether trust income should be distributed to a beneficiary in a particular year. Therefore, this is not a present interest that would qualify a donor's transfers to the trust for the annual $11,000-per-donee gift tax exclusion, unless certain other preconditions were met. This should be reviewed closely with counsel before assuming your gift to a spendthrift trust qualifies for the annual exclusion.

Who is the spendthrift?

A grantor may not be concerned so much that her daughter or son has spendthrift tendencies, as that this child's spouse is the one who is likely to be wildly extravagant or gullible. The grantor may provide that anything she gives or leaves to her child is to be in the form of a life income from a trust, so that the principal cannot get into the hands of the spouse. The remainderperson(s) will be specified as the grantor sees fit—often the grandchildren are named rather than the prodigal spouse.

Encouragement not to be a spendthrift

A grantor may seek to convert a spendthrift trust into an incentive trust, by using the concept of matching funds. A trustee may be empowered to supplement authorized or mandatory support payments with additional trust income equal to the beneficiary's earnings in any year through his own efforts. If the primary beneficiary fails to earn a minimum level, the trustee may consider the penalty of giving the income to others or accumulation with "makeup" provisions. In this way, the income will be accumulated in lean years, but in successful years, the beneficiary will be rewarded. Obviously, there are several possible variations you may wish to explore.

Conclusions and advice

• Check with counsel as to whether a spendthrift trust is valid in your state or is deemed to be a fraud against creditors.

• Consider seeking counsel and advice where spendthrift trusts are allowed and determine the effect of locating the trust corpus in this more friendly jurisdiction.

• A spendthrift trust may be used to protect principal from the beneficiary's spouse.

• The trustee may be empowered to pay out to the spendthrift beneficiary any additional amounts to match what the latter was able to earn by her own efforts.

• Do not seek to protect a beneficiary from claims by the IRS. It can't be done.

• Do not treat transfers to a spendthrift trust as gifts of present interests if the trustee has discretionary powers as to the time of payouts, unless the trust includes and qualifies under the so-called "Crummey power" rule. Generally, this is a trust clause that allows the beneficiary to withdraw certain amounts when a gift is made to the trust. Although the IRS does not agree with this court-made exception to the present interest rule, it has its proponents. However, such a power may be the exact opposite type of power you wish the spendthrift beneficiary to have. Thoroughly consider and discuss the benefits with your advisers.

• Note that many trusts typically include a Crummey power even if it is not a primary purpose of the trust. Some trusts now provide this power, thereby allowing the gift to qualify for the annual gift tax exclusion, yet also offering the grantor or donor the right, upon making each gift, to "opt out" of the power. Should the grantor choose not to give the Crummey notice and make the gift available for withdrawal, he will lose the annual exclusion for that gift. However, the corresponding gain is a sense of security knowing that his gift will remain in trust.

Chapter Fifteen

GENERATION-SKIPPING TRUSTS

A device favored for many years to avoid paying multiple estate taxes on transfers of property along generational lines was a trust that left a life interest to the grantor's children, with either a further life interest or a distribution to grandchildren, great-grandchildren and so on down the line. The major advantage of this "generation-skipping trust" was that it is only a life interest. The value was not taxed in the estate of the grantor's child at that child's death and therefore, was transmitted entirely to the next younger generation, tax free. The rule against perpetuities mentioned earlier could sometimes extend a full century or more before terminating a given trust if at least one of the beneficiaries, alive when the trust was created, was young and healthy.

However, in 1976, Congress imposed a "skip-a-generation" tax, closing the loophole that permitted this kind of tax avoidance. In effect, it made the distribution of trust assets to two or more generations of heirs subject to a tax equal to what the escaped estate tax would have been.

Subsequently, this tax was repealed by a new law retroactive to 1976. Now the 2001 tax law effectively increases the generation-skipping exemption as the applicable exclusion amount increases. In addition, several other changes of substance are contained in the 2001 tax law. Because of the complexity of the provisions and the confusing legislative history, it is advisable to discuss specific problems with competent professional counsel if you are contemplating such a generation-skipping arrangement. Transfers to one's spouse are not covered by the tax because the spouses are considered to be of the same generation, regardless of differences in age.

There is a flat-rate tax on both (1) transfers under a trust or similar arrangement involving benefit sharing by more than one generation below that of the grantor and (2) direct beneficiaries more than one generation below that of the grantor (that is, which skip generations). This tax is imposed on taxable terminations and taxable distributions (including distributions of income) under generation-skipping arrangements. A skip person must be a "natural person" whose generation assignment is two or more generations younger than that of the transferor. Taxable beneficiaries include only persons having interests in property (as opposed to powers over it).

If the use of trust property to satisfy any obligation of support arising by reason of state law is discretionary or is made pursuant to any state law substantially equivalent to the Uniform Gifts to Minors Act, it will be disregarded in determining whether a portion may be distributed to, or for the benefit of, a person other than the beneficiary of the gift. (See Chapter Twenty-Five, "The Uniform Gifts to Minors Act.") Thus, a parent is not treated as having an interest in a trust if the trust instrument requires that trust assets be used to discharge a support obligation.

Rules similar to those governing the deduction of administration expenses, indebtedness and taxes for income and estate purposes have been extended to the generation-skipping tax. Thus, these amounts are generally not deductible in determining taxable income unless an election is made not to deduct these amounts in determining the taxable amount subject to the generation-skipping tax.

There is a specific exemption of $1,100,000 per transferor in 2001 and under the 2001 tax law, this remains unchanged through 2003 (indexed for inflation). Transfers in excess of that amount are subject to tax at the maximum gift and estate tax rate. Transfers after December 31, 2003, will receive an exemption equal to the amount of that year's estate tax applicable exclusion amount. If an individual makes a direct skip gift during his life, any unused portion of the exemption is deemed to be allocated to the transferred property unless a proper election is made to the contrary. Several changes have been made in the new 2001 tax law regarding deemed allocations, even allowing some retroactive allocations. In addition, you may include a new provision in your trust document giving the trustee the power to sever the trusts into two trusts which mirror the "inclusion ratio" and may provide added benefit to all concerned. Also, the annual $11,000-per-year donee exclusion is available and therefore not subject to the tax. There is also a limited exception for trusts. However, to qualify for the trust exception, assets of a trust that terminates on the beneficiary's death must be includable in the beneficiary's estate.

Property transferred to an incompetent person after August 3, 1990, is now subject to the generation-skipping tax. Further, a credit against the generation-skipping transfer tax is permitted equal to 5% of any state taxes on generation-skipping transfers. The most important concept, however, is that this is a tax levied after the estate tax has been assessed and paid. It taxes the balance actually passing to the prohibited generation.

Other considerations

There are circumstances under which an individual may find it necessary to provide a life income to a beneficiary through a trust, the property to go to persons in a second younger generation on the death of the income beneficiary. Obviously, this will mean imposition of the generation-skipping transfer tax when the life tenant dies. But there are times when the tax consequences should be ignored.

If a person is concerned about the generation-skipping transfer tax, he might provide for his second generation of beneficiaries through life insurance. Or, he could establish separate trusts for the children and the grandchildren.

Planning, planning and more planning

It is important to remember that each person receives the exemption. Therefore, married grandparents could each establish a generation-skipping trust. They could effectively pass a total of $2,200,000 to their grandchildren, assuming their own children did not need these funds or were wealthy in their own right. We sometimes lose sight of this exemption, and clients become emotionally tied to what their children will say or feel. Note, however, that often these same dollars are taxed in both your estate and that of your children. There is sometimes less than 30% left when you consider the potential of two estate taxes at the 45% rate (taxed when the last grandparent dies and passes the property to the children, and then taxed again when the child and his spouse die, passing it on to the grandchild).

As American taxpayers begin to spend more time in this planning arena and as their wealth increases, the desire to provide for successive generations will increase correspondingly. The fact that several states have already moved in the direction of allowing the so-called dynasty trusts is a clear indication that they will be utilized. This will mean that the exemption will also be used more frequently.

Conclusions and advice

• Do not assume that skip-a-generation trusts are inadvisable merely because a transfer tax must be paid. The trust may still be highly desirable for nontax reasons.

• Do not tie up your assets in trust for an extended period of time without advice. Many states have laws against perpetuities. They may allow you to make provision only for the extent of a life or lives already in being at the time the trust is created, plus 21 years after all of their deaths.

• A dozen or so states impose a generation-skipping tax.

• Under the 2001 tax law, the estate tax rates and exemptions have changed in the taxpayer's favor, resulting in a lower overall GST tax. Also, there have been several other changes involving generation-skipping trusts in the new law. While this is still a very complex area, these changes have been positive.

• In cases where a parent predeceases the transferor, there is an exception to the tax on skips when lineal descendants inherit. The 1997 tax law expanded this to collateral heirs, provided there are no living lineal descendants.

Chapter Sixteen

THE SHORT-TERM TRUST AND ITS RELATIVES VS. THE IRS

Generally, the IRS does not favor attempts to assign income from higher to lower bracketed taxpayers, which trusts are often used to accomplish. The so-called "kiddie tax" and the grantor trust rules (Code Sections 671–679) are two weapons in the IRS's arsenal to combat abuses.

The short-term trust

Prior to the Tax Reform Act of 1986, the short-term trust was useful because it allowed a donor to part with property and its income during a period when the person was in a high tax bracket and didn't need the income. At the end of a period of time (more than 10 years minimum), the trust ended and the property returned to the donor. Such a trust was considered a benevolent boomerang that could return when needed.

Generally, in the case of transfers in trust made after March 1, 1986, the income of a trust is taxed to its grantor if the trust principal will return to her or her spouse at any time. An exception is provided where the principal may return only after the death of an income beneficiary of the trust who is a minor (under 21) and a lineal descendant of the grantor. Also, an exception to this rule is made for certain trusts created under a binding property settlement entered into before March 1, 1986.

This type of plan involves what is sometimes called a "come-back" or "give-and-keep" trust. An individual transfers income-producing properties, such as securities or real estate, to a trust for the benefit of someone else—a person or an institution—who will receive all the income. At the end of the stated duration of the trust, the trust terminates and the remaining principal goes to a predetermined party or parties.

A grantor may be treated as the owner of a trust in which she has a reversionary interest in either the principal or income—and be taxed on the income. This can happen if, at the time the trust is created, the grantor's interest will or may be reasonably expected to take effect in repossession or enjoyment. If, for example, there is any significant possibility that interests or powers may become effective in the grantor and there is more than a 5% possibility that any of the proscribed powers or interests will revert or be enjoyed by the grantor after the transfer, the rule will apply. For this purpose, the possibility that an interest may return to the grantor or her spouse solely under intestacy laws is to be ignored.

The value of the reversionary interest, if any, is determined by comparing the actuarial possibility that a transferred right might be subject to return to the grantor—for example, if the grantee should die before the grantor does. The possibility of any reversionary interest can be eliminated entirely by provision that upon the death of the grantee, any remaining interest will go to named contingent or secondary parties, such as a nonprofit organization.

The transfer of property to a short-term trust may result in federal gift tax based on the value of the life income transferred to the life tenant. The gift tax applies to the total value of the property transferred, not merely to the value of the income interest, because it will vary. In addition, the $11,000-per-donee annual gift tax exclusion is not available, as this applies only to property of ascertainable value.

The grantor of a short-term trust that is still in existence at the time of her death has something of value when she dies. Therefore, it will be includable in her gross estate. Her estate will not include the full value of the property she has transferred, because she has no ownership of the income interest. The value of the property is reduced by the actuarial value of the right to the income possessed by the income beneficiary at the time of the grantor's death. The reversionary right possessed by the decedent at the time of her death must be discounted, because the principal that will return to the estate after the trust terminates (for example, 13 years later) must reflect the fact that a dollar paid 13 years hence will be worth less than a dollar paid today.

For the most part, short-term trusts are no longer used except in those circumstances where the grantor knows the downside. In fact, when they are used, they are often called "grantor trusts" (see below). Yet there may be situations which warrant the use of this vehicle. More importantly, however, be aware of the trap that this formerly desirable vehicle now presents.

A reverse of the short-term trust which still remains an effective tool is the grantor retained interest trust (GRIT). Its purpose is to produce estate tax savings, and currently the grantor retained annuity trust (GRAT) and the grantor retained unitrust (GRUT) are allowed "split-interest" trusts.

Under Internal Revenue Code Section 2702, a grantor who reserves the right to receive fixed amounts annually for a term of years which need not be life (GRAT) may successfully keep the remainder interest out of her estate. Likewise, a GRUT provides for a fixed annual payment of a percentage of the trust's assets, and again allows the remainder to pass outside of the grantor's estate.

A further exception to Section 2702 regarding split gifts involves the personal residence GRIT. This is a valuable tool for the intrafamily wealth transfer concept, as is a variation commonly referred to as a qualified personal residence trust (QPRT).

Each of these trusts consists of complex documents designed to help in the overall estate plan. They allow the grantor to plan her current living needs and estate together. These trusts allow her to retain the income or use of her home for a period of time or until death while removing them from her gross estate for tax purposes. They must be drafted precisely by a qualified draftsperson. If these trusts are appropriate from your estate planning point of view, they can be extremely beneficial.

Business, equipment and family residence trusts

Oftentimes, the unschooled taxpayer is ill-advised with schemes using trusts as a tool to generate supposed tax benefits. The business or equipment (lease) trust is designed to generate deductions, while the family residence trust purportedly generates a step-up in the basis of the residence.

The IRS has many tools to combat these devices, including Code Section 262 providing for nondeductibility of personal expenses, the age-old "substance over form" argument and the grantor trust rules (see below). As we have said previously, it is best to have an expert team by your side before entering the trust arena. You would be well advised to ask anyone trying to sell you on such a scheme if the plan received advance approval from the IRS or if the plan has been labeled an "abusive trust arrangement" by the IRS in its Cumulative Bulletin Notice 97-24.

The grantor trust rules and a defective trust

The grantor trust rules (Code Sections 671–679) are generally seen as stumbling blocks to income tax savings. Essentially, they trigger a tax to the grantor of the trust's income if any of a certain broad category of rights are retained by the grantor. These include reversion of a short-term trust as discussed earlier, power to control who receives the beneficial enjoyment of the trust, power to revoke or return the trust corpus, power to distribute income to the grantor and retention of certain important administrative powers.

Sometimes, it is beneficial to knowingly set up a trust where the income will be taxed to the grantor. Due to the compressed trust income tax brackets, it may be favorable to be taxed at the individual rates, if, for example, the goal is to remove the asset from the grantor's estate. This is the so-called "defective" grantor trust. If drafted properly, it obtains both the lower individual tax rate and successfully removes the asset from the grantor's estate.

Conclusions and advice

• In setting up a short-term or any other split-interest trust, consider carefully whether you can do without the income or the asset. Take into account every economic, social and personal factor you can imagine, including loss of your employment, health and/or severe economic reverses.

• The trust principal cannot revert to the grantor or to her spouse.

• If your goal is income or estate tax savings, the trust must be irrevocable. You can't change it.

• Consult an experienced professional before establishing any trust.

• Do not retain any powers involving the trust arrangement. This is very often the trap people find themselves unknowingly caught in. Specifically, ask your draftsperson if there are any such retained powers.

• The demise of the use of short-term trusts to save family income taxes does not eliminate them completely as an effective tool. Sometimes, it may be desirable to set up a trust even when you know you'll be taxed on its income. For example, income may be accumulated for a minor and taxed at the grantor's rate as opposed to the higher trust bracket. The income-producing property you transfer to this trust is owned by the trustee you have named. This type of trust need not in fact be, or classified as, a "short-term trust," but is usually called a "grantor trust." Because of the income and estate tax consequences, the decision to create such a trust should be made only after thoughtful and well-counseled considerations. Note that in this type of trust, several rights may be reserved for the grantor and her spouse. Upon your death, the property goes to, or continues to be held for, the persons you have selected to be the recipients without the undue delay, expense and publicity of probate.

• The use of the GRIT has been eroded due to special valuation rules; however, the GRAT and GRUT are still valuable tools, as are charitable remainder trusts. (See Chapter Seventeen, "Charitable Remainder Trusts.")

CHARITABLE REMAINDER TRUSTS

A husband who wishes to provide an income for life to a designated party, such as his spouse, may also have specific requirements. He chooses not to give her income-producing properties, for she may not want the responsibility of investments and fund management. Nor does he want her to own the properties outright at the time of her death in the event she bequeaths them to persons he does not choose. Instead, when his principal beneficiary dies, he would like to have the assets go to his favorite charity or hospital, or to his alma mater. He'd like this even better if he could benefit from tax deductions. If he plans properly, he can accomplish all of his goals.

Charitable deductions

For federal income, gift and estate tax purposes, a deduction is allowed for a charitable gift of a remainder interest in a trust where there is a noncharitable income beneficiary if the trust is either a charitable remainder annuity trust or a charitable remainder unitrust. The amount receivable each year by the income beneficiary must be either a stated dollar amount or a fixed percentage of the value of the trust property.

The grantor is entitled to a federal income tax deduction for the actuarial value of the remainder interest that will pass to the designated charitable organization. This deduction is taken in the tax year of the transfer to the trust. When the grantor dies, the value of the remainder interest passing to the charitable organization is deductible as a charitable bequest for federal estate tax purposes.

What the income beneficiary receives

An annuity trust must be required by the trust instrument to distribute at least 5% of the net fair market value of its assets each year, as valued at the time of the donor's contribution. Income payments must be made at least annually.

A unitrust must be required by the trust instrument to distribute yearly at least 5% of the net fair market value of its assets, valued annually, or the amount of the trust income, excluding capital gains, whichever is lower.

In valuing the amount of the charitable contribution, the deduction is computed on the assumption that the income beneficiary of the trust will receive the amounts specified. No provision may exist for payments to noncharitable beneficiaries of amounts other than the stated annuity or fixed percentage amount. Principal may not be diverted under any circumstances to a noncharitable beneficiary.

Available options

The income interest in the case of both forms of trust may be either for a term of years or for the life of the income beneficiary. A charitable annuity trust or unitrust may have more than one noncharitable beneficiary if the interest of such beneficiary is either for a term of years, not to exceed 20, or is for the life of the beneficiary. An individual who was not living at the time of creation of the trust, however, may not be an income beneficiary of a charitable remainder trust.

The governing instrument of a unitrust may provide that, when the trust income is less than the required payment to the noncharitable income beneficiary, the trust need distribute to him only the amount of the trust income. The deficiencies in income distributions in this case (that is, where the trust income was less than the stated amount payable to the income beneficiary) may be made up in later years when the trust income exceeds the amount otherwise payable to the income beneficiary for that year. The determination of what constitutes trust income is made under the applicable state law and may not include such items as capital gains, which must be allocated to the trust principal.

Federal income tax treatment

Under either an annuity trust or a unitrust, amounts paid to the income beneficiary are treated as consisting of the following:

1. Ordinary income, to the extent of the trust's ordinary income for the taxable year and its undistributed ordinary income from prior years.

2. Capital gains, to the extent of the trust's capital gains for the year and undistributed capital gains (determined on a cumulative net basis) from prior years.

3. Other income (such as state bond interest), to the extent of the trust's other income for the year and its undistributed other income from prior years.

4. Distribution of principal.

A charitable remainder trust that qualifies as an annuity trust or a unitrust is exempt from federal income tax except on what may be characterized as unrelated business income from sources outside the stated purpose of the trust. *Example:* Rent or royalties from a subsidiary of a business interest acquired by the trust.

Pooled-income funds

One type of gift of a charitable remainder interest in trust involves a transfer of property to a pooled-income fund. This is a trust to which a person has transferred property, giving an irrevocable remainder interest in the property to a public charity and retaining an income interest in the property for the life of one or more beneficiaries living at the time of the transfer. There are a number of restrictions on a pooled-income fund, including the following:

• The fund must commingle the property transferred to it with properties transferred to it under similar circumstances by other persons.

• The fund may have no investments in tax-exempt securities.

• No donor or income beneficiary may be a trustee of the fund, and the fund must be maintained by the charitable organization to which the remainder interest is given.

108

- Each person with a life interest in the pooled-income fund must receive an annual income determined by the trust's rate of return for the year.

A pooled-income fund won't qualify if it includes amounts received under types of arrangements other than those described above; however, a pooled-income fund that is commingled with other, larger groups of assets for investment purposes may have a separate accounting for the fund's assets.

The amount of the charitable contribution deduction allowed the donor upon transfer of the property to a pooled-income fund is determined by valuing the interest income on the basis of the highest annual rate of return earned by the fund in any of the three years preceding the transfer. If a fund has not been in existence for this period of time, the rate of return is 1% less than the highest annual average of the monthly rates (prescribed by Code Section 7520(a)(2)) for the three calendar years immediately preceding the year in which the fund is created.

Giving up the charitable deduction

It was noted above that the charitable deduction is allowed only if there is no right of invasion—that is, no right to use principal for the benefit of the noncharitable income beneficiary. But, on occasion, it may be desirable to allow for a right of invasion in order to achieve other objectives, even though the tax advantage is lost. Obviously, this decision should be made only with competent advice.

Conclusions and advice

- Despite changes in the tax law, you can still obtain both income and estate tax charitable deductions for gifts to a charitable remainder trust. But the rules and conditions under which this is possible are strict; seek guidance from an attorney, accountant or trust officer.

- Trust income is based on actuarial factors, so advice on the computation is important.

- Consult counsel on what constitutes trust income in a particular state.

• Do not provide for the use of principal to meet the needs of the non-charitable income beneficiary.

• Do not overlook the possible advantage of naming more than one life beneficiary or more than one charity as the remainder interest holders.

• The 1997 tax law contained two major provisions dealing with charitable remainder trusts. First, it provided that the maximum annual payout from an annuity trust cannot exceed 50% of the initial value and for a unitrust, 50% of the annual fair market value. Second, both types of trusts are subject to tests which, in essence, require the charity to receive, at a minimum, a 10% benefit.

• The tax law also carves out an exception to the requirements mandating a trust document when dealing with gifts of a personal residence or farm. Here a donor can, without a trust, contribute such property to the charity and reserve a life use for the donor and his spouse. The gift must be irrevocable.

• Charitable trusts also offer an excellent opportunity for those who have assets with substantially appreciated values and low income returns. The charitable trust can sell these assets tax free and invest the full value received in assets that yield higher rates of return.

Chapter Eighteen

WHERE THE SURVIVING SPOUSE CAN'T TOUCH ANYTHING BUT INCOME

The idea of transferring a complete interest in a substantial part of one's wealth to a surviving spouse troubles many thoughtful individuals planning the disposition of his estate. Perhaps the spouse is too financially unsophisticated to be given control over property that is intended to provide support and comfort for life. Perhaps the survivor doesn't want the responsibilities involved in property ownership and management. Maybe the person believes that the spouse will be prey to fortune hunters or swindlers. The obvious solution would be to give merely a life interest in income, without the headaches and nuisances of ownership. Since 1982, the deceased has been able to do just that, provided the interest is a qualifying life interest in qualified terminable interest property (referred to by the acronym "QTIP"), and the executor elects irrevocably to claim the marital deduction for all or a portion of such property. For example, if (in 2002) the fiduciary makes a QTIP election with respect to $1 million of a $2 million trust, he has thereby elected to claim the marital deduction with respect to only the $1 million. Possibly the balance will use up the unified credit and/or skip a generation.

Qualified terminable interest property provides an elective deduction

The executor may elect to claim the marital deduction for qualified terminable interest property. Such property may or may not be an interest in a trust. Very frequently, however, a trust is used to achieve the desired result. The surviving spouse must have a qualified life interest in the property, which means that income from the property must be paid to her at least annually. If there is a trust, the trustee may have the discretionary right to use the principal for the surviving spouse's benefit. But neither the trustee, the spouse nor anyone else may have the power to appoint the property itself to anyone during the spouse's lifetime. However, the power to appoint the property upon the spouse's death may, but need not be, included in the trust.

Under a properly established QTIP trust, a life interest granted to a surviving spouse is not automatically treated as a qualified terminable interest that is not taxable in the estate. Rather, the estate is permitted to make a QTIP election to defer the payment of estate taxes. If the estate so elects, the QTIP property is then treated as if passing outright from the decedent to the surviving spouse. Because such treatment brings the trust property within the confines of the unlimited marital deduction, the property is not taxed in the decedent's estate.

Where the QTIP requirements are met, the entire remaining proceeds (a life income interest and the remainder of the underlying QTIP) is treated as passing to the surviving spouse and qualifies for the marital deduction. To the extent that it is not consumed or disposed of during the surviving spouse's life, the value of the entire remaining property is included for tax purposes in the gross estate of the surviving spouse.

A QTIP interest may be created by a lifetime gift as well as at death. If so created, the donor makes the election to have the interest qualify for the marital deduction.

If QTIP qualifies for the marital deduction, it must be subject to tax in the estate of the second spouse to die. To make sure such taxation occurs, the law levies a tax on the underlying property even if the surviving spouse gives away her income interest. At that point, the unified transfer tax on the property itself becomes due.

The QTIP device provides a very flexible tool for minimizing taxes on both estates. If a QTIP interest is present, the executor can elect to claim the marital deduction for only that portion of the property that exceeds the amount of property subject to the unified credit (now also called interchangeably either the exemption equivalent amount or the applicable exclusion amount). Since much property may pass to the surviving spouse outside the will—such as jointly owned property, insurance or employee plan benefits—the executor can take into account all such property when making his election.

The transfer to a spouse of an interest in a joint and survivor annuity in which only the spouse has the right to receive any payments prior to the death of the last spouse to die qualifies for the marital deduction under the QTIP rules. Such transfer, however, does not qualify if either the donor or the executor, as the case may be, irrevocably elects out of QTIP treatment.

A joint and survivor annuity is treated as qualifying under the QTIP rule only if the annuity is includable in the decedent's estate as an annuity. Thus, an annuity created by the decedent's will does not qualify.

The QTIP interests must be created with great care to make sure they are in perfect agreement with the requirements and regulations of the law. This places a burden on the executor and makes it more important than ever that this fiduciary be chosen with care.

Other considerations

The QTIP device does not mean that the older marital deduction trust, in which the surviving spouse received not only an income interest but other rights involving the trust principal, is not still viable. For example, the right to withdraw principal and the right to decide who would receive the principal after the survivor's death continue to be effective provisions. If properly drawn, such a trust still qualifies for the marital deduction. It does, however, lack the flexibility that allows an executor to decide whether, and how much of, the trust should get the marital deduction. This fact, together with the increasing exemption equivalent amounts of the 2001 tax law, may make QTIP trusts a preferable tool for your estate planner.

There are some reasons why the QTIP election may seem unattractive. Your executor may not be familiar with the procedure. If the executor makes the election, it cannot subsequently be revoked. Also the surviving spouse may, in effect, cancel the executor's election. The amount of property the survivor consumes will affect the amount left after the survivor dies. In effect, an individual has no assurance that the property will be distributed in line with what she had in mind and she is therefore surrendering some of her options.

In addition, it may be easier to finance two partial estate taxes (on the death of the wife and, perhaps much later, upon the death of the surviving husband) than to pay what may be a far higher tax on the second death, when the survivor's property plus the unconsumed portion of the wife's assets also may be taxable. The tax rates that would be in effect when the second spouse dies are also unpredictable, as are the values of the property due to appreciation and inflation. Yet additional time has been purchased to plan, make gifts and decide what disposition is to be made of each spouse's property.

An individual considering the use of the QTIP alternative would be well advised to consult a competent professional, and review their estate with all of the potential changes of the new 2001 tax law.

Couple a life interest with dispositive powers

A plan may also give the surviving spouse life income in trust, as well as other powers, i.e., a testamentary power of appointment, without the possibility of wasting or losing the principal. This still eliminates the duties of property administration and maintains the benefit of the marital deduction, while providing some flexibility. Below are some guidelines.

The ground rules

The marital deduction is not lost when a surviving spouse is given a life interest in income from a trust meeting the following conditions:

1. The surviving spouse must be entitled for life to all of the income from the entire trust property. It is not necessary but often stated that the trustee may also distribute principal to or for the benefit of the surviving spouse.

2. The income must be payable annually or at more frequent intervals, and distributed currently to the surviving spouse. In one case, the governing trust instrument provided for the income each year to be paid quarterly during the specified following years. The marital deduction was forfeited because of the mandatory delay of at least a year before income could be paid out. Payment of income was not considered current.

3. The surviving spouse may also be given a general testamentary power of appointment over the principal of the entire trust property. A "power of appointment," for this purpose, means the right to control the ultimate disposition of designated property, that is, the trust principal remaining when the surviving spouse dies. (See Chapter Forty-Seven, "Powers of Appointment.") The crucial point is that the surviving spouse may be given the right to name in his will the person who will get the trust property after his death, without in any way being restricted by conditions imposed by his late wife when she transferred the property to the trust. In order for the property passing under the instrument to qualify for the marital deduction, the power of appointment must be in existence at the time the property itself passes. This means that it must be absolute and unconditional. If the husband chooses not to exercise his power to direct who will receive the property upon his death, the power will lapse and the trust usually designates a recipient in this event without losing the marital deduction.

4. No other person can have the power to appoint any part of the interest to any person other than the surviving spouse.

5. This also means that the power must be exercisable by the surviving spouse alone and in all events. One decedent's will gave his wife the right to dispose of the property as she saw fit. But she was incompetent and therefore unable to enter into a legal transaction without a guardian. Accordingly, her power of appointment over the property was not exercisable "alone and in all events," and the marital deduction wasn't allowed to the husband's estate.

With respect to persons dying after December 31, 1983, no marital deduction is allowed for any claim against a surviving spouse's estate for an interest for which a QTIP property election was made by the first spouse to die. This is important in second marriage situations.

Surviving spouse can't be under restraints

In one case, the decedent provided that his wife would receive the trust income for life, with a right to stipulate in her will who would get any remaining trust principal. But he further provided that if she attempted to assign her right to the trust income, her absolute right to the trust income would cease and the trustee would provide her with whatever income was, in the trustee's sole discretion, necessary for her support. The husband wanted to protect the trust from any effort by the wife to divert income to other persons. Provisions like this may spell disaster, even though here the estate was entitled to the marital deduction. The trustee could use principal only if he agreed to her "requests," which she was not required to make. Since principal could be diverted to others during the wife's lifetime only by her initiative, this power did not curtail the right given to her by her husband's will to designate the recipients of any remaining amount of principal when she died.

Faulty wording can be fatal

One individual, after certain bequests, left the remainder of his property in trust for the benefit of his wife. The trust instrument provided that she was entitled to support and maintenance for life, not to "all of the income" from the residue of the estate. Nor was it specified that she would be entitled to the income "annually or at more frequent intervals." This careless draftsmanship of the will resulted in forfeiture of the marital deduction.

Impact of state law

In some states, a widow is not permitted to designate her own estate or her creditors as parties who can receive the trust principal. As a result, she does not have the power to determine who is to get the principal in all instances, and the marital deduction may be lost without proper drafting.

Conclusions and advice

- To qualify for the marital deduction without placing property at the disposition of a surviving spouse who may not be able or willing to care for it, provide for a qualified terminable interest in your will or trust. This device will give your executor flexibility in deciding what portion of this interest should qualify for the marital deduction and what portion should be included in your taxable estate.

- Remember that a trust providing your spouse with a life income and the right to dispose of the remaining principal will qualify for the marital deduction.

- Do not attempt to qualify life income for the marital deduction without getting advice from experienced counsel on the technical ground rules.

- Consider the total tax bill payable by your estate and that of your spouse. It is important that each of you get the full benefit of the unified estate and gift tax credit.

- The marital deduction can apply to gift tax as well as estate tax. As noted previously under 2001 tax law, the gift tax will not be repealed in 2010.

- Even after the 2001 tax law there is an interplay between the unified credit exemption equivalent amount and the marital deduction, regardless of whether you use a QTIP trust or not. It is important to underscore that formula clauses are often used to arrive at the exemption equivalent trust amount. As the credit increases, even the QTIP or marital trust amount will correspondingly decrease. This should only be done with the advice of counsel and with full understanding.

Chapter Nineteen

THE GREAT DEBATE

In previous chapters, we have emphasized the most effective transfer of assets from one person to another. We have yet to touch on the concept of lifetime giving, as the text to this point has centered around the passage of assets upon death.

Without considering taxation, the passage of assets on death can be accomplished through vehicles as simple as having a joint savings account with the right of survivorship or stock certificates in two names with similar survivorship rights. Alternatively and, of course, of greater complexity, transfer might be made through a last will and testament, or through a trust established either during one's lifetime (living or *inter vivos* trusts) or in the will (a testamentary trust).

Living trusts can be irrevocable (you cannot change them) or revocable (which you can change or revoke). The former are most often used to reduce the estate, estate taxes and estate tax marginal rate by making gifts to trusts created for the benefit of others. However, the donor loses all control over the assets in the trust. Such trusts are often used in conjunction with a gifting program and/or the use of life insurance.

Revocable trusts, however, are more often used as a "will substitute" or as a "complement to your will." If properly drafted, they can achieve the same estate tax savings as your will and the irrevocable trust. They cannot, however, achieve the gifting advantages of the irrevocable trust. Usually, the grantor of the trust is the sole or one of the trustee(s) of the revocable trust. The trust is often funded with current assets, or maybe a "dry" or "stand-by" trust is used. There should always be a complementary will which, in most cases, "pours over" remaining assets to the trust upon the death of the person who created the trust (or, if coupled with a power of attorney, incompetency can trigger the funding).

The principal reasons for the use of revocable trusts as a will substitute are (1) to avoid probate fees, expenses and delays, (2) to reduce other fees, principally administration and attorney's fees, (3) privacy from the curious public and (4) to ease asset transfer. Those who favor the use of revocable trusts want you to believe that submission of your estate and/or trust to the jurisdiction of the probate court will raise all of these implied problems.

Here is a more complete list of reasons usually cited to convince (sometimes scare) clients to consider using a revocable trust:

1. Privacy: Usually, there is little or no court supervision, therefore others will not know your family business. Of course, because of this lack of court supervision, you lose an often needed referee.

2. Delay: Probate is typically a lengthy system to be avoided to the benefit of your heirs. Yet, in most situations, such delay does no financial harm.

3. Less expensive: By avoiding probate, you avoid its fees and usually some or all attorney and accounting fees. However, these fees are small in comparison to estate taxes and legal fees, when there is no court supervision.

4. With a trust there is no disruption of a vital income stream. In truth, there is usually some delay with most probate systems.

5. With a funded operating trust, the settlor/grantor can see what is happening and is likely to happen after his death, and has an opportunity to make changes in his trust documents.

6. The trust provides a receptacle for estate assets and death benefits which, as the probate court need not be involved, may begin immediately to be paid out upon death.

7. Trusts may amass assets from different states into one vehicle (called ancillary estates), thereby avoiding multijurisdictional probate. This is a substantial benefit.

8. With a trust, you can choose a state with a trust-friendly jurisdiction. Some states are more trust friendly than others.

9. With a trust, businesses can continue to run without interruption. This can also be accomplished by and through your will.

10. Trusts can facilitate gifts to charities in states where there are limitations on such gifts in your will.

11. A living trust relieves the grantor of the burden of investment management. This is especially important if the grantor becomes infirm and the trustee can assume a greater fiduciary role.

12. Trusts can actually help out the estate by advancing it funds.

13. Trusts are somewhat less vulnerable to attack from disgruntled heirs than a last will and testament. Generally, a court challenge of a trust is also more costly (usually brought in a court of greater jurisdiction than probate courts) and, therefore, trusts don't seem to be overturned as easily as wills.

14. Trusts have less judicial supervision, which may not necessarily be a benefit.

15. There are fewer accounting and administrative requirements if the document so provides.

16. Depending on the state, a trust can protect assets from creditors.

17. Most importantly, in many states, the use of wills has become outdated for certain clients and situations. Your situation may very well be one of them.

The other side of the debate

For years, estate planning professionals have been debating whether wills or trusts are better documents to transfer your assets upon death.

Each individual has a unique situation relative to family makeup, expenses, financial assets and goals. You come from different states and different employment situations, and therefore you must humanize and personalize the process. What is best for you can only be decided by a professional who is willing to prepare documents of either nature (some won't, and you should ask that question). After you have heard the pros and cons of each (wills vs. trusts) and have asked the costs, ask your adviser what most people in situations similar to yours do in your particular state. This may be very telling.

We emphasize the word "your" to remind readers that their document should be drafted to their personal requirements. As you have seen, there are virtually dozens of options to consider in compiling the right trust components. There is no cookie-cutter, one-size-fits-all form. You must be very cautious to avoid them, regardless of what scare tactics people use or how much they tell you that you can save.

Unfortunately, some individuals shade and distort the truth for their advantage. Some even prey upon the elderly, making wild promises and charging exorbitant amounts for relatively simple documents. In one recent case, a group using a logo similar to the AARP swept into a northeastern state and defrauded many citizens of thousands of dollars before the attorney general could react.

The con artists cited many of the reasons we have described and even charged one couple $4,900 for "canned documents" that were prepared in a far-western state based upon its laws. These documents neither conformed to the law of the clients' state, nor would they have saved the couple one cent. Even the deed that was prepared would not have passed title, as it was defective under state statute. Unfortunately, the couple lost their money because of unscrupulous misrepresentations about what may have been a legitimate concern.

While there are valid and viable reasons to use revocable trusts, it is most important to seek competent advice from an attorney who specializes in this area and can tailor documents to suit your situation. Be sure to ask her to outline all of the estimated fees and expenses for both approaches (will and revocable trust), i.e., What will it cost me to put into place a will vs. a trust? What about the charges upon my death? Which is most beneficial to my heirs, whether there is a dispute or if everything runs smoothly? What do most people with my size of estate and family situation do? Who oversees a will vs. a revocable trust?

You may be surprised to know that in a recent article from a respected national newsletter, the research authors found little difference in the expenses or frequency of use of either format. Further, it suggested that the fear of the "dreaded costs and delays" of the probate court system was generally not justified. Again, it is important to match the right tools with the situation at hand.

Conclusions and advice

• Do not assume what you do today is either all inclusive or everlasting. As your life changes, so do your needs. Review your plan periodically.

• Do not assume that avoiding probate court or using a revocable trust is right for you. It may not be. Seek competent counsel.

• Many have found that lack of court supervision for revocable trusts can be costly. Many beneficiaries feel their interests are not properly protected. Some states are even considering statutes to require some minimal oversight. You might consider adding one provision to your trust allowing the trustee to submit the trust to the jurisdiction of the court if the trustee deems this appropriate. As noted previously, the American Bar Association is in the process of recommending a uniform law to address many of these concerns. Ask your attorney if your state has adopted a version of this recommended law.

Section IV: Lifetime Gifts & Elder Planning
Chapter Twenty

ELDER PLANNING: A STRATEGIC OVERVIEW

As we have stated, an increasing segment of our population faces the issue of living to an advanced age. These individuals must manage their own financial and health needs. Further, assuming they have amassed some assets, they wish to preserve this wealth for their own use, and also pass on as much as possible to their children, loved ones or favored charities. What they fear most, and what their children and family fear for them, is substantial depletion of their assets to cover the costs of long-term health care.

Of course, this sounds no different from the goal of estate planning, but with the twist of advanced age and incapacity. The unknown factor is not the person's demise, but rather his long-term health-care needs. The potential for incurring long-term medical care or nursing home fees not covered by ordinary health insurance or the Medicare and Medicaid systems is high. For many individuals, such expenses are likely to deplete sizable amounts of their estate.

There are other problems besides asset depletion. Who can make decisions for you or your elderly parent? What documents are needed? What about medical decisions? At what point should these documents be executed and put in effect? How does a child broach the subject with the parent(s)?

For example, suppose you have started a gifting program by setting up a trust, which has purchased life insurance. The trust now depends on annual contributions (gifts) to pay the premiums. Now suppose you are disabled in an automobile accident. What will happen to the estate plan you so effectively worked out? Your estate may have sufficient assets to fund the trust, but will your trust obtain the needed funds to pay the premiums and under what authority will this money pass to the trustee?

Before answering these questions, we make three general points. Often it is the adult children who must take the lead and help their parent(s) plan for the future. As their parents approach their twilight year, regardless of how able they have been in the past, they may need help. That little hint from a loving child may be the key that unlocks a door his parents would not willingly pass through. Yes, sometimes it may be difficult emotionally for the child, or the child may even be accused of meddling or worse. However, just as your parents cared for you when you may not have appreciated their advice, you may have to do the same in their later years. That is not a license to take total control, but to be the one who ensures that it gets done.

Secondly, it is never too early to execute many of the documents that we describe. You never know when you may be in a disabling automobile or sporting accident.

Finally, as you will see, part of the overall discussion in this chapter deals with lifetime gifting. Gifting and elder planning are interrelated. For those of you who may be starting later in life or who are trying to urge your parents to begin, this is sometimes a "hard sell." Don't give up, however, as gifting is an important ingredient in the mix.

Available tools

The following list comprises the most widely used tools in the areas of elder and/or disability planning. We've included the concept of disability in this section. Disabilities occur with greater regularity in the elderly, but they are certainly not limited to any age group. Each state has different laws and therefore it is likely that your particular jurisdiction may have different types of names for such instruments, which your adviser will counsel you on. However, here is what you should be considering at a minimum:

• Durable general power of attorney. This grants someone the right to act on your behalf and survives your incompetency. It should include a specific grant to make gifts from all assets, including assets held in trust (for tax purposes, gifts to the holder of the power are limited). The power should also grant the right to transfer real estate if the principal (person granting the power) and the agent (holder of the power) are spouses.

• Springing durable power of attorney. This is usually the same as a general power but is used in cases when you only wish the power to come into effect upon one or more triggering events (e.g., your disability, hospitalization).

• Living wills (sometimes referred to as advance directives). This document indicates your desires regarding medical treatment, including extraordinary measures, in the event of an illness and your inability or incapacity to advise your doctor as to your wishes.

• Health-care agent or proxy. This tool enables you to appoint a decision maker if you are incapable of making your own health-care decisions.

• Advanced conservator appointments. In some states, you may designate your choice of a conservator should one be needed. A conservator is a court appointee who generally has limited powers to act on your behalf. Note, however, that a power of attorney may prove less cumbersome than a court appointed and supervised conservator.

• Joint banking accounts. Such accounts often "bridge the gap" between the time when money is needed and the time when all of the necessary appointments are made. Often elderly clients are advised to have both their operating account and at least one other major account in joint names. However, see Chapter Twenty-Two for the consequences of this ownership.

• Estate planning questionnaire and other vital information. (See Appendices A, B and C.) These data sheets are a must. Your family must be able to locate your key documents and understand the complexities of your estate. All too often, as people age, they begin to "clean house." Many a will and trust have been thrown out by a well-intentioned but slightly forgetful person who assumed that a family member or attorney had all their important documents. Before tossing something, please double-check.

• Lifetime gifts. As suggested, this is an important area that will be discussed in greater detail in the chapters that follow.

• Disability insurance. Although somewhat costly in comparison to life insurance, this is clearly an area to consider in view of your current financial needs and responsibilities.

• Long-term-care insurance. This also will be discussed in greater detail. It is designed to help pay for all or a portion of your long-term-care needs, including stays in a nursing home.

• Trusts. There are a group of trusts and trust provisions that may be well suited to the area of elder law. Your adviser will be able to better direct you toward those on which you should concentrate. Some are highlighted below.

• Helpful agencies. Do not discount the help you can receive from groups, agencies and/or state and local commissions. While you should always review their advice with your counselors, such advice is generally helpful, topical and offered at little or no charge. For example, many communities have a senior center and a commission on aging. The Alzheimer's associations and, of course, the AARP also have a wealth of information. They can be excellent resources, although their information is generalized and you must seek counsel for your specific situation. Also, the National Academy of Elder Law Attorneys (NAELA) can help you find an attorney in your area that specializes in elder law. See page 128 for its address and phone numbers.

Lifetime gifts

Having identified the documents needed to help you, your family and your counselors over the hurdles, we turn to your assets. There are many benefits to making lifetime gifts which we will discuss in the chapters to come. One critical benefit is the fact that legitimate gifting lowers the amount of assets available to creditors. Additionally, having fewer assets may better position you for programs that are restricted to those with assets below certain limits.

Some criticize this approach on the basis that such action is in some way not fair play or in good faith but we take fervent issue with this reasoning. As long as you, your family and your planning team stay within the rules of law written by the various controlling authorities, you have no duty to remain unprotected. One famous jurist once said that a taxpayer had every right to minimize his tax burden within the legal bounds of the Tax Code. No less can be said for elder law planning.

As we will show, the government does restrict your right to make gifts and subsequently apply for benefits. In the case of Title XIX benefits (which pay for nursing homes for those who have no assets), there are disqualification periods. In the case of outright gifts, the disqualification period is 36 months, and for gifts to a trust, it is 60 months. The disqualification periods, however, are based upon a complicated formula, and your adviser will have to use your specific variables to determine your exact disqualification period.

A related question seems to be whether or not a parent should give her home (and/or other assets) to her children. If so, should it be an outright gift or should the parent retain a life use? This question invariably comes up when an estate planner speaks to an elderly audience. Clients are often told by well-meaning friends that they made such a gift, and it was simple to do and very cheap.

However, it may be neither simple nor inexpensive. The planner must open up discussions with the client in the following areas:

• Gifting rules and gift tax potentials.

• Impact of retained rights of residency on estate taxes.

• Disqualification periods for Title XIX purposes from the date when a gift is made (see below for Title XIX discussion).

• Children's ownership and their creditors, deaths, divorces and/or disagreements.

• Loss of capital gains exclusion ($250,000 for a single person, $500,000 for a married couple) on the sale of a personal residence and the resulting tax when children sell the home.

• Possible increases in real estate taxes and insurance due to loss of elder exemptions and owner occupancy rates.

• Possible concern by the bank which holds a mortgage on the property.

These are obviously dangerous waters. The rules are complicated and, to some degree, apply differently in each state. For example, the federal and state Medicaid program was established under Title XIX of the Social Security Act in 1965 and deals with gifting and the disqualification period. In part, the program funds the cost of nursing home care for individuals who cannot pay due to a lack of assets and income. It is administered by each state, and each state has its own variations to the regulations. As noted, when gifts are made, the donor is usually disqualified from the program for a period of time based upon a formula. Therefore, making such a gift could disqualify you for a substantial period. The client must understand this, and have calculated the disqualification period prior to making the gift.

With proper planning, however, substantial assets can be both given away to children/grandchildren and saved and protected from needless loss. Such gifting programs, if designed by a professional, will not run afoul of the tangled web of regulations. Of paramount importance is the fact that there is more misinformation about what can and cannot be done under the rules of the Title XIX program than in any other area of elder law and estate planning. Therefore, you are strongly advised to seek competent counsel. You may wish to check with NAELA, 1604 N. Country Club Rd., Tucson, AZ 85716-3102 (telephone 520-881-4005; TDD 520-326-2467) for a recommendation of a qualified attorney in your area.

Long-term-care insurance

Another method of protecting against the possible depletion of your estate from the substantial cost of long-term health care would be to purchase insurance. There are many different policies and possible coverage options. Also, there are several different state rules that may apply. You should, therefore, check with counselors in your state before discussing a policy or making a purchase.

There are several important concepts here. First, you should know your state's rules before you make a purchase. Second, it would be most desirable that the benefits you purchase be enjoyed in another state if you decide to move. Finally, the company from which you purchase your policy should be a top-rated insurance provider. Remember, you may not need this coverage for many years to come. Choosing a highly rated company will increase the likelihood that it will still be in existence at the time of your future claim. Seek out a number of highly recommended insurance professionals and get several quotes from each.

The use of trusts

Trusts are used in a variety of ways by the elderly. First, they provide for their offspring and reduce the size of their estate. These trusts have been discussed in other chapters. You should, however, be aware of the disqualification rule and how gifts to such trusts are considered. A second area is for children or grandchildren with special needs. Finally, trusts set up for either the elderly person or their spouse can take the form of living or testamentary trusts.

• Special needs trust. If you are considering leaving a significant amount to a person who is either infirm or disabled, and that person is receiving benefits such as SSI (Supplemental Security Income), you might want to use a surrogate. In effect, you would leave it outright or in trust to another person (say, a sibling of the intended recipient) with whom you have a nonbinding understanding that the funds will be used exclusively for the well-being of the person you intended. Obviously, this requires faith and trust in the person you choose, and you must also be prepared for the eventuality that this plan may not work.

For larger amounts, a special needs trust can be established by a third party (usually a parent or grandparent) for the benefit of a disabled child. There is also another type we do not discuss in detail, in which the disabled person uses her own assets to set up the trust.

The special needs trust must be very carefully drafted in order not to disqualify the beneficiary from the benefits she may currently enjoy. The beneficiary can have no right to compel distributions of the trust or to revoke the trust. The trustee must have sole discretion in this regard and, if so, the trust assets will not be considered "available" to the beneficiary and thus will not potentially disqualify her from benefits.

Note that states differ regarding who the residuary beneficiary may be upon the death of the current beneficiary. It is also important that the trustee know the SSI rules and limit distribution to those expenditures that are appropriate under these rules; otherwise, the beneficiary's SSI qualification may be in jeopardy.

Obviously, these are sophisticated, highly technical legal documents. They can be of great benefit to the disabled individual regardless of their age if they do not risk disqualifying that individual from receipt of very important benefits. Seek the advice of competent counsel before considering such documents.

• Revocable trusts. One very common misconception is that the use of a revocable trust will protect assets from creditors, including expenses related to the costs of long-term care. Unfortunately, this is not the case.

Where the trust is revocable, for Medicaid purposes, there has been no transfer. Therefore, the assets are still available to the grantor, and the entire corpus of a revocable trust is considered an available resource and is used in the determination of one's eligibility for benefits. In addition, in many states, creditors can also reach these assets.

• Irrevocable trusts. The following discussion of irrevocable trusts speaks in terms of general rules. As noted, each state is given latitude in determining its policy and/or how it interprets and enforces the federal regulations. Therefore, the rules set forth below may not be applicable in all states. Before entering the arena of trusts and Title XIX planning, you are urged to exercise extreme caution and to test each concept against the rules applicable in your state.

We have found that seniors tend to consider transfers to their children/grandchildren as gifts, whether they are made in the form of an outright transfer or through a trust. However, if they transfer assets to a trust in which they retain some interest, there is an air of protection added to their ultimate desire for benevolence.

Irrevocable trusts in which the grantor and/or the grantor's spouse has only an income interest are allowed under the 1993 federal law. This law updated and changed the rules regarding trusts. There can, however, be no access to principal. If this standard is met, then the principal is considered an unavailable asset for calculating eligibility for Title XIX purposes. This is the general rule, but the income interest alone may, in some states, cause disqualification.

There are many other reasons why an income-only trust might be considered opposed to an outright transfer to the children, especially in a situation where estate tax is not an issue. First, there may be the issue of maintaining a degree of control as well as risk avoidance. Also, the client may be in a lower tax bracket. Sometimes, putting the assets in the children's name disqualifies them from needed college aid for their own children's education.

There are also other issues to be considered in deciding to utilize an income-only trust. If the grantor reserves the right to the income of the trust, its entire value would be taxed in his estate. This could be very significant, especially if the principal appreciates substantially.

Remember, also, that for Title XIX purposes there are different disqualification periods for gifts. For an outright gift, it is a 36-month period, while for a gift to a trust, there is a 60-month period of disqualification. These are thorny issues and must be thoroughly discussed with competent counsel before deciding if this trust suits your purposes. Much will depend on your state law and how it views income-only trusts.

• Miller trusts. In 1990, the Colorado Federal District Court, in the case of *Miller v. Ibarra* (746 F. Supp. 19; D. Colo. 1990), upheld an individual's right to assign excess income to an irrevocable trust in order to reduce his own income level to below the Medicaid cap and gain eligibility. The 1993 law sanctioned this type of trust and thus made these arrangements viable. They are known as qualified income trusts or income assignment trusts. The rules and structure are complicated, and they cannot be used in all states, so check with your adviser.

• Sole benefit trust. The spousal annuity trust (SAT) and the disability annuity trust (DAT) function very much like an annuity for the spouse not in long-term care, commonly referred to as the "community spouse." The assets are transferred to an irrevocable trust for the sole benefit of that spouse.

The assets in the trust are then paid out to the beneficiary on an actuarial basis. There is no penalty period for the transferor; however, there is some question whether the trust is an available asset of the beneficiary.

• Testamentary trust. Testamentary trusts, i.e., those contained in your will, seemed to have escaped the wrath against trusts levied in the 1993 law. It has generally been thought that if the decedent's will created a trust for her spouse or child which did not provide an invasion right exercisable by the beneficiary, the trust would not be considered an available asset.

Therefore, it has been quite common for estate planners, even where estate tax is not an issue, to split a married couple's assets. Each would own half of the assets, and each will would set up a testamentary trust for the other upon the first death.

The theory is to save at least half of the assets. Even if gifting were being used, the trust would protect one-half of what was left. This concept seems to still be valid, although it has been challenged at the lower administrative level in at least one state. As always, your adviser can best tell you of its current status in your state.

Conclusions and advice

• Elder law and planning is an emerging area and is often neglected by parent and child alike. The sooner you start, the better position you will be in.

• There are many health-related, as well as power-granting, documents you should have in place. Do them now, not later. We can cite many examples of healthy young adults who were going about their normal activities, participating in sports or simply driving home from work who meet some malady. Failure to have these documents in place may prove both tragic and financially disastrous.

• Not all attorneys are qualified elder law attorneys. Nor are all estate planners qualified in the area of elder law. Call NAELA for a reference in your area.

• Gifting is a key part of estate and elder planning. Decide with your adviser whether the gift should be outright or to a trust.

• Long-term care may include home health care, assisted living, adult day care, respite care and nursing home care. In 1997, it was estimated that the average American male would spend approximately $57,000 on this care and a female, $125,000. Remember, costs have increased considerably since then.

• Virtually all states have passed some laws and regulations relating to long-term-care insurance. Due to the wide range of interpretations of Title XIX regulations, you must seek competent advice to help choose a policy that meets both your needs and the regulations of your state. Also, remember to ask if it is transportable to the state in which you plan to retire.

• Trusts and elder law are a field filled with land mines. If you want to give assets to a trust and retain benefits for yourself and/or your spouse, consider this very carefully. Seek counsel who is thoroughly versed in this area and who receives periodic updates of the changes in the regulations at both the state and federal level.

Chapter Twenty-One

GIFTS HAVE
MANY ADVANTAGES

Prior to 1977, the federal gift tax rate was only three-fourths of the federal estate tax rate at each value bracket. This differential encouraged the making of lifetime gifts, rather than property dispositions upon a person's demise. Now the tax rates are the same, and there is a unified credit for both taxes. That has led to a general tendency to think, "Why should I give away property now, when the tax impact will be no greater if I hold on to what's mine until I die? The longer I keep my properties, the longer I can keep my options open." In addition, the 2001 tax law did not repeal the gift tax in 2010 as it did with the estate tax. The theory presumably was to avoid massive transfers of wealth on a tax-free basis before the sunset provision returns the estate and gift tax rates to their 2001 levels. The 2010 top gift tax rate is slated to be 35 percent.

Why lifetime transfers may be more attractive than transfers upon death

Thus, there is some superficial appeal to this thought of holding on to your property. But there are persuasive tax and other reasons for making lifetime transfers rather than waiting until one's death. Here are the principal reasons:

1. If property seems likely to appreciate in value, a current transfer will have less gift tax impact now than it would if made later when the fair market value is higher. Also, if the property is retained and held until death, all of the appreciation will be taxable in the estate.

2. Some property automatically becomes more valuable each year. For example, if you give away a policy of insurance on your life, gift tax is based

upon the interpolated terminal reserve, which for practical purposes may be thought of as the cash surrender value. Assuming that you do not borrow against the policy, the reserve that is the basis for gift tax value will increase each year. The longer you wait to give away the policy, the higher the gift tax will be. At death, the entire proceeds can be included.

3. The donor can reduce current federal income tax by making transfers of income-producing properties to beneficiaries, who are presumably in a lower tax bracket.

4. In many situations, a present gift of property will save the donor all liability for state or local property taxes. Many localities have intangible property taxes on securities, receivables and sometimes bank accounts.

5. A present gift of property can save the donor administration, custody and insurance expenses, plus the chores of property ownership.

6. There is an annual gift tax exclusion of up to $11,000 per donee, which can be doubled to as much as $22,000 if both spouses consent to the making of a gift (gift-splitting) to that donee. The sooner such a program starts, the more money can be given away free of tax.

7. The gift tax marital deduction allows all transfers to a US citizen spouse to be free of tax liability. There is a $110,000 annual exclusion for gifts to a noncitizen spouse in the case of transfers that would qualify for the marital deduction if the donee were a US citizen. A transfer to a noncitizen spouse that creates a joint tenancy is treated as consideration belonging to the surviving noncitizen spouse if the transfer would have constituted an executable gift. Accordingly, the amount of joint tenancy property included in the estate of the first spouse to die is reduced proportionately by the amount of the gift.

8. Gain on the sale of appreciated-value property can be avoided by selling the property to a beneficiary at cost, making a gift of the balance.

9. Gifts can be made of property that has appreciated in value, so that the donor is relieved of the gain on which he would have to pay tax if he sold the property (real or personal).

10. Lifetime gifts can reduce the cost of administering what will eventually be the donor's gross estate, since executor's fees are customarily based upon the size of the estate.

11. Lifetime transfers can minimize the chance of loss of the donor's property. A physician might be sued for malpractice in an amount exceeding his liability insurance coverage, which would make his other property subject to creditors' claims. Bona fide gifts to beneficiaries would protect this property.

12. A donor's current dispositions might better represent what he wants to do than transfers made at a time when he might lack today's acumen and ability to resist external pressures.

13. By making modest gifts of income-producing property or business interests at this time, a donor gains the opportunity to see how responsibly his beneficiaries behave in the management of this property. If they prove unable to handle the property, he could modify his thinking. He could amend his will or trusts and provide that all future gifts (lifetime and death) be in trust with a knowledgeable trustee.

14. Lifetime gifts can be made with the assurance of privacy. No one will learn about them other than the donees themselves and the IRS, which is bound by law to keep tax information confidential. What is left to anyone by will, on the other hand, is hardly a secret, since wills are available in probate courts or other designated offices where others can read them.

15. Gifts made at the present time won't be held up in probate proceedings or by the slowness of an executor.

16. Gifts made at the present time can afford the donor the psychological satisfaction of seeing his beneficiaries enjoy them.

17. As noted in Chapter Twenty, lifetime gifts may place an elderly person in a better position vis-à-vis various federal, state and local programs that are available to seniors. Depending on the size of your estate, you should discuss with your adviser whether such gifts should be made annually or in one lump sum. From an estate and gift tax standpoint, you may use your unified credit

during your lifetime. The advantage may be that you begin, and therefore finish, any Title XIX disqualification or penalty period sooner. This is a crucial point which should not be overlooked.

18. Using your annual exclusion through the vehicle of your insurance trust, with a Crummey power, is a common technique.

19. Gifts to charities offer multiple benefits. You receive not only an income tax deduction but also the satisfaction of helping your favorite charities. You also reduce the size of your estate.

Conclusions and advice

- Remember that your children, grandchildren or parents may possess something of great tax value: Low income tax brackets. But unearned income of a child under 14 in excess of $1,500 per year (in 2001) can now be taxed at the parents' top marginal tax rates. (See Item 16 in Chapter Two, "Hidden Traps in Estate Planning.") Also includable in a parent's gross estate on death is the value of property which the parent transferred to an existing enterprise (or assets from that enterprise) to another asset in which a child owns a disproportionately large share of potential appreciation and in which the parent retains an income interest or other rights causing inclusions.

- Be certain that your gifts are complete, or the property may in fact, end up in your gross estate. Comply with state laws, for example, requiring that real estate transfers be in written form and recorded in the appropriate land records. Most states require this.

- Have you retained control over property that you have transferred?

- Generally, we don't know when we are going to die. But lifetime gifts may be planned in light of what we do know. For example, a routine annual physical checkup may alert someone to accelerate his gift program with deliberate speed.

- Be careful not to make gifts of income-producing properties if doing so would leave you without adequate income. Anticipate your needs in light of inflation, and presume that, as you get older, medical expenses will increase— unless you carry an excellent major-medical insurance policy.

• Do not make gifts that will relieve you of a legal obligation without being aware of all the tax consequences. If you make a gift of income-producing property to a trust for the benefit of your minor child, and this income is used to provide maintenance and support of the child, you have been relieved of a legal obligation. You may be taxed on the income, and the trust principal may end up in your gross estate. Make other arrangements for the child's support requirements and be careful to prohibit such use.

• Do not make lifetime gifts after you have used up your unified estate and gift tax credit unless you thoroughly explore the tax consequences. This would be equivalent to prepayment of estate taxes.

• If a marriage appears to be strained, a husband and wife should not make taxable split gifts. This could result in one spouse being held responsible for the entire gift tax liability, even if some or all of the property really had belonged to the other spouse.

• Always seek advice as there are many traps. For example, if a person has an annuity payable to him for the remainder of his life, and he has this changed to a contract calling for payments (in a lesser amount) to himself and a named person (such as his daughter) for as long a period as she may outlive him, he has made a taxable gift to her.

• If you are thinking about a trust and there are possible generation-skipping features, ask your counselor about the new provisions allowed under the 2001 tax law. In particular, you may want to give your trustee the right/power of severance (to split the trust into two for the same beneficiaries) as granted under the 2001 tax law. This may prove very helpful.

• Recently many tax figures that were indexed for inflation were adjusted by Rev. Proc. 2001-59. These include the upward adjustments of the annual exclusion per donee from $10,000 to $11,000, the annual gifts to a noncitizen spouse from $103,000 to $110,000 and the GST exemption from $1,060,000 to $1.1 million per estate.

Chapter Twenty-Two

CHOICE OF FORMS OF OWNERSHIP

The manner in which property is owned is most meaningful for estate planning purposes. It affects the passage of property when an owner dies, it may insulate part of the value from creditor claims and there are federal estate, gift and income tax implications. In addition, the creation of joint ownership may be both a gift as well as a useful tool in other situations such as planning with your elderly parent(s).

At the time of a person's death, the value of all the property she owns is included in her gross estate. If her interest in a property is actually and demonstrably less than 100%, only the applicable portion of its value will be included in her estate. Joint ownership can therefore reduce the amount of the estate tax if you can prove the actual interest owned.

Why property may be held in joint ownership

There are various justifications for owning property with someone else:

1. Fait accompli. Property may have been acquired by two or more persons, so that form of ownership represents the fact. *Examples:* Each of the purchasers of an asset supplied some of the funds; or the property was acquired jointly by gift, as when a bride and groom are given a house or securities by one set of parents.

2. Protection. An individual wishes to make certain that upon his death the property will go to designated parties without the risk of someone else claiming the assets. A husband may wish the residence to go to his wife, without interference from the children. Or a mother may set up a joint bank account with her daughter so that the money in the account will unquestionably be the daughter's even if a son claims a portion after the mother's death.

3. Avoidance of probate. Joint ownership of property with a survivorship provision will avoid the delay, expense and publicity involved in probate. Under a survivorship provision, upon the death of a co-owner, his interest automatically passes to the surviving co-owner(s). The dispositions of a will are open to an inquisitive public when the document is filed. By contrast, few know what property passes to whom under a survivorship clause in most personal property situations and even in a real property deed.

In the case of decedents who died after December 31, 1981, where a husband and wife owned property in joint tenancy with a right of survivorship, the estate of the first spouse to die includes one-half of the value of the property, regardless of which spouse furnished the consideration for its acquisition. At first blush, this appears to be good news for married couples, as it eliminates the sometimes impossible job of endeavoring to trace the financial history of the property and prove the relative contribution of each spouse. On the other hand, the first spouse to die may have paid little if any of the cost, so that her gross estate may include half the value of property that had been obtained through the work or purchase of the survivor. Where property has increased in value since acquisition, the tax cost or basis for determining gain or loss on subsequent sale by the surviving spouse will, in the case of inherited property, be valued in an altogether different and somewhat controversial manner under the 2001 tax law.

Here is a brief comparison of the old and new rules. Under the old rule the property would be valued at the time of death or six months later, if elected by the executor. Where the husband dies first, his assumed one-half of the property will have this value as a stepped-up basis inherited by his surviving spouse, while her assumed one-half will have its cost as its basis.

Under the 2001 law, beginning in 2010 the step-up rule will be repealed and replaced with a modified carryover basis rule. In essence, the heir will receive the decedent's current basis instead of the current law's step-up to the date-of-death fair-market value. However, as a partial replacement, executors will be able to increase the basis of estate property by up to $1.3 million or $3 million in the case of property passing to a surviving spouse.

The problems with this law are many. First is the need for meticulous record keeping and the transference of this knowledge to the executor. Then there is the fair allocation of the step-up ($1.3 or $3 million) among heirs. Many have claimed that this will put executors in extremely difficult positions causing fees and possible litigation to increase due to disputes. This does not even begin to mention the problem of lost or poor record keeping by the decedent.

In all, the new law will change the calculation of the cost basis of property inherited from a decedent, whether it is a full interest or a joint interest. If more than one-half of the property is proven to be the husband's, then a greater part (perhaps all) of the property will receive a stepped-up basis only until 2010. Note, where the 50-50 split provided by the Economic Recovery Tax Act of 1981 is not what the parties want, consideration should be given to changing these proportions by such means as interspousal gifts, which can now be regarded as tax free under most circumstances.

4. Debt. In some states, certain jointly owned property is beyond the reach of the creditors of a deceased co-owner.

5. Trust-funding mechanism. When an insurance trust has been used as part of a person's estate plan and there is either a death or disability, there is the possibility that the premiums will not be paid. This becomes an even greater concern if the spouse is not the beneficiary of the trust (i.e., the trust holds insurance which presumably benefits children of a first marriage). If the trustee is one of the children, as is often the case, then a joint account can be set up to pay the premiums. While there is no legally binding agreement with the child/trustee to use the funds for this purpose, it is a simple way of handling the problem. A better way, of course, would be to make a specific bequest in your will to the trust.

Joint ownership isn't always desirable

There are some disadvantages in joint ownership of property:

1. A major shortcoming of joint ownership is that on the death of one co-owner, where the co-owners are not married, the IRS considers that the decedent really owned all of the property and includes its full value in the decedent's gross estate. This leaves it to the executor to prove the extent to which all of this property wasn't the decedent's. In the absence of adequate proof, the total value of property in which the decedent was only one co-owner frequently winds up in his gross estate even though the other co-owner(s) may actually have paid for their interests with their own funds. Proof of who furnished how much of the consideration many years ago is difficult, especially if the property was acquired piecemeal. This rule no longer applies to joint interests of husband and wife. However, for others it can have substantial estate tax ramifications.

2. The death of a co-owner may make all of the property unavailable to the survivor for a time. For example, in the case of a joint bank account, in some states the funds are frozen by the bank upon the death of a co-owner until the tax authorities unfreeze the account. Sale of property held in joint ownership with a decedent may entail similar problems.

3. There can be serious practical problems in selling one's interest in property if co-owners are opposed to the idea.

4. If two or more persons jointly own property, such as a business, the IRS can shut down the entire enterprise for nonpayment of taxes by one co-owner.

5. If a husband and wife own property jointly, and there is a divorce, or even if there are marital difficulties that haven't gone that far, management and administration of the joint property can prove difficult.

6. Where certain types of property are owned jointly, one owner can be seriously involved financially because of an act of the co-owner. For example, if a mother and son own an automobile jointly and he gets involved in an accident resulting in more damages than the insurance covers, she is confronted with the liability because the accident was caused by her property.

7. When there is a joint bank account, one spouse cannot logically argue that she didn't know what was in the account. This greatly weakens any claim, for example, that if the husband omits income from a joint return, the wife is not subject to tax, penalty and interest on the unreported income because she is an innocent spouse.

Forms of joint ownership

These are the principal forms of joint ownership of property:

1. Joint tenancy. Each of the parties has an undivided interest in the entire property, so that if one owner dies, the survivor(s) owns the property. Each party reports the income from his portion. The parties need not be married.

2. Tenancy in common. Each person owns a specified portion of the property. Upon the death of one party, her interest goes to her estate rather than to the surviving co-owner(s).

3. Tenancy by the entirety. This form of ownership applies only to legally married couples, and in some states it applies only to real estate. Each spouse has an undivided interest in the entire property, and on the death of one spouse, the survivor doesn't succeed to the decedent's right and title because he already had it. Half of the value of the property goes to the estate of the first to die. Upon sale of the property by the couple, gain or loss is divided between the spouses.

Federal gift tax

Federal gift tax may apply to the creation or termination of a joint ownership arrangement. In general, if a person is given an interest in property without paying for it, or the consideration paid is less than the value of what is received, gift tax is owed. If a father opens a joint bank account with his daughter, providing all the funds for it, or if he sets up a joint brokerage account to which he supplies all of the securities and cash, he has not made a taxable gift until such time as she withdraws or makes use of what he has put into the joint account.

Except for spouses, where two persons hold real property as joint tenants (realty tenancies by the entirety or joint tenancies with right of survivorship), there is a taxable gift if one party contributed more of the purchase price than the other did. A gift also results if a joint tenancy is terminated and the proceeds of the sale of the property are divided among the parties in unequal amounts.

Federal income tax

Where co-owned property is sold, each co-owner generally has gain or loss measured by the difference between his/her basis (tax cost) in the property and his/her share of the realization.

Deaths in common disaster

When two joint tenants die under circumstances where it is impossible to determine the sequence of deaths, the property so held is generally distributable one-half as if one co-owner had survived and one-half as if the other co-owner had survived. (See Chapter Eight, "Simultaneous Deaths of Spouses.")

Conclusions and advice

• Unmarried co-owners should be prepared to show that the decedent had not furnished all of the consideration for the purchase of property by documenting what the co-owners had furnished of their own funds.

• Where husband and wife own property jointly, make provisions for the disposition of the property in case both spouses die simultaneously.

• Do not use joint ownership as a sole substitute for a will. Very likely, all property won't be jointly owned, and in the absence of a will, such other property is distributable according to the state's law of intestacy. In addition, a will or trust is far more flexible and is subject to modification as family structure and other circumstances change.

• Do not use joint ownership if there is reason to believe that the co-owners, such as a husband and wife, are having difficulties or are likely to divorce.

Chapter Twenty-Three

TAKING ADVANTAGE OF THE ANNUAL EXCLUSION

Lifetime transfers of property are subject to the same tax rates as transfers at death. But the first $11,000 (as indexed for future inflation) of gifts to any single donee in each calendar year is excluded from taxable lifetime transfers. If the donor's spouse elects to share in the gift, the annual exclusion can be brought up to $22,000 per donee (gift splitting). Additionally, the new 2001 tax law has added what might be classified as several beneficial education-based exclusions, credits and deductions. These will be discussed in later chapters. However, parents and grandparents often combine their gifting plan with the education expense needs for their children and grandchildren.

Eligibility for the annual exclusion

Gifts are eligible for this annual exclusion if they fulfill the following conditions: The value of the interest transferred must be reasonably certain, and what is transferred must be a present, as opposed to a future, interest. A gift without reasonably ascertainable value might be a transfer of an income interest in shares of a family corporation at a time when dividends could not be paid and the shares could not be sold or otherwise converted into cash. Similarly, the transfer of a franchise would not be excludable if its value could not be determined because of unpredictable income, which itself was subject to various restrictions. Most gifts can be valued or appraised; be attentive to having a qualified appraisal when there is no accepted fair market value.

To qualify as a present interest, a gift must carry an unrestricted right to the immediate use, possession or enjoyment of the property or its income (for example, income from certain land for the remainder of the donee's life or for a specified number of years). A promise to make a gift in the future is not a present interest, even though the promise may be an enforceable one. A future interest is one that is to commence in use, possession or enjoyment at some later date or time. The decisive factor is when the donee receives possession or enjoyment of the property—not when he receives title.

The gift of a life insurance policy where the donee has no rights until the death of the insured is a future interest and is not excludable from taxable gifts. However, when the donee owns the policy, or a trust is the donee and it owns the policy, this is a completed gift of a present interest provided the donor gave up all rights to the policy. Similarly, if a donor conveys real estate to a donee but reserves the right to the rentals for as long as he lives, then the gift is of a future interest. The donee's possession and enjoyment of the land is postponed until the death of the donor. However, the donor may later release this to complete the gift.

When a spouse is not a US citizen

The $11,000 annual exclusion is not available where the donor spouse is a US citizen but the donee spouse is not. In the case of transfers that would qualify for the marital deduction if the donee were a US citizen, there is a $110,000 annual exclusion for such transfers by gift to a noncitizen spouse. For example, a gift in trust does not qualify for the $110,000 annual exclusion unless it is within one of the exceptions to the terminable interest rule. In other words, a trust that qualifies for the marital deduction will also qualify for the $110,000 annual exclusion. This rule applies to gifts made after June 29, 1989.

A nonresident is entitled to a marital deduction or annual exclusion for gift tax purposes in the same circumstances as a US citizen or resident. Thus, gifts from a nonresident noncitizen to a US citizen spouse qualify for the marital deduction. In addition, each year the first $110,000 in gifts from a nonresident noncitizen to a noncitizen spouse is not taxed, as long as the gifts would qualify for the marital deduction if the donee were a US citizen. However, the deduction and annual exclusion apply only if the property is subject to US gift tax.

Unutilized exclusions are forfeited

Unlike charitable contributions and business losses, unutilized gift tax exclusions cannot be carried over for use in a later year's computations. If the annual exclusion is not fully utilized in any single year, it is forfeited forever. The earlier you start an annual gift program, the greater the potential dollar benefits of the annual exclusion. If you lack the cash to make gifts in a particular year, borrow money for the purpose. Further, the gift need not be in cash if property with a determinable value is given for immediate enjoyment.

Available donees

There is no limit on the number of beneficiaries who may receive gifts subject to the annual exclusion. Multiple donees could build up the amount of the exclusion indefinitely. In the case of gifts to a properly drafted trust, the beneficiaries are the donees. Transfers to several trusts for the benefit of the same beneficiary, however, permit only one $11,000 exclusion that year. If gifts are made to the donor's son, to the wife of the donor's son and to the married couple jointly, there are only two exclusions, as only two individuals are involved. In one case, each of two brothers made gifts at the same time to his own children and to his brother's children (the donor's nieces and nephews), but the gifts to the nieces and nephews didn't qualify as separate exclusions, being regarded in this situation as indirect gifts to each donor's own children.

Gifts to minors may qualify as present interests

Under appropriate circumstances, a gift to or for the benefit of a minor child qualifies as a gift of a present interest even though the child does not actually have the use, possession or enjoyment of the gift. There must be a provision that the property and any income from it may be expended by or for the benefit of the donee before he reaches age 21 and will to the extent not so expended either pass to the child on reaching 21 or be payable to the child's estate or to properly designated persons in case the minor dies before age 21.

This is an important concept, especially with the trusts that you may create. Your estate planner will undoubtedly recommend that while a child is a minor (or under 21) income from the trust be accumulated at the trustee's discretion. Gifts to a trust so drafted would not qualify for the annual exclusion, unless the trust also provides that the child upon reaching this age has a right to withdraw, not only the accumulated income, but also the principal. This is an extremely important provision, as it preserves the exclusions. (See Chapter Twenty-Four, "Gifts to Minors Can Qualify for the Annual Exclusion.") In most cases, this does not present a problem, as children can usually understand the detriment of withdrawing the funds, especially if it will have a negative impact on future expectations.

Gift splitting

The amount of the annual gift tax exclusion can in effect be doubled to as much as $22,000 per donee per year if the proper election is made. A gift by one spouse to someone other than his/her spouse may be treated as made one-half by each spouse, but only if each was a citizen or resident of the US at the time of the gift. This split-gift election can be made only on the federal gift tax return filed by the 15th day of the fourth month following the close of the year in which the gift is made. Consent may not be signified after the IRS sends a notice of deficiency with respect to tax for the year to either spouse.

Once the gift tax return is filed, even if the consent has been overlooked because of an error of judgment or lack of knowledge, it cannot be given in any other way. In a few isolated instances, courts have allowed gift splitting even where the election had not been made on the required form, on the grounds that proper gift-splitting consents had been filed on returns for the preceding years, and in this particular year, the donor's accountant testified that his clients told him that they intended their gifts to be split. But don't count on receiving this lenient treatment from a court.

The only acceptable way to make the split-gift election is for the spouse to sign the return and to check the block headed "Yes" on Form 709, United States

Gift Tax Return, in response to the question, "Do you consent to have the gifts made by you and by your spouse to third parties during the calendar year considered as made one-half by each of you?" If no gift tax return is filed for any reason, clearly no election can be made. Where the consent is effective for the entire year, all gifts made by husband or wife to third parties during that year must be treated in the same way.

Recapitalization in order to utilize the annual exclusion

An individual may feel that he must sacrifice the annual gift tax exclusion if substantially all of his wealth is tied up in his closely held corporation. He doesn't want to give away his stock because its voting power is essential to him in controlling the enterprise. But a gift to take advantage of the exclusion is possible. He can cause a recapitalization to be effected from his present one-class voting stock into voting and nonvoting shares. The latter can then be given away as he sees fit—for example, by presents each year of enough of the nonvoting stock to meet the annual exclusion rules. (See Chapter Twenty-Eight, "Using a Family Business to Transfer Assets.")

Conclusions and advice

• Start your gift program as soon as possible in order to maximize the number of annual exclusions.

• The exclusion is effectively doubled if your spouse consents to participate in gift splitting, even if in fact your spouse has no property to give away or does not contribute to the gift. File a gift tax return and both must sign.

• Recapitalization of a corporation you own may allow you to give away shares without loss of control. Or, use short-term borrowing.

• Gifts of future interests do not qualify for the annual exclusion, except in the case of gifts to a trust where the Crummey rules apply and are followed.

• Reciprocal or cross-gifts don't provide additional exclusions.

• Annual gifts to grandchildren may avoid a generation-skipping tax at a later date and do not reduce your specific generation-skipping exemption.

Chapter Twenty-Four

GIFTS TO MINORS CAN QUALIFY FOR THE ANNUAL EXCLUSION

As noted, the first $11,000 of gifts to any individual in a given year is not subject to federal gift tax, nor does it use up any of the unified credit for gift and estate taxes. But this annual exclusion applies only to gifts of present interests—that is, where there is an unrestricted right to the immediate use, possession or enjoyment of the property given. The exclusion doesn't apply to the gift of a future interest. This would appear to eliminate the exclusion for gifts to minor children, who, for legal or practical reasons, are in no position to handle the immediate right to do as they please with a gift of cash, diamonds, postage stamps or antiques. A special provision in the tax law, however, permits the annual gift tax exclusion even in cases when a minor child may not be able to get her hands on the property, or determine what is going to be done with it, for many years.

Start your gift program when children are still young

Careful adherence to this rule means that you can begin to take advantage of the annual exclusion when a baby is born, giving away substantial amounts free of tax by the time the child reaches age 21, without fear that the recipient will squander or misuse the property while still financially unsophisticated. Of course, this advantage is multiplied when gifts are made to several minor children or grandchildren each year.

If a gift is legitimate and outright, the annual gift tax exclusion isn't lost merely because the named recipient is a minor. But a minor may have no legal capacity as to the subject matter of the gift, so it must be made for her benefit

—that is, to a trustee, guardian or custodian. There is no gift if the donor has not actually relinquished the property. It isn't necessary that the property or its income actually be expended by or for the benefit of the minor during her period of minority, as long as all amounts not expended will pass to her when she reaches her 21st birthday. Should she die before that time, the property must be distributed to her estate or in accordance with her valid instructions on the subject.

Chapter Twenty-Five will examine the Uniform Gift to Minors Act. This is a custodial arrangement allowed by each state in order to facilitate gifts to minors.

Below we describe the requirements for ensuring that your annual gifts to your trust will qualify for the annual exclusion.

Gifts to minors treated as present interests

Here are the ground rules. A transfer for the benefit of someone who hasn't reached age 21 on the date of the gift will qualify for the annual gift tax exclusion (even though the property is beyond her grasp) if the conditions of the transfer meet all three of the following requirements:

1. Property is transferred to a trust for the benefit of a minor, and the trustee is given sole discretion, without substantial restriction, to decide whether and how to use the money on behalf of the minor. Both the property itself and its income may be expended for the benefit of the donee on or before she reaches her 21st birthday, but it could be the donor's firm intention and expectation that no part of the gift will be touched before the minor reaches 21. In any case, it is not the minor who decides whether the gift may be expended by or for her. The phrase "may be expended" can refer to a mere grant of power to expend the trust funds or even to a probability that the funds will be used by or on behalf of the minor.

In one case, the court found that there was no substantial restriction on the trustee's discretion where he was authorized to spend trust money on the minor's behalf to cover costs and expenses "not otherwise adequately provided for." This kind of transaction, which arises from the minor's need, is unlikely to be treated as a future interest ineligible for the annual exclusion. On the other hand, expenditures on the minor's behalf to be made only in the case of accident, illness or other emergency would create restrictions on the trustee's discretion substantial enough to bar the annual exclusion.

2. Any portion of the property (trust principal) and its income not disposed of under #1 will pass to the child when she reaches age 21.

3. If the minor dies before turning 21, any portion of the property and its income not disposed of under #1 will be payable either to the minor's estate or in accordance with other directions she has given in a will. If, under state law, a minor does not have the legal right to make a will or otherwise dispose of property, the property will be distributed according to that state's laws of intestacy. Customarily, the assets would go to her next of kin, according to the state's definition of what that means.

A transfer will satisfy the above conditions even if:

a. The minor, upon reaching age 21, has the right to extend the terms of the trust, which may very well be the expectation.

b. The trust instrument contains provisions for disposition of the property in case the donee should die intestate.

Lower age for reaching majority in some states

Allowance of the annual exclusion is not affected in states that have lowered the age of majority from 21 to 18 and require property to be distributed to a donee when she reaches age 18.

You can't correct previous gifts

A trust agreement or other arrangement that does not include the three main requirements cannot be amended retroactively to obtain the annual gift tax exclusion. Correction of a faulty document is impossible for federal tax purposes in this case, even where state law may permit it.

Distribution at age 21

Most clients are quite gratified and willingly agree to the provision that income be accumulated for beneficiaries who are minors. On occasion, some do not even want to give the trustee discretionary rights to distribute income and/or principal to the minor even when limited to ascertainable standards such as education, health, maintenance and reasonable support. However, very often they object to the requirement that all accumulated income and remaining principal be distributable upon the date when the beneficiary attains the age of 21 or sooner dies. Usually, their desire is to keep this property in trust for substantially longer periods.

While there are no guarantees that all will work out as planned, many advisers suggest that this is not a valid reason not to proceed with the gifting plan. The trust provisions usually will require the trustee to notify the beneficiary of her withdrawal rights and grant her some modest time (30 days at least) to withdraw. If the trustee and the grantor (and, if different, the parents) have laid a proper groundwork and explained the benefits of retaining the trust arrangement, then most often the child will simply let the matter lie and the trust will stay where it is. Also, she may understand that there may be more funds to come if she "plays the game," so to speak. Certainly, there is the potential that the child could "take the trust funds and run," but this usually is the least of all evils given the size of the estate tax.

Conclusions and advice

- Start a program of gifts to your children or grandchildren as soon as possible in order to take maximum advantage of the annual exclusions. The fact that the minor is a very young child need not be a deterrent.

- You must let go of the property completely, even though the minor can't touch it.

- Use a trust or other separate entity for gifts to minors in order to show your complete divestiture. But, if you use a trust, unearned income of a child under 14 in excess of $1,500 in 2002 is taxed at the parents' top tax rate.

• Do not make gifts to minors in the form of future interests. You and your attorney should carefully discuss gifts to trusts and whether they qualify for the annual exclusion by means of the so-called Crummey power.

• Do not count on getting back the property you have given to your minor child if she dies before reaching age 21. True, you may be next of kin, but the minor, unless she is under the age of majority, might have taken steps that would frustrate this.

• Do not entrust your company's lawyer with the responsibility for setting up this arrangement. State law is involved in various respects, such as the age for attaining majority and what constitutes a gift. Use of an attorney who is familiar with your state's estate and trust laws, as well as tax law, is always advisable.

• If parents establish a custodial account for their minor child, but she will have control over the funds when she reaches the state's age of legal maturity (usually 18), the account then in the minor's name will reduce the amount of college financial aid that might otherwise be available to her.

• In addition to the annual exclusion of $11,000 per year, you are also allowed an unlimited exclusion for direct payments for tuition for education at nursery, elementary, secondary and foreign schools, as well as traditional university study. This is particularly attractive to grandparents and is often coupled with a Crummey trust in their gifting plan. Additionally, as noted, the 2001 tax law expanded several features and established new initiatives to help stem the tide of the rising cost of education.

• Recently many tax figures which were indexed for inflation were adjusted by Rev. Proc. 2001-59. These include the upward adjustments of the annual exclusion per donee from $10,000 to $11,000, the annual allowable gifts to a noncitizen spouse from $103,000 to $110,000 and the GST exemption from $1,060,000 to $1.1 million per estate.

Chapter Twenty-Five

THE UNIFORM GIFTS TO MINORS ACT

For many years, making gifts to minors in the form of securities has presented a difficult problem. The act of gifting is simple enough, but what happens later if the minor chooses to sell the securities? A minor has the power to repudiate contracts or to disaffirm sales upon attaining majority, which is age 21 in some states but younger in others. As a result, brokers, banks or other parties are reluctant to buy securities from minors. Their reasoning is, if the market value of the securities goes down after the sale, the minor could choose to let it stand. But if the market value rises, he might repudiate the sale upon reaching majority. The New York Stock Exchange, interested in the unhampered purchase of securities, was largely responsible for passage of the Uniform Gifts to Minors Act, which, with some variations, has now been adopted by every state.

Ground rules for uniform gifts to minors

These laws eliminate the usual requirement that a trust be set up or a guardian appointed when a minor is to be the donee of a gift. Instead, an adult custodian is named. The donor should not name himself as custodian, or the property will be included in his gross estate if he dies before the minor reaches 21. (One benefit of a custodianship: Setting it up is cheaper and simpler than setting up a trust.) Title to the gifted property rests absolutely with the minor. The custodian has sole discretion to apply as much of the principal or income for the benefit of the minor as he sees fit. Principal and income that are not used are to be delivered to the minor/donee upon her reaching majority or, if the state allows, age 21. Sales of securities may be made only by the custodian, eliminating the problem of sales by a minor.

In the case of registered securities, delivery need not be made to the custodian, provided they are registered in his name followed by the words "as custodian for (name of minor) under the (name of enacting state) Uniform Gifts to Minors Act." In the case of unregistered securities, a donor must deliver them to the designated custodian with a statement of gift in the following form, signed by the donor and the custodian:

> "Gift under the (name of enacting state) Uniform Gifts to Minors Act. I, (name of donor), hereby deliver to (name of custodian) as custodian for (name of minor) under the (name of enacting state) Uniform Gifts to Minors Act, the following security(ies): (Insert a description of the security or securities delivered)."

Gift tax treatment for securities and other gifts

A transfer of securities to a minor under the Uniform Gifts to Minors Act constitutes a completed gift for federal tax purposes at the time the transfer is made. It qualifies for the annual gift exclusion of up to $11,000 per donee, and gift splitting can increase this to $22,000. No taxable gift occurs for federal gift tax purposes by reason of a subsequent resignation of the custodian or termination of the custodianship.

An adult may, during his lifetime, make a gift of a life insurance policy, an annuity contract or cash to someone who is a minor on the date of the gift. A gift of a life insurance policy or annuity contract can be made by having the ownership of the policy or contract registered with the issuing insurance company in the name of the custodian, followed by the words "as custodian for (name of minor) under the (name of enacting state) Uniform Gifts to Minors Act." If the gift is cash, it is delivered to a domestic financial institution or broker for credit to an account in the name of the custodian, followed by the words "as custodian for (name of minor) under the (name of enacting state) Uniform Gifts to Minors Act."

A donor who makes a gift to a minor must do everything possible to put the gift in the possession and control of the custodian. But neither the donor's failure to comply with the requirements nor his designation of an ineligible person (for example, another minor) as custodian, nor renunciation by the person designated as custodian, affects the completion of the gift. What could be affected is the donor's own tax liability if he has not properly parted with all interest in the property. In that case, the property may be includable in his own gross estate when he dies, since he has not effectively parted with the assets. A transfer made under the Uniform Gifts to Minors Act is irrevocable.

Income tax treatment

Income derived from property transferred under the Uniform Gifts to Minors Act is taxable to the minor donee. But to the extent that the income is used in the discharge or satisfaction of a legal obligation of any person to support or maintain a minor, it is taxable to that person. For example, a father has a legal obligation to support his minor child. If income earned by securities in a custodianship he created is used to provide support for the child, the father is taxed. (See Chapter Two, "Hidden Traps in Estate Planning.")

Estate tax treatment

The value of property transferred to a minor under the Uniform Gifts to Minors Act is includable in the gross estate of the donor for federal estate tax purposes if he appoints himself custodian and dies while serving in that capacity and before the donee attains the age of majority. In all other circumstances, custodial property is includable only in the gross estate of the minor donee.

Successor custodian

Usually, only an adult member of the minor's family, a guardian of the minor or a trust company is eligible to become successor custodian. A custodian may designate his successor by executing and dating an instrument of designation before a witness other than the successor. This instrument of designation may, but does not have to, contain the successor's signature. If he doesn't designate his successor in this manner before he dies and if the minor has reached the age of 14, in some states, the minor may designate a successor custodian by executing an instrument of designation before a witness other than the successor.

Pros and cons

The Uniform Gifts to Minors Act presents an easy, cost-effective way to commence a gifting program to a minor child. The rights, duties and obligations of the custodian and the minor are a matter of state law. The donor has very few choices available to him in terms of fashioning the document. When he attains the age of majority or 21, ownership of the assets must pass to the minor, who is now an adult.

Many estate planners recommend that such accounts are appropriate if either (1) the amounts will be relatively small, (2) the number of recipients is small, or (3) the funds will definitely be disbursed for college. In these cases, the use of a trust may be a needless expenditure. Of course, if the converse is true (i.e., larger amounts, several beneficiaries and/or intent to preserve principal are present), then a trust may be the preferred document.

Conclusions and advice

• You can remove property from your gross estate by transferring it under the Uniform Gifts to Minors Act without that property being under the minor's control. As a result, potential buyers won't be deterred by fears of repudiation when the minor attains majority.

• Use the Uniform Gifts to Minors Act for properties and securities.

• Consult a lawyer who is familiar with the laws in your state.

• You do not have to set up a trust for the benefit of your minor child if a custodianship will accomplish the same result at less cost.

• Beware of being both the donor and the custodian on an account set up under the Uniform Gifts to Minors Act. The account may be taxed in your estate.

• Gifts made under the Uniform Gifts to Minors Act are irrevocable.

Chapter Twenty-Six

USE OF NET GIFTS

A would-be donor who wants to give property away might be deterred from making lifetime gifts because of the prospect of owing federal gift tax if the gift is in excess of the annual exclusion or if the unified gift and estate tax credit has already been used up. Alternatively, she may not want to exhaust the entire credit at this time, as required, but she may prefer to reserve some of it for the future. So she fails to make gifts for these reasons:

1. She may be unwilling to pay the gift tax at present, reasoning that she isn't going to pay the estate tax after she dies. Rather, her beneficiaries will pay, so that estate assets going to them will be decreased by the estate tax.

2. She may not be able to pay the gift tax despite her wealth as her assets may not be liquid. Her wealth is tied up in assets, which might be disadvantageous to liquidate.

3. One who has to sell assets in order to pay the gift tax is likely to have to pay income tax on the sale, especially in inflationary times.

4. There is always the chance the estate tax will be permanently eliminated after 2010.

The advantage of net gifts

The donor's reluctance to pay gift taxes can be reduced through transfers of properties to beneficiaries, subject to the condition that they pay the federal gift taxes. A gift conditioned on the payment of federal gift tax by the donee is termed a "net gift."

There are several advantages to this procedure:

• The donor has reduced her ultimate gross estate, should the estate tax be retained.

• If the gift is of income-producing assets, she reduces her annual state and federal income taxes.

• She may save state and local property taxes, tangible and intangible, on property she no longer owns, as well as care, maintenance and insurance costs.

• The gift tax paid by the donee(s) is based on a lower figure than would be the case if the donor had paid the tax.

The net gift is computed by reducing the gross value of the gift by the amount of the tax the donee must pay in order to receive the gift. The gift tax actually paid is based on this reduced value.

Will the donee(s) be willing to pay the federal gift tax as a condition of getting the property? The answer is almost invariably yes, if the situation is understood. The donee may be anxious to get the property instead of waiting until the donor's death. If an intended donee refuses to pay the gift tax, the property may never become his. We now have the possibility of depletion due to stays in nursing homes or long-term-care facilities or the donor may feel compelled to dispose of the property immediately, such as might be the case with burdensome real estate. She will select a more accommodating donee. Alternatively, the owner may decide to give the assets to an approved charitable organization, creating an income tax deduction in the year of the contribution. When presented with possibilities like these, the intended donee is likely to agree to pay the gift tax.

When a donee is obliged to pay the gift tax because of the conditions of the transfer, the donee may deduct the amount of the tax from the value of the gift subject to tax. This may require the use of an algebraic computation. The Internal Revenue Service can help with the computation, but the IRS should be asked for assistance well in advance of the return due date.

Proof that the gift was on a net basis

In order to achieve this favorable tax treatment—that is, payment of federal gift tax on only the difference between the property's value and the amount of gift tax that would ordinarily be imposed—it must be clearly established that the tax payment by the donee was an express condition of the transfer.

One transfer was considered to be a net gift where the donee's signed letters prepared by the donor's lawyer, stating: "We have further been informed that this gift is being made subject to my paying the gift tax on same. This letter can be taken as my acceptance of the proposed condition of the gift, and I agree to accept as my share of the gift tax an amount computed by your tax counsel."

This procedure may be used when an individual creates a trust for the benefit of someone else, such as her daughter. She transfers assets to the trust, subject to the condition that the trustee pay the federal gift tax. In one example, the trust instrument contained this language: "This gift is on the express condition that the trustee report and pay out of the trust estate all gift taxes...imposed upon donor by virtue of this gift."

Income and estate tax consequences

The donor's unified credit must be exhausted before the donee can be liable for the tax (IRS Rev. Rul. 81-223, 1981-2CB 189). This limits the usefulness of the net gift, as the tax is levied against the donor and, under the 2001 tax law, the unified credit effective equivalent amount increases significantly. Also, it is a general principle of federal income taxation that when a solvent person is relieved of indebtedness, she has taxable income to that extent, since her financial condition has improved. In the case of a net gift, the donor has made a transfer of property, but the donee, by paying the federal gift tax, directly or indirectly, has relieved the donor of paying this tax. If the recipient of a gift pays the federal gift tax legally imposed on the donor, the donor has an income tax liability to the extent the discharge of her liability for gift tax actually paid by the donee exceeds the donor's adjusted basis in the gift property. Under a tax court decision, the donor's gross estate includes the gift tax paid by the donee if the death occurs within three years of the payment. Finally, some states have their own gift tax. Agreements by the donee to pay the gift taxes raises several questions that need to be reviewed with your adviser.

Conclusions and advice

• If you wish to take advantage of net gift treatment, thoroughly review the merits/consequences of the donee's written agreement to pay.

• The donee must make certain that a federal gift tax return is filed and any tax due gets paid. Otherwise, the donee may lose the property in order to satisfy federal taxes owed by the donor. If the transfer was not demonstrably a gift (and failure to file a gift tax return suggests that it was not), the property may still be regarded as the donor's, subject to claims against the donor.

• Do not refuse a donor's gift conditioned upon your paying the gift tax without careful reflection. Your refusal could cost you the property.

• Do not assume that the donee is going to pay the tax. Make sure he does. A donee may be completely unaware of what's required, and the donor might be called upon to pay an unpaid tax resulting from the gift.

• Predetermine with your accountant the state and federal estate and income tax consequences. If the gift tax paid by the donee exceeds the donor's adjusted basis in the property and the donor is relieved of any liability, there may be an income tax accruing to the donor.

• As a footnote to all gifts, the 1997 tax law closed the door on a favorite IRS trick. If a gift is adequately disclosed on a gift tax return, even if no tax was owed due to the unified credit, the IRS may not revalue the gift on the donor's death if the gift tax statute of limitations has passed.

• If you are considering such a gift, seek counsel to discuss the best timing. On the one hand, the property will be in your estate, possibly subject to estate taxation and subject to creditors (i.e., long-term health-care providers) while on the other hand, transfer may be less costly due to an increase in the unified credit. However, you might be paying a needless tax.

Chapter Twenty-Seven

SALE AND LEASEBACK; GIFT AND LEASEBACK

With proper planning, an individual can reduce his potential gross estate by immediately disposing of property that he owns and uses in his trade or profession. However, he can retain the business use of this property, and simultaneously achieve income tax and other advantages, if the transaction is properly structured. The mechanism for this is a sale and leaseback. Somewhat analogous to the sale and leaseback is another type of arrangement, the gift and leaseback.

The sale-and-leaseback arrangement would have been most affected by the complete repeal of the estate tax, principally because the end result is elimination of the asset from your estate. Without estate tax, this goal would not be important, especially if the asset was a desirable one to keep in your portfolio. However, if your desire is to build wealth for other family members, then the gift and leaseback, as well as our other suggestions in this chapter, may also serve you well regardless of the status of the estate tax law. Notably, under the 2001 tax law, both of these arrangements remain viable if your estate is at the levels and tax concern that warrant such a discussion with your estate planner.

Nature of a sale-and-leaseback transaction

Under a sale and leaseback, business property is sold, most advisedly to a completely independent party, here called "the investor" for the sake of simplicity. At the same time, the original owner leases back this property, usually for a period of years. When he dies, the value of the property will not be includable in his gross estate, for he doesn't own it. But he has continued to have the use of somebody else's property in return for the payment of rent, which for federal income tax purposes is deductible as a business expense.

A sale and leaseback with an unrelated party can be structured to meet the tax—and other—preferences of both parties.

The seller (the original owner of the business property) has these principal alternatives:

1. If his property has appreciated in value, he can sell it at cost, thereby avoiding tax on the appreciation. As the investor has acquired the property at a bargain price, the simultaneous leaseback will call for this differential to be balanced out by means of a low rental for the life of the lease. In such arrangements between unrelated parties, the one who pays too much or too little in terms of fair market value will have this differential adjusted in the form of adjusted rental payments, so that what each party gives and gets over the life of the lease is substantially equivalent. The terms take into account the fact that an interest factor balances present payment of purchase price with rental payments over a period of years. For example, if the leaseback is for a period of 20 years, there are tables that disclose the present value of a dollar payable in 20 years.

2. Where the original owner sells his property at a loss and then leases it back, he is entitled to deduct a loss for tax purposes.

3. Property may be sold by the original owner for more than market value if he is in a low tax bracket or if he is operating at a loss. In such circumstances, the gain is not important to him taxwise. But the simultaneous leaseback will provide for a high rental to compensate the buyer for the inflated price.

4. If the property includes land, the original owner would not have been able to deduct depreciation. But after the leaseback, he deducts the rent paid on both the land and the building. He is, moreover, rid of the problems and nuisance of depreciation records and disputes that often occur with the IRS.

Sale-and-leaseback transactions increase the seller's liquidity. Added liquidity can be used for several purposes. You can commence a gifting program or leverage your assets by setting up a trust and using your new-found cash to fund the purchase of much-needed life insurance. The concept is that you have potentially eliminated a key asset from your estate which might also have presented a valuation and/or liquidation problem for your executors. Now you can concentrate on how best to place these substitute assets out of the reach of the revenue agents and your potential creditors.

A sale and leaseback is not recognized for tax purposes by the Internal Revenue Service if the original owner retains any rights in the property other than the use of it in return for the payment of rent. The transaction must be a genuine sale. But, in a 1979 decision, a court recognized as bona fide a sale and leaseback in which the original owner had been granted an option to repurchase the property by the investor.

The parties must be unrelated

For reasons we discussed, the original owner may be selling the property for more or less than its fair market value and, in consequence, paying rent that is higher or lower than a customary sale or a conventional lease. But as long as the parties are not related and the transaction is not a sham, but rather one of substance, then these arrangements are acceptable for tax purposes. Unrelated parties can bargain in an unconventional manner as long as each party achieves his own purposes without regard to what the other is seeking. But avoid transactions of this nature with related parties. Even if a party sells to and then leases back property from a related party at the identical terms offered by an outside party, the Internal Revenue Service will predictably rule that where assets are sold to a related party at an off-market price, or rented at an unrealistic figure in terms of standard practices, the consideration or expense can be readjusted for tax purposes. That is, if the rent paid to a related party is more than would have been charged on a standard lease, the excess can be disallowed as a deduction.

Nature of a gift-and-leaseback transaction

Less common than the sale and leaseback is the gift and leaseback. This transaction may involve related parties if the terms are set at arm's length, or it may involve a charitable organization.

A father may own property that he uses in his business or profession. For example, a physician owns the building in which he practices, which also contains costly medical equipment. He gives the property to his children, reducing his ultimate gross estate. But he needs these facilities for his practice, so he immediately leases them back. His annual rental payments are deductible as business expenses. The income, received by children over age 14, will presumably be taxed at a much lower rate than the doctor's.

To gain the tax advantages from situations like this, it is vital that the original owner really let go of the property and that the rental payments be fair to the children, who may not be able to bargain for an equitable rental. For this reason, it would be advisable for the physician to transfer the property in trust for the benefit of his children. The trustee(s) should be completely independent of the domination of the original owner, so that they can negotiate a fair rental that is in the children's interest. All too frequently, transactions of this kind are not recognized for tax purposes because the original owner set the rent, or served as trustee, or selected trustees who really represented the grantor and not the beneficiaries. For example, the transaction wasn't recognized for tax purposes where the trustees were the three persons whom the original owner regarded most highly: His lawyer, his accountant and himself. The two professionals merely acquiesced in whatever their long-time client wanted. The property was thus includable in his gross estate.

Where a gift and leaseback involves the owner's children, the rental payments he makes cannot be used to discharge his legal obligation of supporting minor children. This would result in taxable income to the grantor.

Motivation for transaction

The motivation for the transaction—even if it takes advantage of a tax opportunity—is immaterial if the donor retains no control over the property.

Conclusions and advice

• To find an independent investor for a sale and leaseback, read brokers' advertisements in the financial sections of newspapers.

• Let go of the property and reacquire an interest solely as tenant. Do not attempt to make any unilateral modification of the arrangement.

• When property is given or sold to one's minor children, use a trust with a truly independent trustee. Avoid preferential leaseback terms.

• Do not enter into a sale and leaseback with a related party even on terms identical to those offered by an outside party. Remember, the IRS has the luxury of reviewing these techniques retrospectively and examines these transactions very closely. Therefore, each step should be taken at "arm's length and in a bona fide manner." Further, you should consult with an accountant and attorney who are familiar with the Tax Code before proceeding with either of these arrangements.

• A variation of these methods is to have a trust benefitting family members or a partnership made up of family members to buy the asset initially. Then the taxpayer leases it from the trust or partnership. As above, the IRS looks closely for "sham transactions," so be sure to have an arm's length, bona fide purchase and fair rental value lease. However, consider the benefits of building wealth in other family members. Your business needs the asset and yet this arrangement allows you to not only give an income stream to your family members, but also to build an asset portfolio in their trust or partnership.

• The sale and leaseback can generate much-needed liquidity which can be used for many other purposes, including gifting. The gift-and-leaseback can benefit others, including aging parents, children and charities.

Chapter Twenty-Eight

USING A FAMILY BUSINESS TO TRANSFER ASSETS

We have discussed the desirability of a regular program of gift giving to intended beneficiaries. However, often an individual's assets will not be in the form of cash, which can easily be given away in any amount at any time. So, if there are several beneficiaries, it will be difficult to give each one the desired, undivided, fractional interest in a piece of real estate, an active business or a valuable collection. Nor is it likely that beneficiaries receiving undivided fractional interests in property of this kind will be able to handle them properly. Each might have their own idea of how the property should be managed, whether it should be sold, for how much and when, etc. Also, a prospective buyer of the property would be reluctant to negotiate with a variety of co-owners who might have different objectives.

A solution to this common problem is to give each beneficiary the proportion of the property you have selected for them while keeping actual ownership and management of the property in the hands of a responsible manager. The manager should not be you, for if you haven't really let go of the property, its value will be includable in your estate when you die.

Nonfragmented transfers

The plan: Transfer selected properties to a newly formed family business in return for an interest therein. Then you can give or bequeath to each beneficiary the desired number of shares or percentage interest, at one time or over a period of years, in order to take advantage of the annual gift tax exclusions (see also final point of this chapter). Here are the advantages:

1. Property can be given away currently, even though it is not possible or feasible to fragment these assets.

2. Property can be given away in whatever amounts are desirable each year, such as $11,000 per donee (or $22,000, if you can gift split), or any other desired figure. Instead of transferring to a particular beneficiary, say, a one-seventh interest in a piece of land, they can be given whatever percentage amount of equity your accountant computes is worth $11,000/$22,000 or whatever figure is desired.

3. A beneficiary should have confidence that her interest in property will not be lessened in value because of a co-owner's irresponsible behavior. The business entity should have as its executive a person of judgment and capacity. The chief executive will make the decisions, subject to ratification when required by a majority of the owners.

4. In the marketplace, the whole is customarily worth more than the sum of its parts. A beneficiary who owns an undivided fractional interest in property possesses a part. The business entity possesses the whole.

Tax-free transfer to a corporation

Ordinarily, if an individual owns property that has appreciated in value, she has a taxable gain when she disposes of it, such as by sale or exchange. But she can avoid present recognition of taxable gain on the transfer of her property to a corporation solely in return for its stock if she owns at least 80% of the stock immediately after the transfer. For the present purpose, it would be advisable that she receive all of the stock. She still owns the property at this point, although the form of ownership has been changed from direct to indirect. That is, she owns the stock of the corporation that owns the property. Transfers to limited liability companies and partnerships can also be accomplished on a tax-free basis in much the same manner.

Therefore, if a husband and wife, or other plural parties, transfer assets to such a business entity in return for all of its stock or ownership interests, this is a transfer to an entity that is collectively controlled by the transferors immediately after the transaction and is tax free. But the Internal Revenue Service has the power to investigate whether the interest the transferors receive is substantially in proportion to the value of the properties transferred. If not, there may be tax due. For example, a father and son individually transfer assets to a corporation, each receiving 50% of the stock. But if the property the father transferred was worth more than twice the property the son transferred, the IRS may query why the father didn't receive two-thirds of the stock. A gift tax could be imposed on the grounds that the father in effect got 66⅔% of the stock since he provided 66⅔% of the property and then gave the son 16⅔% as a taxable gift so that father and son each ended up with 50% of the stock.

The person transferring stock to a controlled corporation must receive corporate stock in return for it. The tax law does not disqualify tax-free treatment where property transferred to a controlled corporation isn't solely for stock. But if the individual transferring the property to the corporation receives not only its stock, but also any other property, he has a taxable gain in an amount not in excess of the fair market value of the other property he receives.

Choosing the business entity

Properly done, assets can be transferred tax free to a corporation (C or S) as well as a partnership (general or limited) or to the newly created limited liability company (LLC) or limited liability partnership (LLP). These are relatively new business entities which have gained recognition in most states. Ask your attorney if your state allows the LLC/LLP, as they offer both the tax advantages of a partnership, as well as the insulation from personal liability that a corporation offers its shareholders (liability shield).

Your estate planners can help you with your choice. Consult your accountant regarding this decision, as there are many tax ramifications to the various choices. For example, with the advent of the LLC and LLP, some advisers believe there are very few reasons to ever again use a corporation or partnership for a small, family owned business. However, we always avoid such blanket statements and encourage considered consultations with your accountant and attorney.

There are two other points of note regarding the family owned business. First, if you intend to give a portion to minors, you can either use the Uniform Gifts to Minors Act or a separate trust to hold the minor's share/interest. We prefer the latter choice. Second, in determining the value of your gift, your accountant will likely take what is known as a "minority discount." This concept allows your accountant to reduce the value of your gift because the donee does not control the business, and therefore, his shares are worth less. With the value reduced, you may effectively increase the size of your annual gift (by anywhere from 10% to 25%). No such discount can be received with a cash gift. Note, however, that this is a double-edged sword. While many planners use the minority discount to increase the size of the annual gift, the IRS reviews such discounts quite rigorously. Therefore, be reasonably conservative and have your accountant prepared to justify any discount percentage used. Remember, all gifts, including holiday and birthday gifts, are added to your gift tax return for that year, and you could very well be put over the $11,000/22,000 limit.

Income tax consequences

Even though the transfer of property to a controlled business entity can be structured on a tax-free basis, there could be income tax consequences. For example, an individual may transfer her office building to the corporation in return for its stock. If the building carries a mortgage substantially in excess of her adjusted cost basis, she has taxable gain to the extent that the mortgage debt transferred to the corporation exceeds this adjusted cost basis in the assets. She has been relieved of liabilities higher than the amount of assets disposed of. Her financial position was improved by this amount.

Release from personal liability is the equivalent of taxable gain. It doesn't matter for this purpose whether this individual transferred to the business entity property subject to a liability in excess of her basis or whether the entity assumed her liabilities. However, the tax law does not treat the assumption of ordinary trade payables as triggering income to the extent that such payables would be deductible by the transferor.

The property transferred to the controlled business entity has the same tax basis in the hands of the new business as it had in the individual's hands. If the property consists of capital assets, the length of time the individual owned them and the time the new family business later owns them are added together to establish whether the gain or loss resulting from a subsequent sale by the business is long or short term.

Conclusions and advice

• Have restrictions as to transferability stamped upon stock certificates or other forms of evidence of ownership so that beneficiaries don't transfer property that may be worth far more if outsiders aren't brought into the picture.

• A transfer to a controlled corporation is tax free only where the transferor or transferors collectively own at least 80% of the stock immediately after the transfer. They should, therefore, not have any legal obligation to dispose of any of the shares at the time of the transfer. Be aware that tax-free organizations and reorganizations are both complicated and highly regulated by the IRS. Therefore, be sure to seek the advice of competent counsel.

• Do not select assets subject to liabilities in excess of the donor's adjusted basis. This may cause an unexpected tax.

• Many of these techniques have also been used with both partnerships and limited partnerships. The IRS allows for the creation of an entity known as a limited liability company or a limited liability partnership, which might also be considered. Most states have adopted legislation to allow the creation of such entities. Essentially, they take advantage of the favorable tax treatment afforded to partnerships while enjoying the limited liability shield granted corporations. An LLC or LLP may very well be the entity of choice over the corporation.

• Often the interest of minor children in these family owned businesses are held in trust. This provides another layer of protection.

172

Chapter Twenty-Nine

INTEGRATING KEY CONCEPTS

The preceding chapters have concentrated on the various components that make up the estate planner's "bag of tricks." Certainly, there are others, as well as fads that come and go—some good, some mere shams. Also, as Congress changes the tax laws, professional advisers look for loopholes and new approaches. Therefore, keeping up-to-date and performing periodic reviews, as required by the 2001 tax law, are always advisable.

At this time, it is prudent to look at the concept of integration. An effective estate plan consists of key components that are integrated with one another, in which the components themselves may change from time to time.

Examples of integrating concepts

In the preceding chapters we have outlined several key concepts. They should not be viewed in a vacuum. We encourage each individual, married couple and family unit to utilize as many of the techniques as may be appropriate within their overall plan. The techniques may be integrated to accomplish more than one desired result. For example:

• Suppose you decide to make gifts to your children, but, after many years of such gifting, you still have a sizable estate. Those gifts (see Chapter Twenty-One) may be coupled with the use of trusts (see Chapter Twelve) which can then buy additional life insurance (see Chapter Thirty-One) to help pay the expected tax.

• Gifts to your grandchildren might encompass both the use of your generation-skipping exemption (see Chapter Fifteen) and the use of the Uniform Gifts to Minors Act (see Chapter Twenty-Five).

• Most important for a married couple is the integration and use of the unified credit exemption equivalent amount ($1 million in 2002) and the marital deduction (see Chapter Four) with the possible inclusion of a second-to-die (or survivorship) life insurance trust. If done properly, a married couple could expect to (1) pass everything on the first death virtually tax free in most states, (2) pass at least the total of two unified credits tax free on the second death ($2 million if both die in 2002) and (3) pay whatever tax there is with cheap dollars, if life insurance were purchased and properly held (i.e., $500,000 of insurance may have cost the couple only $100,000 over their lives).

• The use of life insurance, retirement plans and other employee benefits play an important role in your estate plan. Insurance and retirement plans can provide the cash needed to fund trusts and/or provide for your survivors. Therefore, they must be considered as part of your integrated plan. We'll discuss these plans in detail later on in the text.

• If you own low-income-producing assets that have appreciated in value, consider a charitable remainder trust. The trustee can sell the asset without the capital gain and invest the proceeds in higher-yielding stock. You (and your spouse) can receive the income from the higher-yielding assets for the remainder of your lives. You may use some of this new-found income to purchase a last-to-die policy for the children. The cash from the policy will act as a replacement for the "assets" that the charity (and not the children) receives upon your death.

• Owners of small businesses should consider integrating many different wealth-building and estate-planning tools. Allow your executor to continue the business after your death. Also, if you have partners or own the business with others, a buy–sell agreement (funded with life insurance) is an important safeguard.

• Incentives can be useful tools. Sometimes we have the luxury of being able to help others, whether it be a charity, family member or friend. Many clients prefer to attach some helpful "strings" to this aid. These strings may be a matching grant for gifts to charities or a match of W-2 wages for gifts to relatives or friends. If you are not inclined to impose strings, you may follow

174

the example of others who prefer to simply be remembered by donating to their alma mater with an established chair or foundation in their name. Individual foundations are now more prevalent than ever.

• Another helpful area of integration, even in modest estates, is the use of testamentary trusts (trusts contained in a will; see Chapter Twelve) to insulate assets from creditors, especially nursing homes. Each year, more adults enter nursing homes paying fees of staggering proportions. Under current federal law, if your will leaves amounts in a properly drafted trust for a loved one who ultimately is placed in a nursing home, these funds are not considered an "available asset." Therefore, they cannot be depleted by the home's charges, and often result in the patient's qualification for substantial state and federal benefits (called Title XIX).

• It is also essential to consider the execution of certain health-related documents while formulating your estate plan. Living wills (sometimes called "advance directives" on your health care) also can deal with the removal of life-support systems. Health-care proxies usually appoint a person to make such decisions if you are incapable. Durable powers of attorney (which survive one's incompetency) are quite helpful, but must be well thought out. In today's society, elder law and elder law planning have become an increasingly important part of one's overall plan. Don't forget them.

The estate planning life cycle

As we proceed through our personal, financial and family lives, situations change. Therefore, our estate, health and elder planning also need to change. Different concepts or tools may be more relevant at different phases of your estate planning cycle. Be prepared to add, change and/or delete these as needed.

One accountant explained this concept to a client as follows: "When you are young, just starting out with maybe a spouse and a child or two, you can't afford life insurance, so you buy cheap term coverage. As you move into your mid-life years, you are concerned with building wealth and you may move more toward whole life, yet still maintain some term coverage. Finally, as you look toward retirement, you are concerned with asset and wealth preservation and you begin to think about last-to-die policies and insurance trusts." In our opinion, this was a perfect summary of how the cycle works, plans change and integration occurs on an ongoing basis.

Another area where the life cycle plays an important role is with your fiduciaries. Young parents are concerned about proper guardians for minor children and faithful trustees of their funds. However, in later years, the children may become your trustees, health-care proxies and holders of your power of attorney.

Generally, your estate planner will counsel you to keep your questionnaire (see Appendix A) and your two fact sheets (see Appendices B and C) current and to review these on at least an annual basis. Also, review your estate plan and documents with your planner every three years, or more often if there is a major change in the tax law such as the recent 2001 tax law. If you move to another state or there is a significant change in your own family or financial situation, you should also consider reviewing your plan.

Conclusions and advice

• As your life changes, so do your needs. Review your plan periodically.

• Many of the tools available to you can be used in conjunction with one another. Sometimes a creative planner can give you an added degree of protection (for example, putting a child's interest in the family business into a trust).

• There are many business-related benefits, retirement plans and insurance plans which also need to be considered in your overall plan.

• If you own a small business, consider not only the need for business succession, but also life insurance to pay large business debts. If you have partners, you definitely will want a buy–sell agreement. Your will or trust should certainly also provide for a potential continuation-of-business arrangement.

LIFE INSURANCE & EMPLOYEE BENEFITS: A POTENT MIXTURE

Too often clients look at estate planning from a singular point of view: "Preserve, maintain, utilize and finally pass along as much as you can."

Along the way, younger to middle-aged clients especially are concerned with wealth accumulation. What assets or products are the most desirable for them to own? What employee benefits will mature most beneficially in the long run?

The concept of the estate planning life cycle envisions that you plan for the totality of life's events. In what stage of the cycle are you currently? What are your current needs and goals? What do you think they will be in five years? By doing this, you will change your plan as your needs and goals change. And the nature of these changes will include not just your will and trust, but also things such as insurance and employee benefits. Additionally, such introspection will cause you to consider your employment and the benefits it may offer.

Why insurance?

There can be no question that the nature of insurance is based on a peculiar relationship which we believe can be a win-win situation for you and your heirs. An insurance company is betting that something tragic is not going to happen to you, for which they charge you a premium. You, in return, are betting that something tragic may happen to you. You hedge the bet by paying this premium.

Some people do not willingly purchase insurance. Yet every estate planner has had a client who was forced to sell the family home or business due to inadequate insurance coverage. Those are unhappy times, and while it easily answers the "why" of insurance coverage, many clients are never convinced of the necessity. Many people do not like to face their own mortality and many more have not had the product and pricing properly explained by a true professional.

What types of insurance?

Generally, estate planners deal with three types of insurance coverage. *Life insurance* is the most prominent. *Disability insurance* is often used as a tool to ensure that a family's income stream is not disrupted. Many planners will advise clients in younger age groups that the likelihood of becoming disabled is more probable than dying early. Yet, the earlier you start your life insurance program, the better the premium and the less likely the chance of uninsurability.

The relatively new coverage, *long-term health-care insurance*, is becoming more popular in both the insurance industry and the estate planning field. Long-term health-care policies have many different types of coverage which need to be matched with state regulations as well as those dealing with Title XIX. Therefore, you must have advice from a qualified insurance expert as well as a lawyer specializing in elder law in your state before you purchase any such policy.

A good group of advisers, including your accountant, attorney and insurance agent, will not limit their efforts to these three insurance areas. For example, they may even review your automobile and liability coverage to ensure that these are adequate, or suggest the addition of a liability umbrella. For small-business owners, life insurance also becomes a mainstay in the buy–sell arrangement. (See Chapter Forty-Two.) Therefore, your planners may very well suggest that you look more deeply into additional coverage.

How much is enough?

There is no single answer to this question. You should understand that the insurance industry is quite competitive, with a myriad of products with different pricing structures. As a general rule, term life insurance has lower premiums than whole life. Yet, whole life has the benefits of equity build-up, fixed premiums, guaranteed insurability, and, over time, is less costly than term.

Ideally, you would determine benefits that will be available from all sources, such as Social Security and pensions, if any. Subtract them from the income needed, showing the presumed shortfall. If you can afford the cost, purchase insurance that will give your family income to cover the shortfall. Ideally, interest and dividend income from the insurance payout, invested conservatively (i.e., 4%), will earn an amount equal to the shortfall plus a reasonable increase for inflation. Your surviving spouse should not have to invade the principal or change lifestyle dramatically. The principal should earn enough to make up for the lost earnings. Sometimes this is not possible, but it is a guideline as well as a reason to consider buying less expensive term insurance.

Therefore, identify what your needs are with your advisers. Determine costs, what you can afford and then decide. Buying insurance is a win-win relationship you must undertake for the protection of your family.

Employee benefits

While insurance helps in the event of a catastrophe, employee benefits can provide additions to the wealth accumulation process. There are a wide variety of benefits available, if your employer is willing to offer them. Seek out jobs that provide not only a livable wage but also an attractive array of benefits.

Many employees think of benefits only in terms of health insurance, pension or profit-sharing plans and stock options. Highly paid executives, as well as those who use headhunters, know there are many other benefits.

Some clients mistakenly believe that smaller companies, or closely held or family owned businesses, do not offer such attractive plans. We have found that this is far from the case. Many benefits suit small as well as large businesses. In fact, some are even more suited to smaller or closely held businesses than to larger firms. The key considerations for you as the employee is (1) Are you well thought of or being sought after? and (2) Did you ask?

Some benefits an employee should look for

The following is a list, not an exhaustive one, of employee benefits available in the workplace today. We discuss many of these in the chapters to come. However, all of these benefits are without cost and therefore create wealth for the employee or add nontaxable compensation. When negotiating with a new or current employer for a compensation package, investigate whether the following benefits are offered:

- IRS-qualified pension and profit-sharing plans (noncontributory)
- IRS-qualified cash or deferred arrangements (401[k]s), possibly with employer matching
- Employee stock ownership plans (ESOPs)
- Group health and major medical insurance
- Medical reimbursement plans
- Medical savings accounts (MSAs)
- Cafeteria plans (a choice of several benefits, often including day care)
- Deferred compensation plans (often nonqualified, offered to select employees)
- IRS-qualified incentive stock options
- Phantom stock plans (employee builds cash value account based on phantom equity)
- Nonqualified option plans
- Stock appreciation rights (SARs = you get the increase in share value)
- Cash bonuses
- Group term life insurance
- Executive life insurance
- Split-dollar life insurance plans
- Educational benefits
- Moving expenses
- Below-market loans
- Financial and/or legal counseling
- Dependent-care assistance

- Group long-term care
- Death benefits paid by company
- Postretirement consulting
- Other benefits, i.e., company cars, meals, lodging, expense accounts, etc.

Conclusions and advice

- Do not view your estate plan as complete when your will or trust is done. Review estate and financial planning periodically.

- Insurance is an important tool. Do not rationalize or try to justify lack of coverage you really can afford. Your family may have to live with that decision.

- Always ask your insurance professional to seek several quotes. Even among top-rated companies, there can be wide variances in the premium.

- When you are considering your insurance needs, remember that after your death, your spouse's household expenses do not decrease dramatically. Therefore, without adequate insurance, there is bound to be a drastic change in your spouse's and children's lifestyle.

- Do not be shy about bargaining for additional insurance with your prospective employer.

- Employers are often willing to offer creative packages to well-qualified employees. Do your homework, and do not be afraid to ask for additional benefits.

- Do not be fooled by salary alone. The value of a good benefits package may be considerable and may prove to be a nontaxable benefit which you might be paying for with after-tax dollars in your current job.

- Maximize your employee tax deferral benefits.

Chapter Thirty-One

PLANNING WITH LIFE INSURANCE

There is no easier way to provide an estate after your death than to take out insurance on your life. Also, if you pay the premiums and arrange matters through a trust so that no creditor is able to attach the value of the policy, you are certain to leave an estate. Even the lack of funds can be dealt with. Arrangements can be made with an insurance company—sometimes they are automatic—to pay missed premiums from accumulated cash values or by conversion to another form of insurance.

What is deemed to be life insurance

Most life insurance policies require the applicant to have a physical examination for large amounts of coverage. Smaller policy amounts require the applicant to only fill in a questionnaire. Beware of delays in applying for insurance. The longer the delay, the greater the possibility that rates will increase or you will become uninsurable. Generally, group insurance doesn't call for a physical examination, nor does flight insurance, although the Supreme Court has called the latter a form of life insurance despite the absence of traditional application procedures and an examination. If the insurance company's doctor labels you uninsurable, speak to your insurance adviser about obtaining high-risk or rated insurance. Regardless of your physical condition, you'll probably be able to get some insurance, but at a high premium reflecting the degree of risk the insurance company faces.

Start coverage as early as possible

Unlike other forms of estate building, such as realty or investments, the creation of an estate through life insurance doesn't require the attainment of a degree of business or financial success that might take many years to achieve. The size of an insurance estate depends upon simply how much an individual is willing or able to pay in premiums. (In many situations, insurance premiums are paid by an employer, in whole or in part.) How much insurance you carry may depend on the form of policy you purchase. For the same amount of premium, for example, you can acquire far greater coverage with term insurance than with straight life or endowment forms.

Ask yourself what you are really purchasing, whole life insurance (which includes the building up of cash values, reinvestment and borrowing power, enforced savings, interest conversion privileges) or term insurance (which only provides indemnity on the death of the insured). Whole life is for the person who desires protection for his entire life, while term covers a specified period of time, i.e., 10 or 15 years, or perhaps until your children reach the age of financial independence or your new business has had time to develop.

The federal income tax

In most instances, insurance proceeds payable by reason of the death of the insured are excluded from gross income, whether received by the estate, a beneficiary, a transferee or anyone else. But the interest element in an insurance company's settlement option may be taxable. For example, after the death of the insured, the beneficiary may have selected a settlement option calling for the payment of a certain dollar amount for life. What he receives represents in part an amortized portion of the principal sum to which he is entitled plus interest on the principal that remains with the insurance company. The death benefit or principal is tax free, while the interest paid on the principal is taxable.

The federal estate tax

Unlike other forms of property, none of the value of insurance proceeds needs to be includable in a decedent's gross estate at the time of death. If an individual knows the simple ground rules, insurance proceeds will not be part of his gross estate unless he wants them to be to provided to his executor(s).

There are alternatives to inclusion (a trust) which we believe should be thoroughly reviewed. Yet proceeds of insurance on a decedent's life are includable in his gross estate if (1) he had named the estate or the executor as the beneficiary, (2) he had given away some incident of ownership in the policy within three years of the time of his death or (3) at the moment of his death he had held any incident of ownership of the policy, exercisable either alone or in conjunction with someone else.

The most common forms of incidents of ownership are the right to change the name of the beneficiary, to assign, borrow from or cancel the policy or to pledge the policy in order to obtain a loan or change the dividend options.

Relinquishment of any of these rights within three years of death will not take the proceeds out of the estate. That the decedent had been unable to relinquish these rights is irrelevant. For example, a policy's terms can be changed only by endorsement of the policy itself by the insurance company, but the policy may be physically in the hands of a hostile person, such as an estranged spouse. Or a traveler might purchase flight insurance that automatically names the purchaser as owner; should the plane crash, even if he has had time to change the name of the owner, the proceeds are still part of his gross estate—the three-year rule takes effect in this case.

If insurance on an individual's life is owned by a corporation, and any part of the proceeds is not payable for the benefit of the corporation, any incident of ownership held by the corporation as to part of the proceeds will be attributed to the decedent when he is the sole or controlling stockholder. If he is the controlling stockholder of a corporation owning a policy on his life and the proceeds are payable to his wife, the full proceeds will be included in his estate. If the policy were payable 40% to his wife and 60% to his corporation, 40% of the proceeds would be deemed to be part of his gross estate, and the value of his corporation may be increased. An individual is considered a controlling stockholder for this purpose if at the time of his death more than 50% of the stock was owned by him and by specified close relatives.

184

Reversionary interests

If an individual is required by the terms of a divorce decree to name his ex-wife as the beneficiary of certain policies on his life and to keep them in effect for as long as she lives and has not remarried, he has a reversionary interest in the policies. That is, the policies will revert to him should she die or remarry. If his reversionary interest exceeds 5% of the value of the property immediately before his death, but before the ex-wife dies, its entire value is included in his gross estate. If he had provided that upon her death or remarriage the policies would go to his children or to a charitable organization and not to him, there would be no reversionary interest and hence no problem.

Simultaneous deaths of spouses

Most states have adopted some version of the Uniform Simultaneous Deaths Act. In these states, if two persons die under circumstances where it isn't possible to determine the order of death, such as in an automobile accident, the insured is presumed to have survived the beneficiary. Anticipate this possibility by naming contingent beneficiaries.

Gifts of life insurance

As an individual gets older, his insurance needs may change. His older beneficiaries may have died, and his younger ones may now be financially independent. If built-up cash values are not needed for funding retirement living, he might consider making a gift of policies he owns on his life to his intended beneficiaries. This is a form of gift an individual can make without in any way impoverishing himself, except to the extent of the dividends and cash buildup that are part of certain policies. Here is something the donee can't waste. There is no management problem for the financially unsophisticated. If the unified credit effective equivalent amount has been used up, there will be a federal gift tax based on the interpolated terminal reserve of the policy at the time of the gift. You can get this figure from the insurance company that issued the policy, and you must notify the company to record the change of ownership. The insurance company will notify the Internal Revenue Service of the transfer and of the value of the interpolated terminal reserve. That means the IRS will automatically be looking for your gift tax return.

Insurance trust

An insurance trust may be used to insulate the policies against claims that may arise from creditors of the insured or of the beneficiaries and keep the proceeds out of the estate. If the policies are assigned to a fiduciary for the benefit of named parties, the insured no longer owns them. In an unfunded or dry trust, a person transfers policies on his life to a trust and continues to pay the premiums. A funded trust is one in which the grantor either transfers policies and/or money from time to time to enable the trust to pay the premiums. Another advantage of an insurance trust is that the trustee may be empowered to select the best settlement option offered by the policy terms, taking into account facts and circumstances that were not known to the insured when he transferred the policies. This is another technique to allow someone to make discretionary decisions on how the grantor's wealth will be used after his death.

Vulnerability of your insurance to IRS liens

An individual is likely to believe that if major business reverses or uninsured casualties threaten all of his other assets, he can at least be assured that his family will get the proceeds of insurance on his life. This may be true with other creditors, but not in the case of the Internal Revenue Service. If a decedent owed the IRS taxes, the Service can attach the cash surrender value of any policies he owned on his life. This extends to policies he gave away many years ago if he retained any significant incident of ownership, such as the right to change the name of the beneficiary. If an individual believes the IRS is likely to attach the cash surrender value of life insurance policies he owns or is deemed to own, he should act swiftly. Seek the advice of both your accountant and a well-informed insurance agent. You should try to avoid actions that will lose your benefits to the IRS, yet some possible choices may be taxable events. Also, if you don't pay the premium, the company may take adverse action as well. Competent advice is a must.

Conclusions and advice

- Have your tax adviser check your actual policies to see if you have retained any incidents of ownership. You may no longer need them; you may have forgotten you had the powers; you may never have known that you retained various rights in certain instances. If you retained the right to repurchase a policy you assigned, that is an incident of ownership.

- Review your insurance program regularly in the light of changed needs of beneficiaries, deaths and births. Your insurance should be reanalyzed to consider changes in the tax law and significant court decisions.

- Because of changing age, income requirements and beneficiaries' needs, you may find it advisable to exchange some policies for others that are more attuned to present circumstances. Check with your tax adviser.

- Do not overlook the effects of inflation on inheritance or income. Additional life insurance may be the only viable way of increasing assets or estates to provide for inflation.

- Property owned by one spouse generally passes without estate tax to the surviving spouse under the marital deduction. But when the second spouse dies, to the extent unexpended, the survivor's estate will include the value of the property the first spouse had owned which is then subject to tax. Consider paying this additional estate tax with the proceeds of "second-to-die" insurance on both spouses, taken out and owned by your insurance trust. Since the insurance premiums are based on two persons instead of one, the cost will be much less than if separate policies had been taken out, and the proceeds will pass estate-tax free if held by your insurance trust.

- Consider that statistically the possibility of being disabled may be greater than the chance of an early death. Disability insurance may be the answer.

Chapter Thirty-Two

SPOUSE INSURANCE

Many people know the importance of having a sizable amount of life insurance to protect their spouse and children. But we might neglect something that's just as important: Life insurance on a spouse to provide financial reimbursement for the loss that would result from the spouse's death. Of course, one can never replace a loved one; however, the replacement value of a spouse can be quite significant from a financial perspective.

Tax cost of losing a spouse

Apart from a number of heavy incidental costs (including those of the funeral), often unnoticed resulting tax costs can be lessened by taking out such insurance. In most situations, federal income tax is lower for a married couple filing a joint return. The most extreme example occurs when one spouse has substantially all of the income. The differences would be less spectacular if both spouses had income, especially if these incomes were about the same. Most often, there is a distinct tax advantage if an individual with a sizable income, such as a business executive, files a joint return with someone who has a smaller income, such as a nonworking spouse.

There are, however, some disadvantages to filing a joint return. An executor might want to consider forgoing a joint return, since each party to a joint return can ordinarily be held liable for any tax deficiency, regardless of which party failed to report income. If the survivor was the spouse with the larger income, there will be additional taxes to pay, because the savings resulting from the filing of joint returns have been forfeited. That there is additional tax is not of so much concern to the executor as seeing that the decedent is not charged with income that the survivor might have omitted from the return, as could happen on a joint return.

In the case of the federal estate tax, loss of one's spouse can result in a major tax disadvantage. The largest deduction from the gross estate in the case of married couples is generally the marital deduction. (See Chapter Four, "The Marital Deduction.") If there is no surviving spouse to whom property can pass, there is no marital deduction. The survivor's estate is taxed, but often insurance on the spouse, payable to either a trust or the children, can help pay these taxes.

The death of a spouse also affects the cost basis of jointly owned property. The tax law automatically assumes that half of this property was owned by the co-owner who died first. So half the value of property owned by husband and wife will be includable in the gross estate of the first spouse to die. The surviving spouse will receive a stepped-up basis only for that half of the property received from the decedent (until carryover basis returns in 2010).

The gift tax marital deduction is also lost upon the death of a spouse to the extent that it was not previously utilized. Obviously, the advantage of gift splitting by the spouses is no longer possible after one of them dies.

Other expenses and costs after death of one spouse

The death of a spouse can mean financial stress for the survivor. A non-earning spouse might have to face a considerable drop in his standard of living. After the death of a nonearning spouse, a working parent with a young family would have to pay someone to look after the household and the children.

The solution

Assuming that the surviving spouse would have the additional net tax expense or higher costs resulting from the death of the other, spouse insurance is clearly indicated, in addition to insurance for other purposes. Note, many policies permit a rider covering your spouse as well.

Conclusions and advice

• Make projections of the tax and other continuing expenses you would have should your spouse die before you do. This will indicate the amount of spouse insurance you will require solely for reimbursement purposes.

• Do not take for granted the likelihood that your spouse will outlive you simply because he/she is younger or in better health. Consider a rider on your policy covering your spouse, if possible, or separate coverage.

• "Second-to-die" insurance can be taken out to provide for the following situation: Due to the so-called unlimited marital deduction, property that the wife owned will not be taxed to her estate if she utilizes the marital deduction by giving her husband everything or everything over the unified credit amount. However, when the husband dies, his estate will include both his own property and what escaped tax (marital deduction amount) in his wife's estate. In some cases, this can mean a doubled or even higher combined estate tax. The federal estate tax is payable nine months after a decedent's death, and the tax on the combined assets of both estates (less the value of property meanwhile consumed) could be too large to be paid by only the husband's estate. *Result:* With this insurance, estate assets will be preserved and not have to be liquidated. Also, premiums on "second-to-die" insurance are generally lower than those on individual life policies, because the insurance company does not have to pay off the face value of the policy until the second spouse dies. Consider having either an irrevocable insurance trust or, in some cases, the heirs themselves buy and own this policy. The insurance will be excluded from the second spouse's estate in this way as well.

• Where one spouse is not healthy, consider using an irrevocable trust which insures only the healthy spouse. The cost could be less than a last-to-die policy where one spouse is "rated," and the funds will be held by trust to pay the taxes, regardless of who dies first.

• If health is an issue, consider maximizing your annual gifts to those you've chosen to receive your estate. If your goal is to build a fund to pay estate taxes, use a trust distributable well beyond your life expectancy while granting the trustee the power to loan funds to your executor to pay taxes.

Chapter Thirty-Three

SPLIT-DOLLAR INSURANCE

Employees of smaller businesses or, even more appropriately, closely held family businesses, can often forge many creative arrangements that benefit each party. Insurance is a significant estate planning tool, and the arrangement can be of substantial benefit to the employee and his family.

The plan

Under the procedure commonly referred to as split-dollar life insurance, the employer and employee join in purchasing an insurance contract on the life of the employee. The employer provides the funds to pay that part of the annual premium equal to the increase in the cash surrender value each year, and the employee pays the balance of the annual premium.

When the employee dies, the employer is entitled to receive, out of the proceeds of the policy, an amount equal to the cash surrender value, or at least a sufficient part of it to equal the funds it has provided for the premium payments. The employee has the right to name the beneficiary of the balance of any proceeds payable by reason of his death. In practical effect, although the employee must pay a part of each premium, the employee obtains valuable insurance protection (decreasing each year, but still substantial for a long time) with a relatively small outlay for the protection granted.

Forms of split-dollar life insurance

Two major types of split-dollar arrangements are in use: The endorsement system and the collateral-assignment system. In the endorsement system, the employer owns the policy and is responsible for payment of the annual premiums. The employee is then required to reimburse the employer for his share, if any, of the premiums. Under the collateral-assignment system, the employee in form owns the policy and pays the entire premium on it. The employer makes annual loans to the employee, without interest or below the going rate, of amounts equal to the yearly increase in cash surrender value, but not exceeding the annual premium. The employee executes an assignment of his policy to the employer as collateral for the loans. The loans are generally payable at the termination of employment or on the death of the employee.

Income tax treatment and other uses

The employee receives an economic benefit represented by the amount of annual premium cost that he is relieved of paying and would otherwise have to bear in the absence of this arrangement. The amount to be included in the employee's gross income each year had been changed by IRS Notice 2001–10 which was then repealed by Notice 2002–8. This new Notice 2002–8 gives us guidance on what the final income tax treatment will be. Your insurance agent can help you with this when designing your plan.

There are many variations such as the executive plan called the Split-Supplemental Executive Retirement Plan (Split-SERP) designed to pay deferred compensation. Also a Proprietorship-Purchase Agreement, where a business owner with no heirs to take over, provides a method of arranging for a buyout by a favored employee. There are also methods of funding business continuation.

Essentially the employer finds split-dollar plans advantageous as these plans are employee incentives, which can be selective and granted without IRS approval. The employee in turn can obtain low-cost insurance with possible coverage beyond retirement. Also, if he is a shareholder, it is an attractive way of providing income- and estate-tax-free cash if an irrevocable trust was used.

According to a 1978 ruling by the Internal Revenue Service, the split-dollar tax treatment rules also apply when the owner of the policy is not an employee, but someone else selected by him. This allows the policy to be owned by a trust established by the employee for his intended beneficiaries.

Deductibility

Neither the employer nor the employee is entitled to a tax deduction for premiums on split-dollar life insurance. As far as the employer is concerned, the company will get back the cost of the policy when it is ultimately paid off on the employee's death. In effect, this is a loan by the employer to the employee. The employee receives most of the protection under such an arrangement, but he pays only a small part of the cost and may have only a relatively small tax, even under the guidelines of Notice 2002–8.

Conclusions and advice

• Split-dollar arrangements are quite attractive in smaller or closely held corporations. Seek the advice of competent counsel and an insurance professional, especially due to the uncertainty of the tax law.

• From the employee's standpoint, a split-dollar arrangement provides greater benefits than group life insurance, in spite of the cash outlay. Also, the plan can be individualized, providing more personal planning results.

• In some cases, the policy is owned by a trust for the benefit of the employee's spouse and/or children. This garners additional estate tax advantages which should be explored.

• Insurance has a place with all estate planning tools. The benefits can be significant, whether used in conjunction with employment, wealth preservation, trusts or charitable giving. A word of caution is in order: Be certain that what you are buying meets your needs and is consistent with expected new rules. Reputable agents will act as consultants to review proposals, make recommendations and ensure compliance with new rules, all in your best interest.

Chapter Thirty-Four

HOW TO GET MORE LIFE INSURANCE

The effects of inflation can hurt the mature executive whose life insurance was generous relative to her earnings and her estate planning objectives at the time it was purchased. She expected the proceeds would provide for her spouse or other beneficiaries upon her death.

As her calculation was based upon outdated assumptions and medical expenses, her estate plans must be revised in light of inflation.

Inflation calls for more insurance: Can you still get it?

How is it possible to refinance an estate plan during times of inflation? The classic solution to the problem is to take out additional life insurance. But if the executive is now middle-aged, the cost of additional insurance might be too high, or she may now have a condition that makes her uninsurable. Her business success may have accustomed her family to a higher standard of living.

Life insurance that doesn't require a physical examination is the best possibility. Group insurance costs appreciably less than an individual policy. If the coverage is group term life, there is the important advantage of not having to report as income the premiums paid by her employer on the cost of providing up to $50,000 in coverage, provided the plan doesn't discriminate. (See Chapter Thirty-Eight, "Choosing a Good Retirement Program.") However, this may not be nearly enough.

Within the last few years, the insurance industry has undergone several changes, which have sparked fierce competition. You may be able to secure higher levels of coverage, but not without a physical. Many companies also offer attractive 5-, 10-, 15- and even 20-year fixed-premium term policies. A good insurance agent will be able to guide you through the maze of products out there. Your agent is very concerned with you and can often work around a troublesome health issue. Don't let the fear of being rated keep you from pursuing needed coverage.

Your employer may be able to assist you. The employer may have taken out similar policies for other executives. Through its business relationships, the employer may be able to make arrangements that might not be available to you personally, such as a split-dollar policy. Also, different insurers view health conditions differently.

A new employer can mean new insurance

Another solution is finding an employer with a liberal group term life insurance program. One possibility for an aging executive is to sign up with an executive search agency, the sizable fees of which are tax deductible in most instances. Ascertain that the agency has done its homework, analyzing compensation packages well enough to know about the group insurance plans available from various employers.

An executive should consider many factors before moving to a corporation for its favorable group term insurance program. She will have to learn about the pension or deferred profit-sharing plan, especially those provisions on minimum number of years (if any) before coverage and the rapidity of vesting. (See Chapter Thirty-Six, "Tax-Favored Retirement Benefits.") Ask your executive search agency about corporations that offer the more flexible "cafeteria plans," which allow employees the most benefits and latitude within the plan's legal confines or structure. If group term insurance is one of the benefits in a cafeteria plan, working at such a corporation offers annual reelection of the particular fringe benefits desired, giving the employee a degree of flexibility.

Conversion privilege

If an executive leaves a corporation with a group insurance plan for a corporation with an appreciably less liberal plan, she should find out before leaving whether there is a conversion privilege. Some plans have provisions for someone who leaves a group insurance program to convert her group policy to an individual one, with identical coverage, often without physical examination, at the prevailing rate for individual insurance at the date of conversion. Although that solution could be costly, the executive might regard it as indispensable—the only method of keeping her insurance coverage. Most agents would advise seeking a new term policy.

Conclusions and advice

• Find out from an authoritative source what employer group insurance programs are available at other companies before leaving your present job. Often, this means engaging an executive search agency. Fees paid to such an agency are deductible if you are still employed at the time you pay the fee. Expenses related to employment are in general deductible, as miscellaneous deductions subject to a 2% floor and other rules regarding applicability.

• Question the possibility of converting your group insurance to individual policies before accepting employment with another company.

• Do not consider group insurance as the sole reason for making a change of employment. But it can be an extremely important reason.

• Do not forget the lessons learned elsewhere in this text. Ask about the possibility of a split-dollar arrangement with a new or prospective employer. Also, the employer might consider a deferred compensation arrangement or a group of other benefits that may amount to savings.

• Use the Internet to research insurance values. Also, if you and your friends start a company as an adjunct to your present business, don't forget that this new company may offer some estate planning benefits and possibilities.

• Don't neglect to ask your current employer if it will increase its benefits.

Chapter Thirty-Five

FUNDING YOUR LIFE INSURANCE TRUST

In previous chapters we have discussed the life insurance trust. Usually, these are irrevocable trusts, which actually own the policy. The beneficiaries are often the children or grandchildren of the grantor. Depending on the situation, the spouse can also be a beneficiary. If the policy is owned by a revocable trust, the proceeds will be in the decedent's estate. Therefore, such a trust is generally not concerned with saving estate taxes. This chapter will concentrate on irrevocable living trusts.

If the spouse is a beneficiary, the policy will generally insure only the grantor and be payable upon his death. The proceeds would be held in trust for his surviving widow and would be used for her benefit as well as that of any children. If properly drafted, the remaining balance would not be in the widow's estate upon her later demise and would thus escape taxation.

If the children, grandchildren or others are the sole beneficiaries, then a married couple would likely use a last-to-die policy. Except in cases where one spouse has a health problem, the cost of a last-to-die policy is usually less than a policy on a sole grantor.

Old policies or new?

One of the vestiges of the previous estate tax law prohibits "gifts in contemplation of death" (old language) of existing life insurance policies. In essence, if an existing life insurance policy is transferred to a trust by the grantor and he dies within three years of the transfer, the policy proceeds will be taxed as if it were in his gross estate.

For this reason, your advisers will prefer to use new policies. However, that may not always be possible or the best choice. For example, the grantor may have become uninsurable or there may be substantial penalties if a policy were to be redeemed. Therefore, any decision to use a current policy should be thoroughly reviewed and discussed with your advisers.

As suggested, the preference is for the trustee to apply for and take out a new policy on the life of the grantor. In the case of a last-to-die policy on the lives of both spouses, the grantor(s) will usually fund the trust with a gift of adequate size to pay the initial premium.

Term or whole life insurance?

This is another area where competent advice can mean all the difference, including tremendous savings. The tendency in most estate plans is to use a whole life product. It builds cash surrender value; therefore, your annual gifts will build a form of equity, and better policies that meet their projected returns will usually "self-fund" after a period. This means that, at some point, the policy may generate enough to pay the annual premium or it vanishes.

Your situation may not require a trust for an extended period. You may have business loans to be covered, or you may be concerned about college education for your children. Your estate may have already been properly planned or gifted away and there are only short-term needs (i.e., 10 years to 15 years). Therefore, it may be that a fixed premium term policy or possibly a universal life policy might be the best choice for your needs.

Obviously, there is a substantial difference in cost of the various types of coverage. Therefore, seek advice first from your estate planners (attorney and accountant) and from their highly recommended insurance professionals. Always ask this agent for several quotes from different companies. Avoid quotes over the phone, the Internet and the like. Insurance contracts are simply too complex to be dealt with in this manner.

Paying the premium

Your trustee should own the policy. The trustee should receive the premium notices and the grantor will have to make sufficient gifts to ensure that the trustee will be able to pay each premium as it becomes due. Here it becomes a bit more complicated.

In order for each gift to qualify for the $11,000/$22,000 annual gift tax exclusion per donee, the trust must contain the so-called Crummey power. Each beneficiary of the trust is a potential recipient of an unspecified gift. The Crummey rule requires, and the trust should provide, that each beneficiary first be given notice of the gift. Secondly, each must have the right to withdraw a specified portion thereof (as set forth in the trust document). Each beneficiary is given a certain period of time, usually no less than 30 days, to withdraw his entitlement.

If the respective beneficiary declines or does not notify the trustee to the contrary, the gift remains in the trust and thus the trustee may pay the premium. Due to the withdrawal right, usually specified in the trust to be at least 30 days, no gift should be made at a time when the withdrawal period would fall in the next year. For example, if the withdrawal right was 30 days and a December 15th gift was made, the beneficiary would have until January of the following year to withdraw.

In years before passage of the 2001 tax law, some members of Congress lobbied to put a cap on annual gifting, other than through use of one's unified credit. Figures as low as $60,000 in a lifetime were mentioned. These factions in Congress are still present, and we are skeptical that in 2011 we will have complete repeal of the estate tax.

To reduce the size of one's estate, we often encourage clients to maximize gifts to their trusts. In other words, gifts in excess of the annual premiums are encouraged. In a situation where a last-to-die policy was purchased and the husband passed away and the surviving widow failed to continue the gifting program, the estate plan may fail due to a lack of funds needed for the premium. This situation must be considered, especially if the widow is a second spouse and the beneficiaries are children of the husband's first marriage. In this event, the widow may be unwilling to continue the gifting plan, especially if there is some discord between parties.

Conclusions and advice

• Thoroughly discuss the choices of documents, types of insurance policies and funding needs of any trust with your estate planners.

• Do not put life insurance in a revocable trust unless you understand that the policy proceeds will be taxable in your estate. Consult your attorney.

• As the grantor, you do not pay the premium. Make a gift to the trust and let the trustee pay the premium.

• Making gifts in excess of the premium is advisable.

• Be sure your trust contains the Crummey power, and make sure your trustee notifies the beneficiaries of each gift and that each beneficiary has a right to withdraw. Note that some trusts allow the grantor to opt out of the Crummey notice/power. The effect is that the gift does not qualify for the annual gift tax exclusion and reduces the donor's unified credit. This may be the lesser of two evils if the beneficiary is likely to withdraw, given the opportunity. This may be a good option to consider including in your trust.

• Do not make gifts during a time of the year when the withdrawal right would extend into the next year. This could jeopardize the exclusion.

• You must be sure you have the right product match for you and your estate planning needs. While all agents may sell you insurance, they may not be qualified to help you find the proper match. Ask your attorney and accountant to help you find the right agent for your needs. It is an important responsibility.

• The events of September 11, 2001, and the resulting economic expenditures, make our skepticism about the repeal of the estate tax more strident. Therefore, delay in the planning process may not be in anyone's best interest.

Chapter Thirty-Six

TAX-FAVORED RETIREMENT BENEFITS

An individual derives several advantages from a retirement program financed entirely or in large measure by an employer. Chief among them:

1. In the case of a qualified retirement program (that is, one approved by the Internal Revenue Service), the individual isn't taxed until she receives payment. Her income is almost invariably lower after retirement than when on salary, so the tax impact is lower than if she were taxed each year on the increment of accruals.

2. The employer, within limits set by the tax law, is entitled to immediate tax deductions, making it a desirable benefit to offer.

3. The trust used to administer most qualified retirement plans is set up on a tax-exempt basis for the benefit of employees or their beneficiaries. Consequently, accumulations of income or capital through interest, dividends, rents and capital gains are tax free. An individual saving money for her own retirement would not have comparable tax-exempt accumulation.

In effect, the employee has a substantial savings program, and will not have to rely only on her own capital to see her through the retirement years, because government restrictions and regulations ensure that planned benefits are delivered. This security permits the employee to make dispositions of other property, reducing what would be her gross estate when she dies.

Pension or deferred profit-sharing plan?

The two most popular types of employer-financed retirement programs are the pension plan (also known as a defined-benefits plan) and the deferred profit-sharing plan (also known as a defined-contributions plan). Although each can have provisions for earlier payouts, as in the case of permanent disability, most plans provide benefits at retirement. Reduced payments may be permitted for retirement a few years before the standard targeted retirement age.

It is customarily the employer's decision which type of retirement plan it will provide. Employee choices, if the plan so provides, are:

• Whether to retire at, before or after the company's normal retirement date.

• Whether to participate, if the plan is of the contributory type.

• Whether to take a payout in the form of an annuity or as a lump-sum payment, where the plan allows this choice.

• Whether to take a retirement annuity in the form of a single-life contract for the employee or a survivorship annuity that covers the employee and another designated party, most frequently a spouse.

Plans must provide survivorship coverage for spouses, and if she desires, an employee must affirmatively act to avoid such coverage if she is married. But an individual has a more basic decision as to the form of employer retirement program that will apply to her. She can select an employer on the basis of the latter's retirement program provisions. Of vital concern are whether the employer has a pension or a deferred profit-sharing plan (few have both); the coverage requirements (how long one has to work before becoming qualified under the program); the vesting requirements (what monetary rights accumulate for the individual after specified periods that can't be lost through resignation or dismissal); the possibility of obtaining benefits in a lump sum; the opportunity to transfer accrued benefits to another retirement program without present tax consequences (a rollover); early retirement provisions and what happens if an employee wants to continue working after the stated retirement date. Usually people don't regard a company's retirement program as a major factor in choosing an employer. But the choice has a definite impact on an estate plan. If an employer has a good retirement program, plus a generous medical reimbursement and health plan, the employee is not obliged to retain as much capital to deal with these expenses on her own.

Qualified pension plans

Pension plans are covered by the strict requirements of several federal labor laws and Internal Revenue Code sections. The Employee Retirement Income Security Act of 1974 (ERISA) is the base legislation. Employers, as a competitive measure, have voluntarily adopted plans to meet these rules. A well-informed employee may choose not to take a job with a company that has a nonqualified pension plan which doesn't meet ERISA ground rules. Such a plan provides little assurance that benefits won't go disproportionately to a few favored persons, that the employee will not lose rights if she is discharged before retirement or decides to work elsewhere, that the money will really be there when she retires, that she won't have to wait excessive periods to obtain benefits and that her financial involvement in the plan will not be treated as something she has no right to know about.

Coverage

If a corporation has a qualified retirement plan, the federal tax law defines the minimum percentage of employees who must be covered—that is, benefitted by the plan. Certain employees may be excluded by the terms of a plan, such as those who have worked for the employer for less than a specified length of time or those who work on a part-time or seasonal basis.

The technical requirements of a plan ensuring all possible tax advantages for both employer and employee involve areas over which an employee has no control. There are intricate rules governing the failure of a plan to qualify because of inadequate coverage of the work force, discrimination in favor of highly compensated employees, reduction of benefits because of early retirement, rollovers of an employee's accrued benefits under the plan when she changes employment and tax treatment of a lump-sum distribution of accrued benefits instead of annual payments. An employee may be able to learn these details from the employer's designated representative. Whether the employer actually complies with the highly technical requirements of the law, so that employee benefits really are being safeguarded, is usually something an employee has no way of knowing.

Vesting

Vesting is the irrevocable transfer of the employer's contributions to the retirement fund to the credit of an employee. Various alternatives are available for a qualified plan's provision as to when employee rights become vested. But each covered employee's rights must be fully vested when she reaches the normal or stated retirement age, or when she actually retires. Generally, it is much sooner than this. The 2001 tax law has modified vesting rules in some areas for the betterment of the employee.

Discrimination

A qualified retirement plan must not discriminate in favor of officers, employee stockholders or other highly compensated employees, either in the actual language of the plan or the way in which it operates. The tax law defines what is meant by the term "highly compensated."

Past-service credit

A current pension plan makes provision for retirement benefits based upon salaries for the number of years of coverage under the plan. But an individual may have worked for the company for many years before the plan was adopted. If it so chooses, a corporation may adopt a past-service credit plan. Employees, in addition to credits based upon current service, may be given credits for the number of years, or for a specified number of those years, before the plan went into effect. This can make a considerable difference in the amount of pension benefits available to an employee who worked for the company prior to the time it adopted its pension plan.

Benefits

Under a pension plan (defined-benefit plan), an employee must be able to ascertain what she will actually receive upon retirement at the specified time, but she must assume how many years she will work and what her compensation will be during her remaining years of employment. It is up to the employer to provide the financial means each year, so that when an individual does retire, her benefits will be there. This usually requires elaborate computations by an actuary. In order to make certain that the employer does have the funds in hand, the tax law provides strict penalties for noncompliance.

If the pension plan is underfunded

If an employee becomes entitled to retirement benefits under a qualified pension plan, and the implementing trust or fund lacks the money to honor this commitment, the Pension Benefit Guarantee Corporation, a federal agency, steps in. This corporation is funded by premiums paid by each covered employer. When a corporation's pension fund can't make the required payments because the plan has been underfunded and Pension Benefit Guarantee Corporation funds are used for this purpose, that agency can recover from the employer amounts up to 30% of the company's net worth. In certain situations, an employer might have two or more qualified pension plans, covering different types of employees or functions. Underfunding could subject the employer to reimbursement payments to the Guarantee Corporation of up to 30% of net worth for each such plan. The same penalty applies to a corporation with a defunct subsidiary whose plan was underfunded.

Retirement annuities

When a plan provides for a retirement benefit in the form of an annuity, and the employee has been married for the one-year period ending on the annuity starting date, the plan must provide for a joint and survivor annuity with the employee's spouse. This annuity must be for not less than half of the annuity payable to the participant during the joint lives of the participant and her spouse. But the employee may elect to receive the higher return of a single-life annuity if the spouse consents. The employer must supply the necessary figures so that the employee can have before her the computations for both scenarios. The time for supplying this information varies according to certain specified circumstances. For example, in the case of an employee who leaves her place of employment before age 35, distributions after December 31, 1989, must be made within "a reasonable time."

Protection against mergers

A qualified pension plan must protect participants in the case of a merger of the plan with another plan or the transfer of assets or liabilities from a plan. The value of benefits to the participant and the extent to which the benefits have been funded are protected by comparing what the benefits would have been if the plan had terminated immediately before the merger and what they would have been under the plan had it terminated just after the merger. Postmerger termination benefit may not be less than the premerger termination benefit.

Termination of employment

Consideration of the advantages of pension plans always assumes that the employee will get back more than she puts into the fund. It doesn't always work out that way, however. If she gets back less than she paid in under a contributory plan, for example, because the fund's investments have been unsuccessful, she may, under some plans, deduct the difference as an ordinary loss in the year of the lump-sum distribution to her.

If an employee's services are terminated, she is likely to have accrued benefits. Any payments she receives will constitute taxable income to her. In addition, the accumulation of amounts established to her credit in the fund will no longer be on a tax-free basis if she withdraws them from the tax-exempt trust. The employee can avoid the present tax impact if she elects not to take possession of the funds and rolls them over to an Individual Retirement Account (IRA), or to the qualified pension plan trust of a new employer if that employer agrees, as long as she does so within a certain specified time period. Such a tax-free rollover can be used only once every three years. Note also that rollover rules have been liberalized under the 2001 tax law.

Penalties

Penalties are imposed on the trustees of a qualified pension plan if it violates the strict requirements of the law. The only impact upon the employee is that this tends to ensure that the plan and its implementing fund or trust will be supervised very carefully. On the other hand, rather than face penalties, management may decide that it doesn't want to have a qualified pension plan at all, and this definitely affects the employees.

Deferred profit-sharing plans

Because of a corporation's vulnerability to a levy of up to 30% of net worth in the case of an underfunded plan, plus the personal liabilities in which executives or plan trustees can be involved, many corporations have become disenchanted with qualified pension plans. Instead, they may adopt a deferred profit-sharing plan to provide employee retirement benefits. Such plans are less "dangerous" because there are no minimum funding requirements and no harsh financial consequences in case of underfunding.

The employer may take a specified percentage of its profits each year as a deduction by paying it into its qualified profit-sharing plan (defined-contributions plan). The portion of employer profits to be shared with employees that exceeds this specified percentage in any year is an unallowable deduction, which may be carried forward by the employer for use in future years when the deduction would otherwise be less than the specified percentage.

A deferred profit-sharing plan may provide for the payment of amounts into a fund for ultimate payout to eligible participants. The difference between this and a pension plan is that under the latter, retirement benefits are the amounts called for by the plan itself, subject only to the number of years of coverage and the amount of compensation on which benefits are based. The deferred profit-sharing plan, on the other hand, guarantees no specific annual amount. Even assuming that the funds are available when employees become entitled to them, the amounts available depend upon previous corporate profits. And there is, of course, no way of determining what these profits will be.

"Profits" may be anything defined by the plan itself—for example, book profits, book profits with certain specified adjustments, income exclusive of capital gains, income exclusive of revenues from foreign operations, income as calculated on the federal income tax return. The portion of defined income that is to be shared with the employees via the deferred profit-sharing plan should also be specified—for example, 50% of income above $100,000, or a sliding scale of percentages of corporate income.

Payouts

An employee entitled to deferred profit-sharing plan benefits may receive payment under a unit system. For example, employees' shares may be determined by assigning units for compensation, length of service and age. An employee's share of the employer contribution is that proportion of the entire amount that the number of units assigned to her bears to the total number of units assigned to all employees. In working out the allocation, units are given a dollar value by dividing the total number issued into the total employer contribution.

Unlike a qualified pension plan, an employee gains from the departure of other employees to the extent their interests have not vested. Amounts forfeited by reason of employees' premature departure become available in the total to be shared by the remaining employees. By contrast, the rights of an employee covered by a qualified pension plan don't change, regardless of what happens to other employees or their shares in a retirement program.

What type of plan is better for you

We cannot say categorically whether an employee benefits more from a qualified pension plan or a deferred profit-sharing plan, although there is far more assurance of collecting retirement benefits under a qualified pension plan.

The actual amount of benefits, however, could be far more or less under a deferred profit-sharing plan, depending upon the profit-sharing arrangement, the profits over the years and the number of employees whose interests are forfeited in favor of the remaining employees. A qualified pension plan may provide for past-service credits, an unusual arrangement for deferred profit-sharing plans.

There has been some criticism, chiefly from labor unions, that corporations offering deferred profit-sharing plans may conceal earnings in order not to share them with the rank-and-file employees. But a deferred profit-sharing plan offers this advantage: Employees are apt to work harder, and to eliminate or at least reduce unnecessary expenses and waste. They realize that they will share in any additional profits that result from increased dedication to their jobs.

Top-heavy plans

Special rules apply to "top-heavy" plans—those whose benefits flow to a limited number of shareholders, partners or key employees. Such plans must provide for faster vesting for non-key employees, and minimum benefits or contributions are required for such non-key employees.

The plans won't be able to take Social Security benefits and contributions into account in determining these minimum benefits or contributions. These rules apply to both corporate plans and Keogh-type plans for the self-employed.

Conclusions and advice

• Have an expert in the field compare the pension plans of corporations where you are considering securing employment.

• Insist on an understandable explanation of your corporation's qualified pension plan as required by law (called a Summary Plan Description).

• Do not rely on current indicated pension payouts. The corporation may obtain permission from the Internal Revenue Service to discontinue its plan, for example, because of circumstances that could not reasonably have been foreseen when the plan was adopted. You may have vested rights, but only to accrued benefits and not to the future of the plan.

• The economic climate or a major corporate "restructuring" may mean that the stated plan benefits will shrink or even disappear entirely.

• If a company for which the decedent had worked has gone out of business, the executor should write to the Pension Benefit Guaranty Corporation, Missing Participant Program, 1200 K Street NW, Washington, DC 20005. This program locates plans that have been terminated, or taken over by the agency. The inquiry should include the name, address, telephone number, Social Security number and date of birth of the decedent, the name and location of the employer and any documents issued by the plan.

- Do not rely on the permanency of the language in the present version of the tax law. It could be changed at any time by Congress. The 2001 tax law enacted several beneficial changes to pension laws.

- Lately, so-called salary-reduction arrangements (401[k]s, etc.) have emerged as a favored employee offering. In theses arrangements, the employee voluntarily reduces his pretax salary. The contributions and his earnings build tax free, and some employers elect to match a given percentage of the employee's contribution. Even the youngest of employees should strongly consider participating or request the employer to consider establishing one.

- Employees who have no salary-reduction plan should consider the expanded IRA, Roth IRA and the new educational IRAs (all were either expanded or enacted by the 2001 tax law). Each have different rules and tax advantages. Also, for smaller employers with few employees, the Simplified Employee Pension plans (SEPs) should be considered (also expanded by the 2001 tax law).

- Do not assume qualified plans are only for larger employers. In fact, smaller employers, closely held corporations, LLCs and/or sole proprietorships can take advantage of the benefits offered. There are many opportunities for integration of these into your estate plan. As always, consult your accountant.

- Many retirement plans have been decimated by investments in volatile markets. Be cautious about what your plan (regardless of the type) is invested in.

- When accepting a position, weigh very seriously the question of accepting stock options in lieu of other benefits such as a pension plan. This is especially true if the company stock would be considered highly speculative.

Chapter Thirty-Seven

DEFERRED COMPENSATION ARRANGEMENTS

An individual may be doing very well financially today—but tomorrow, when he retires or when his income tapers off, could be another matter. If he retains his assets in order to live on its income, his gross estate at death will be larger than it needs to be. He won't have the satisfaction of giving properties to his beneficiaries while he is living. And in later years, he may no longer have the capacity to administer or maintain his assets properly.

With careful planning, however, this individual can arrange now to have some of the income he doesn't need today deferred until later years, when it might be taxed at lower rates.

Nature of deferred income

Pension and deferred profit-sharing plans are forms of deferred compensation. (See Chapter Thirty-Six.) Here are some others forms:

Ordinarily, when someone earns income in a particular year, regardless of when he or somebody else actually receives payment, it is taxable in that year if he had access to the money without any substantial restrictions or difficulty. This is called "constructive receipt of income." For example, savings bank interest is taxed in the year earned, even if the depositor never withdrew it. But, if there is a substantial question whether he will ever receive it, an individual hasn't received income. There may be a provision that income earned today will be paid to the employee in 10 years, or upon his retirement, if he has not gone into competition with his employer corporation. Until the specified time of payment, he has no taxable income until it is established whether he has honored his commitment.

Another arrangement may require that part of a person's current income be paid in yearly or other installments until he dies, provided he is available for consultation if requested by the corporation. Only on a year-to-year basis can it be determined whether he has done so, a fact not affected by whether the employer ever asks his advice. The possibility exists that he could forfeit his right to receive the deferred compensation, so he isn't taxed on it until payment is actually made.

Variations to these arrangements, given good faith, trust and a stable business, can provide effective retirement and estate planning tools.

Unfunded compensation: A danger

There is an element of risk in a deferred compensation arrangement if the money is not actually safeguarded by deposits in a trust fund for the employee's benefit or in an escrow account in his name. The risk is that the employer simply won't have the funds to honor it. So, if the deferred compensation plan is not funded, and the employee takes the risk that he might never be paid, the income goes untaxed until actually received.

For example, if there is no forfeiture provision that could cause the employee to lose his right to future payment, and if there is a trust or other arrangement that assures him that the money is available for the payout date, he is taxed in the year his services are performed. But, under one procedure, an employee can be assured that the money will be there without being taxed before receipt. One employee was granted a deferred compensation arrangement to run until he reached age 65 or his employment was terminated. The employer purchased an annuity contract to fund its deferred compensation liability. The annuity contract was owned by the corporation, which was the beneficiary, and the contract was subject to claims of the corporation's general creditors. The employee was taxed only when he received the deferred payments, for he had no interest in the annuity. But he had reason to be confident that he would get his money when it was due, unless the corporation's creditors got there first.

Taxability

A deferred compensation plan postpones taxability until the payment date if the election to defer income is made before the period in which the services are to be rendered. In one instance, a contract provided that each year officers could, before income for the following year was earned, elect irrevocably to defer receipt of specified portions of their salaries, which would then be paid ratably over a 10-year period. A deferred compensation account was set up on the corporate books for each officer who made the election, but the amounts thus deferred were to be satisfied only from general corporate funds, which could have been subject to creditors' claims. The deferred amounts were not taxable to electing officers in the years earned but in the years received.

Key to a contract

In another situation, an employee and a corporation executed a five-year employment contract providing for a stated annual salary and stipulated additional compensation. The additional compensation was to be credited to a bookkeeping reserve account, to be deferred, accumulated and paid in annual installments equal to one-fifth of the amount in reserve as of the close of the year immediately preceding the year of the corporation's payment. Payments were to begin only when the individual (1) terminated full-time employment, (2) became a part-time employee of the corporation or (3) became partially or totally incapacitated. The corporation was merely under a contractual obligation. There was no trust arrangement to ensure that the employee would in fact get the money.

The contract provided that if the employee should fail or refuse to perform his duties, the corporation would be relieved of its obligation to make any further credits to the reserve. It also provided that if he died prior to his receipt in full of the account balance, the remaining balance would be payable to any party he named at the rate of one-fifth per year for five years. The Internal Revenue Service ruled that the additional compensation stipulated under the contract would be taxable to the employee only in the years he actually received installment payments in cash from the amounts credited to his account.

Spurs to performance

Another corporation set up a supplementary retirement plan under which a committee of directors (none of whom was an officer or employee) could award incentive bonuses to selected employees for payment at future dates to be designated by that employee. Employees thus selected had no right to any money until the date they named, and no payment could be made more than 10 years after an employee's normal retirement date. The awards were not funded, nor could they be assigned, although they would be paid to the employee's beneficiary at the time of his death.

Federal estate tax

Federal estate tax problems may arise in the case of a deferred compensation arrangement. In one case, a corporation agreed to make specified payments to an employee on his retirement or to his nominee upon his death. There were certain forfeiture provisions, but they all ended with the employee's death. The value of the payments the corporation was obliged to make to his nominee after his death was included in his gross estate.

But, in another case, nothing was includable in the gross estate of one executive who was covered by an agreement under which the employer corporation undertook to pay specified annuities to the widows of executives who died while still employed. The contract identified each wife by name and the husband had no right to the annuity or any property interest in it. He couldn't alter it or change the name of the beneficiary, because parties to the agreement were only the corporation and the executive's wife as an individual.

Interplay with economic factors

An executive should consider the merits of a deferred compensation plan carefully. He might prefer to take his money today rather than at a time when it will be worth less. If the deferred compensation is not set aside in the individual's name (as in a trust fund), there is a possibility that the money will not be paid when it is due because of poor business conditions. Mounting economic pressures might result in higher tax rates when the individual retires than at present, even if his income is lower.

Conclusions and advice

• Make a deferred compensation arrangement before income is actually earned.

• If income is to be paid to a nominee after the executive's death, specify several persons, such as children or grandchildren, to lessen the tax impact on the payees.

• Consider using a deferred compensation arrangement for someone who seems unable to invest unneeded current income wisely.

• Do not agree to such an arrangement with a corporation that is of questionable financial stature.

• Do not make an arrangement where income is earned currently and is merely made payable in the future for the employee's convenience. If the income is really subject to his command, it is not deferred compensation.

• Beware of financial, personnel, policy or other changes that will imperil future benefits.

• Consider asking the employer to set aside the funds in an asset not earmarked for a particular employee such as investment accounts and insurance products to ensure that the assets will be there.

• If your employer experiences hard times, or if there is serious merger or acquisition talk, consider asking for a "payout."

• Don't be afraid to ask your employer to consider a deferred compensation arrangement for selected employees. These are not "qualified plans," and therefore the employer need not treat everyone the same. In fact, in stable smaller businesses, these plans can provide a significant benefit to select employees especially when the employer actually sets the funds aside.

Chapter Thirty-Eight

CHOOSING A GOOD RETIREMENT PROGRAM

Your employer's fringe benefit program can be an important element in your own estate planning. What will be most important to you and your beneficiaries? It might be insurance coverage on your life or an annuity that will also cover the remaining life of your spouse or other designated beneficiaries. It might be some form of wage continuation plan that could carry on to a specified survivor your salary, or a portion of it, for a stipulated length of time. It might be an education fund that could benefit your children. The list is long.

Weigh the available compensation packages

The compensation package of a valued executive or an employee with especially desired skills might be subject to individual negotiation. Consequently, it is important to ascertain what employer-provided benefits would be most desirable in the implementation of your own estate plan and to bargain from there. Consult with an expert in executive compensation and fringe benefits to learn what kind of package would be most useful to you.

If your employer doesn't offer the type of benefits you have determined best suited for your own income and estate plan, and if you are unable to negotiate for such an arrangement, consider moving to another employer who will supply what you want. To find out what other employers are providing, it may be necessary to engage an executive search agency, which should have such information. The fees can be considerable, but they are tax deductible by an employed executive.

Desirable compensation plans

Choosing an employer-provided benefit that would be of most value to your own situation necessarily involves consideration of its federal tax impact. Ordinarily, the value of what's received as the result of an employer–employee relationship is regarded as additional compensation, taxable as ordinary income. But there are some important exceptions, such as:

1. Group term life insurance. An employee may exclude from gross income the cost of premiums paid by her employer on group term life insurance. The excludable cost cannot exceed the expense of providing $50,000 of such insurance. The employer's plan to provide group term insurance must not discriminate in favor of key employees as to benefits or type and amount of eligibility. If it does, there is no exclusion for the premium cost. If an employer pays for coverage in excess of that figure, there may be some taxable income. But the employee couldn't have obtained such coverage for as low a premium that the employer pays on a group policy. This treatment is not limited to a lump-sum payment of proceeds upon the death of the insured. The employer's master policy may provide that payments be made in other ways: For example, the proceeds could go to the employee's beneficiaries in equal annual or monthly installments over a fixed period of time not to exceed 20 years. Or they could be used to purchase a lifetime annuity. The existence of alternative payout options does not affect the plan's status as a tax-favored group term life insurance policy. Retired employees are treated in the same manner as active employees.

2. Accident and health plans. Premiums paid under an employer's accident and health plan are not includable in gross income. An accident and health plan is an arrangement for payments to employees who are unable to work due to personal injury or illness.

3. Medical insurance and reimbursement plans. Today the cost of private medical insurance coverage is so expensive that employer-sponsored plans are a key nontaxable benefit. Also an employee may exclude from gross income any amounts received—directly or indirectly, by herself, her spouse and her

dependents (according to the terms of the plan)—reimbursement for medical expenses, if these amounts are attributable to payments made by her employer. This includes payments made directly to physicians and hospitals. A medical reimbursement plan for this purpose cannot discriminate in favor of select employees—for example, shareholder employees (owners of more than 10% of the stock) or highly compensated employees. If the plan does discriminate, all or part of the reimbursement becomes taxable compensation. The employee is clearly better off with these tax-free benefits since only medical expenses exceeding 7.5% of her adjusted gross income can be deducted on her federal income tax return.

4. Voluntary Employees' Beneficiary Associations (VEBAs). A VEBA is a special type of tax-exempt organization sanctioned by the IRS. In recent years, VEBAs have become popular and they provide benefits to employees and/or their dependents or designated beneficiaries. Generally, the benefits are limited to the areas of illness, accident, death and other similar benefits, including those to safeguard or improve health or protect against interruption of earning power. VEBAs must also meet nondiscrimination requirements.

Tax-favored benefits

Consider other employer plans in relation to your own estate planning objectives. Even if employer-financed benefits of a particular type are taxable, an employee can still reap a substantial benefit from them. For example, if the employee is in a 30% income tax bracket, only 70% of the employer's cost in providing the benefits will be received tax free by the employee.

A nonmonetary (and nontaxable) benefit might include a prized office location and an "executive" assistant.

Here are some additional employer-provided benefits to consider:

• Life insurance. Many employers participate with employees in securing life insurance. (See Chapter Thirty-Three, "Split-Dollar Insurance.")

• Scholarships. Many corporations make scholarships available to children of employees or fund scholarships for needy individuals, with first preference given to the children of present or past employees. Your children might meet the necessary standards of eligibility.

• Education trusts. A corporation may set up a trust to pay for college or other defined educational expenses of designated key employees. If an employee has several children and the available coverage is less than the trust provides, the employee may choose which child will be covered; if that child leaves college or otherwise becomes ineligible, the employee may name a "replacement" child. There is no taxable income to the employee until payouts are made for the benefit of her children.

• Retirement plans. The corporation may have a pension or deferred profit-sharing plan that provides retirement benefits for employees. In some instances, the spouses or other relatives of the employees may benefit from them as well. (See Chapter Thirty-Six, "Tax-Favored Retirement Benefits.")

• Annuities. The employer may provide a retirement annuity for an employee, or a survivorship annuity covering the employee and her spouse or other beneficiary. (See Chapter Forty-Five, "Annuities.")

• Deferred compensation. Advantageous arrangements may be made with an employer to have a certain portion of the employee's compensation payable after a specified number of years, which may be after the employee retires and is presumably in a lower tax bracket. (See Chapter Thirty-Seven, "Deferred Compensation Arrangements.")

• Interest-free loans. Most economic advantages obtained as the result of an employer–employee relationship are taxed as additional compensation. This is not the case with small interest-free loans which do not exceed $10,000. When interest rates soar, an interest-free loan is an attractive fringe benefit. Find out the employer's policy.

• Stock options and stock purchase plans. These are complex subjects to discuss with your tax adviser. Incentive stock options provide substantial tax benefits as well as increasing your chance to own part of the business. Before entering upon a stock option plan, find out if it qualifies for tax benefits and what the conditions are in the event of your death. Will exercising the option make you subject to the alternative minimum tax? Will the option granted to you be exercisable by your spouse if you die before exercising it? If you purchase stock in a closely held corporation, will your executors have to sell it back to the corporation at the time of your death under a formula or at a price that might be undesirable, such as original cost? Is the stock subject to a buy–sell agreement? (See Chapter Forty-Two, "Buy–Sell Agreements.")

- Directors' and officers' liability insurance. Such premiums, although paid by the employer corporation, are not regarded as income taxable to the employee. The existence of such a policy could save an individual or an estate considerable expense in the event of an unfortunate business decision or act.

- Extended working period. Will your employer permit you to work beyond the company's stated mandatory retirement age? Will employer-provided fringe benefits be added to your compensation after normal retirement age? Can you get assurance that you'll be retained as a part-time consultant after you retire?

Conclusions and advice

- Keep abreast of changes in your employer's benefit package. Check your own objectives regularly. Your economic circumstances, as well as the employer corporation's executives, vary from time to time.

- Find out if an employer fringe benefit plan is discriminatory. If it is, all tax benefits to you may be lost even though you were not responsible for the discriminatory practice.

- Executive search agency fees and moving expenses are deductible in many instances. Check with tax counsel to find out whether your costs in finding and accepting employment with an employer that has more attractive fringe benefits are deductible for income tax purposes.

- Do not assume that higher salary must be the most desirable form of compensation. Consider the after-tax effects.

- Do not assume that all group insurance premiums are excludable from gross income for up to $50,000 of coverage. This applies only to group term life insurance.

• An employee who is covered by certain kinds of retirement plans can choose to have part of her compensation contributed by her employer to a retirement fund rather than paid to her. These amounts are called elective deferrals, because she may choose (elect) to set aside the money and defer the income tax on the amount until it is distributed to her. These elective deferrals include deferred contributions to cash or deferral arrangements (known as Section 401[k] plans). Because these contributions are considered to be made by the employer, the employee is taxed on any payments she receives from the retirement fund unless she properly rolls over the payments into a qualified IRA rollover account. (For an explanation of this, speak to your tax adviser or see IRS Publication 575.) Generally, an employee may not defer more than a total of $11,000 in 2002, which increases by $1,000 per year until reaching $15,000 in 2006 for all qualified plans by which she is covered. There are some exceptions for employees also covered by #457 plans and a "catch-up" for employees over age 50. They can contribute an extra $1,000 to their 401(k), which increases by $1,000 per year until it reaches $5,000 in 2006.

• An employment contract providing that the employer will pay benefits to an employee's spouse in the event the employee dies while still on the payroll has become much more attractive. In 1992, the IRS reversed its prior position and now holds that this is not to be treated as a taxable gift to the spouse.

• Consider, also, the discussion on split-dollar insurance in Chapter Thirty-Three. Many employers use this tool, especially in closely held corporations.

• Thoughtfully consider all of the employer's offerings. Do not discount performance shares, stock appreciation rights (SARs), medical savings accounts (MSAs), company-provided meals, lodging, education and health facilities. Many larger companies even offer financial counseling, legal assistance and day care. Of course, the traditional expense account and a company car may also provide substantial nontaxable benefits. The employment market is most competitive, and you may be surprised at what is available if you ask.

THE FAMILY BUSINESS AS A MECHANISM TO PASS WEALTH

As noted in Section V, there are several potential benefits that can be offered to an employee to help him amass wealth. Chapter Twenty-Eight outlined the potential of taking existing assets and establishing a business with the thought of giving away parts of the new entity. Here we consider using the free enterprise system to create wealth not only in your family (your children, parents and siblings) but possibly for friends and other relatives as well.

One mechanism to pass on wealth is the family or closely held business. In the past, when the work force was typically employed by a small group of large moguls, ownership opportunity in a family business was very limited. Farmers were the principal exception. In general, in the early part of the 20th century, small family businesses were limited in size and scope.

Today, however, the family or closely held business (the terms are used interchangeably) has taken on a new dimension. There are still family farms, but many more people have opened family enterprises—from restaurants to clothiers to contractors. The Internet has spawned many new closely held businesses. The employee of the 21st century has the option not only of working for someone but also of starting his own business. Further, if the business is started with the plan to admit other family members or close friends, one can effectively pass wealth from one generation to another without gift or estate tax, regardless of the somewhat uncertain state of affairs involving both laws at the present under the 2001 tax act.

Consider the airline pilot who invests in real estate during his off hours, starting slowly and with limited capital. He makes his children and his wife his partners. As the business grows, so does their wealth. And what about the computer programmer who sets up a Web hosting site in his basement? The business, owned by the programmer and his family, operates with his knowledge and expertise, and may grow into a valuable entity to be purchased by a larger company.

What type of entity should I use?

Until recently, the types of entities for organizing family businesses were somewhat limited. They consisted of the C corporation that protected the owners from liability, but was harsh from a tax standpoint. The IRS later developed the S corporation that again protected the owners' personal assets from liability and yet was less harsh taxwise, but not ideal.

At the other end of the spectrum, the partnership was the best tax choice, but the partners could be held personally liable for the debts of the entity. In other words, it lacked the corporate liability shield. The limited partnership and its cousin, the family limited partnership, were developed to take some of the liability sting away. In a limited partnership, only the general partner is fully liable for the debts of the partnership. The limited partners are liable only up to the amount of their investment.

There were variations to this, such as a joint venture or a limited partnership where the general partner was a shell corporation. However, no entity was generally accepted as preferred. The choice often came down to a question of liability, tax benefits, how well you could protect yourself and how much you had to lose.

Within the last few years, the concept of the *limited liability company* (LLC) and *limited liability partnership* (LLP) was presented to the IRS. This is a new entity, created by state law, where the owners (called *members*) are essentially partners for tax purposes. Yet, they are also given the liability shield by state statute, just as a shareholder of a corporation is.

The IRS was asked to approve the concept and tax the entity as if it were a partnership. Surprisingly, the IRS agreed. From that point, the floodgates opened and most states have now adopted a version of a statute to allow the LLC/LLP. Most allow a single-person LLC/LLP which, of course, is contrary to the concept of a partnership, which requires more than one person. In any event, this entity seems to offer the best of both worlds (tax benefits and liability shield) and is often used for the family business along with a family limited partnership as a mechanism to pass wealth. Corporations are less often used in smaller settings.

How does it work?

First and foremost, discuss your plans and ideas with your accountant and attorney. They can advise you which entity to choose, how best to capitalize (fund) the entity, who should own the entity initially and, assuming this is your goal, develop and commence a gifting program.

If you have young children, you may wish to put their portion of the entity into a trust for them. Therefore, let us say you will own 40%, your wife, 40% and the trust for your children, 20%. Obviously, you can choose any percentages you wish, but you must do so within the gifting rules.

Suppose in this example, there is a small two-family home on the corner of an important intersection, and you can purchase it for $100,000. The rental income would easily justify a $50,000 mortgage, and you believe the property will greatly appreciate. Our example assumes you have the balance of the purchase price.

First, you would create a trust for your children with a $10,000 gift. Then, you would create the family business with you and your wife each contributing $20,000 and the trust would contribute the remaining $10,000. The business now has the necessary funds to purchase the property. It does so with the bank's $50,000 mortgage.

In later years, the business will have rental income. If you guessed correctly and the property has appreciated to $500,000, that's a handsome gain for your children without much assistance from you other than the initial gift, your good judgment and management each year. With such a success you would continue the venture in another area. Obviously, these numbers are examples only, yet many individuals use this concept of leverage to a much greater degree. Remember, however, the goal is to build wealth, not create debt.

The possibilities for small family business are endless. Not too many years ago, the top federal income tax bracket was 70%. Some clients, adding state income tax, wonder why they should work if they pay more than 70¢ on every dollar to the government. One reason is to build wealth in and for your children or other family members by creating family businesses and working in and through them. In some cases, the solution is to work for your relatives, friends or favorite charity after providing for yourself and your family. We can attest to the fact that this has worked for countless taxpayers.

Conclusions and advice

• Do not be deterred from the concept of wealth transfers through a family or closely held business. Setting up such a business is usually not that costly.

• Using leverage, you can often invest in assets such as real estate. If you own a property with other family members, as you pay down the mortgage and (hopefully) the property appreciates, you will build wealth in other family members' names. You may also find that you will have created full-time employment positions for family members.

• Discuss the best choice of entity with your accountant and your attorney. Remember, many of the entities require you to file, by law, certain paperwork. Do not try to save on these fees and do it yourself. It may backfire, and you may find your business does not exist.

• Use the family business interest to attain your annual gifting goals. Speak to your accountant to make sure of the value of the gift and that there will be no debt-forgiveness income. However, you can give a percentage interest in the business and also take a minority discount to increase the amount you give away. This allows you to make a substantial gift without using cash or marketable securities.

Chapter Forty

RECAPITALIZING A CORPORATION

If a substantial portion of an individual's assets consists of stock in a closely held corporation, the tax consequences of her eventual death should be minimized by one or more of several available plans. If this person plans to reduce the amount of her future gross estate, she should consider making gifts of assets to her beneficiaries. Additionally, or alternatively, she may make gifts to approved charitable organizations currently for deductions on her federal income tax return. Or, she can make charitable bequests that will constitute deductions in arriving at her taxable estate.

Where retention of control seems to rule out stock gifts

The making of such gifts, contributions or charitable bequests is a standard method of reducing one's gross estate at the time of death. In the case of a significant stock interest in a closely held corporation, the idea is usually unattractive. Possession of all, most or even a large portion of the voting stock of a corporation enables a person to control—or at least participate in the control of—her business. She doesn't want to give up this control or dilute it to any meaningful degree. Her control of the company's voting stock enables her to make business decisions, name the company's directors and executives, choose her successors and have a major role in setting her own salary, bonus and fringe benefits. She wants to retain the stock, even if it means paying unnecessarily high estate and perhaps income taxes.

Here is a practical alternative that is useful when, as usually happens, a closely held corporation has only one class of stock outstanding. The plan is equally attractive if the corporation is capitalized with common stock that carries the voting power, plus preferred stock.

Recapitalization offers opportunities

The directors can vote to have a recapitalization from the existing one-class stock into two new classes of stock, voting and nonvoting. If there are both common and preferred shares outstanding, the recapitalization will involve a reshuffling from the old common into new common of two types, which may be identical except that only one of these classes has voting power. An attorney can easily take care of the formalities of recapitalization. This can be a "Type E" tax-free reorganization in which the shareholders will not have to pay federal income tax when they surrender their old shares and receive new ones.

When a major stockholder's shares are exchanged for the new ones—for example, old one-class voting stock for new voting common shares and new non-voting common shares—the tax value of her investment in the shares of the corporation remains exactly as it was before the recapitalization. But the basis of her investment now is apportioned between the new voting stock and the new nonvoting stock. The services of an experienced accountant are usually necessary to apportion the tax cost and value of the investment between the new voting and the new nonvoting shares.

The stockholder will keep her new voting shares, for they represent a control over the corporation that, understandably, she doesn't want to relinquish. She gives the nonvoting shares to her beneficiaries, perhaps in gifts over a period of years in order to minimize the tax on these gifts through the annual gift tax exclusion and husband–wife split gifts. (See Chapter Twenty-One, "Gifts Have Many Advantages.")

This tax-free recapitalization into voting and nonvoting shares assures that an important stockholder retains what is probably the most important thing to her: the voting control of—or at least a voting interest in—the corporation. What she will then have in her gross estate when she dies is only that portion of the stock's total value that has been apportioned by the accountant to the voting stock, assuming the accountant has used a generally accepted procedure. Usually, this is the total value of the individual's investment in the company, apportioned between voting and nonvoting shares on the basis of their respective values. For example, suppose the voting stock represented 40% and nonvoting stock 60% of the value of the new capitalization. The value of the nonvoting stock which the individual gives away before her death won't be part of her gross estate when she dies. Therefore, she has managed to reduce her estate without any loss of control of the corporation.

Why stop at one recapitalization?

This method need not be regarded as a one-time benefit. In a later year, if inflation or the corporation's financial success has brought the value of the stockholder's new voting stock to a figure that would swell the value of her gross estate unduly, there can be a second recapitalization. This will once more bring down the value of the voting stock by apportioning of total value between the existing stock and the new nonvoting stock.

Other uses of recapitalizations

A recapitalization may also be utilized to bring down the value, and therefore the price, of voting stock so that some of it can be sold to employees at an affordable price. This would provide them with incentive to remain with the company and to work more energetically for its success, as they now own a piece of the action.

A decedent's gross estate includes the value of stock transferred to an irrevocable trust in which she retained no benefit to herself, if she continued to own, directly or indirectly, shares possessing at least 20% of the corporation's voting rights. A recapitalization might be used so that she received both voting and nonvoting stock, thereby enabling her to transfer nonvoting stock to the trust. This is risky, and current IRS positions must be closely reviewed.

As shareholders who are actively in control of a company get older, a recapitalization from the existing one-class voting stock will enable the more mature shareholders to receive preferred stock with its relatively safe fixed dividend. The voting common stock could go to younger persons assuming greater responsibilities in the corporation and who should be entitled to the stock's appreciation or the higher dividends.

As a person ages or her health deteriorates, a recapitalization may be used to protect the voting stock interest she chooses to retain in the corporation to assure her salary determination and the like. New voting stock can be made available to proven executives who will take over increasing responsibilities so that the corporation won't suffer from the aging shareholder's diminishing capabilities. Meanwhile, her investment is protected.

Recapitalization and the marital deduction

An individual may direct in her will that her one-class stock go to her husband and children in specified amounts. The will may further provide that when she dies, a recapitalization will be effected under stipulated terms, so that her husband's shares will be replaced with preferred stock of equal value. In one such situation, the preferred stock received by a surviving widow qualified for the marital deduction. (See Chapter Four, "The Marital Deduction.") This was true even though the preferred stock did not exist at the moment of the husband's death, the recapitalization remaining unimplemented until after he died. The widow's preferred stock interest had been created by his will and, therefore, passed from the decedent to her.

Recapitalization may be at the bidding of a third party

Sometimes it is necessary to recapitalize in order to preserve the value of an inherited bequest. For example, a decedent might have left to her husband or children a valuable automobile distributorship franchise that she owned and operated. Frequently, such a franchise agreement provides that upon the death of the principal operator, the franchise will be canceled by the manufacturer unless the principal is succeeded by an experienced person acceptable to the manufacturer. Usually, the distributor's spouse and children will not be acceptable. So there is a recapitalization, the family getting preferred or nonvoting common stock as well as a minority interest in the voting stock. Most of the voting stock is made available to persons who are acceptable to the manufacturer and appear likely to keep the franchise operating successfully. Without this recapitalization, a valuable franchise may be lost.

Without a similar arrangement, a bank sometimes refuses to continue or extend a credit agreement to a corporation on the death of its guiding spirit.

Conclusions and advice

• Use experienced tax counsel in structuring a corporate recapitalization. The IRS looks closely at valuation "estate tax freezes," and the rules can be quite complex. A knowledgeable accountant should allocate the tax basis and value between the new stock issues.

• Tax-free recapitalizations may be utilized several times throughout the years to obtain the benefits described in this chapter.

• Do not confine the advantages of a tax-free recapitalization to estate planning benefits. Such a recapitalization may also be utilized for present tax benefits, to induce key employees to remain with the company, as well as to assure the renewal of corporate franchises and bank-credit agreements.

• Do not assume that all recapitalizations are tax free; they aren't. Professional guidance is advisable to assure tax-free status.

• Restructuring can bring in parties with whom you do not wish to associate for either business or personal purposes.

• Under the 1997 tax law, family owned businesses, which comprise a statutory set percentage of an estate and which pass to certain qualified heirs, are entitled to an extra deduction over the then-applicable unified credit. The total credit is limited to $1,300,000, but this has been repealed as of 2004 (see Appendix D). Also liberalized by the 2001 tax law for qualifying estates, the federal estate tax may be paid in installments when closely held businesses comprise a given percentage of the estate.

• Also consider combining your corporate stock with other "family oriented" entities such as a limited partnership, LLC/LLP and/or a family trust. Not only can multiple entities provide attractive estate planning opportunities, but they also can create and maintain wealth in other family members.

Chapter Forty-One

REDEMPTION OF STOCK TO PAY DEATH TAXES

The death of someone who owns all or a large proportion of the shares of a closely held corporation can present serious problems: What is to be done with his stock? Furthermore, where does the executor find the cash to pay probate expenses and death taxes?

Money will be required to pay bills as well as the federal estate tax and the requirements of the beneficiaries under the will. The family or other beneficiaries may prefer to receive cash rather than an investment in a business that they don't understand or lack the experience to direct. The remaining shareholders of the corporation, if there are any, might be disinclined to accept as co-owners the spouse, children or other relatives of the decedent. Banks and other parties with which the corporation has been dealing may be unwilling to deal with an enterprise with unproven persons in positions of authority. Employees are apt to be demoralized at the thought of having outsiders outrank them.

As noted in Chapter Thirty-Nine, your corporation may be either a C corporation or an S corporation. Many older family or closely held businesses were started before the advent of the S corporation or the LLC, and, therefore, it is not uncommon to find substantial wealth held in C corporations.

Unfortunately, with a C corporation, earnings that are not distributed are retained and, as a general rule, if the corporation buys back only a small portion of a shareholder's stock and there are retained earnings, the IRS classifies the purchase as a dividend. What would normally be a capital gain is deemed to be a dividend and thus ordinary income to the decedent's estate.

Therefore, if an executor were to sell some of the decedent's stock back to the corporation in order to pay taxes, etc., this could cause dividend treatment. However, this result can be avoided if the conditions outlined in this chapter can be met.

The need to sell a decedent's stock

In many instances, the obvious choice would be for the executor or the beneficiaries to sell their stock. But to whom, and at what price? Shares of a closely held corporation are a highly unmarketable commodity—who knows the true state of the organization or the value of the stock? This is especially important if, as often happens, there has never been a thorough examination of the books by an independent certified public accountant. If the decedent's stock represented less than a controlling interest in the corporation, the problem of marketability becomes even more serious. Who would buy stock in a closely held corporation where the buyer wouldn't be able to apply his own expertise and ingenuity to the business because the other shareholders might resent an outsider?

So, if the executor or beneficiaries could find a potential buyer at all, the price might be distressingly low.

Corporation's purchase of a decedent's shares may be a dividend, unless...

The logical market for the decedent's shares would be the corporation itself. But federal income tax law provides that any money flowing from a corporation to a shareholder when the company has sufficient earnings and profits to pay a dividend will be taxed as a dividend—that is, as ordinary income and not as capital gain. There are a few specific exceptions to this rule: for example, when all of a stockholder's stock is acquired and he completely terminates his relationship with the corporation. This would be the case when a shareholder dies, of course, but the rule also provides that all shares of certain closely related persons must be taken into account in determining whether the redemption satisfies other highly technical rules. So this solution is not available in some situations where the decedent's immediate family members also own a portion of the stock.

A ready purchaser for a decedent's stock

There is a method by which a decedent's stock may be purchased by the issuing corporation without dividend implications to the seller. But to put this method into operation after the shareholder's death, planning is necessary.

Federal tax law provides that the proceeds of a sale of stock to the corporation will not be taxed as a dividend to the extent that the money is used to pay death taxes and the estate's administrative expenses. Any amount paid by the corporation to the seller in excess of this amount will be taxed as a dividend. Under the Tax Reform Act of 1986, none of the excess amount of the redemption will be treated as capital gain, unless it qualifies under another Tax Code section. But if it qualifies, it is treated as a sale of stock, meaning that the proceeds will be reduced for tax purposes by the basis (usually cost) of the stock, instead of being fully taxable as a dividend.

The tax law refers to this sale of stock back to the issuing corporation as a "distribution in redemption of stock to pay death taxes." But the stock doesn't actually have to be redeemed in the ordinary sense—that is, canceled by the corporation. For this purpose, it is immaterial what happens to the shares after the company buys them back.

A crucial test

However, even if the proceeds of redemption are used only for such costs, there is another paramount consideration. For the purchase of its own stock by the corporation not to result in a dividend to the estate or beneficiaries, the value of the stock included in the decedent's gross estate must exceed 35% of the total value of the gross estate beyond expenses, obligations, taxes and losses of the estate.

In applying this percentage test, the value of all of the decedent's stock in the corporation is considered—not merely the value of the shares of the particular class of stock to be redeemed, such as voting common stock. Accordingly, if the total value of both the common and preferred stock of a corporation owned by an estate meets the percentage test, but neither common nor preferred stock alone meets it, the redemption of either class up to the permissible limitation qualifies for nondividend treatment.

Sometimes a decedent's shares in any one corporation won't qualify for this 35% rule because his investments took the form of substantial holdings in several companies. Where the estate includes stock of two or more corporations, in each of which the decedent had a 20% or greater interest, these companies may be regarded as a single corporation for this purpose.

The redemption by the corporation must be made within three years and 90 days after the filing date of the federal estate tax return. If the executor and the Internal Revenue Service are not in agreement about the amount of tax payable, the permissible period for redemption of stock is extended until 60 days after the decision of the tax court becomes final. Whichever party loses it can appeal to a higher court, so the appeals procedure can keep the redemption period open for a considerable period of time. For this reason, an executor may not know how much stock to present to the corporation for redemption without dividend implications. When the estate tax return is filed, enough stock to pay the indicated tax and administrative expenses may be redeemed. If the IRS or a court subsequently decides that more tax is due, additional shares can be redeemed without dividend implications as long as it is within the aforementioned time limits.

To reap the benefits of the advice in this chapter, the executor should understand that stock must be redeemed within the permissible period; it does no good if one learns about it too late. In one case, a judge declared, "It would appear to me...that in a given circumstance it would not be untoward for an agent of the IRS to point out to a taxpayer that there is a benefit [in redeeming stock to pay death taxes] that could be taken advantage of...." But don't count on getting such a suggestion.

In determining whether a decedent owned sufficient shares in a particular corporation to qualify for nondividend treatment, only the value of shares owned directly by him is taken into account. Accordingly, in ascertaining whether a decedent owned more than 35% of the stock of Corporation A, do not include any shares of A which were owned by Corporation B, even if the decedent owned 90% of the stock of Corporation B. But any shares owned by a trust the decedent created will be included, if he is deemed to have retained at the time of his death such a degree of control over the trust that he hadn't let go of the property transferred to it.

Funding

A certain amount of planning is necessary to take advantage of this provision of the tax law. Sufficient funds must be available so that the corporation will be able to buy the stock if and when it is presented for redemption. This funding is frequently arranged by taking out insurance on shareholders' lives just for this purpose. (See Chapter Forty-Two, "Buy–Sell Agreements.") Or, a corporation might be able to borrow money to redeem a shareholder's stock at the time of his death if it has not retained income for that purpose.

If the corporation retains earnings that have been earmarked to redeem a decedent's shares under circumstances that qualify as a redemption of stock to pay death taxes, the retained earnings are not subject to the accumulated earnings tax on undistributed profits for that tax year. However, you would be well advised to document this fact in your corporate minutes. In other words, state that the earnings are being retained for this purpose as well as other potential expenditures, such as a large capital building project.

Advance planning

An accountant should check the figures periodically to ascertain whether a shareholder's stock interest in a particular corporation exceeds 35% of his adjusted gross estate. This is the portion of his estate necessary to take advantage of the nondividend treatment discussed in this chapter. That means

(1) estimating the approximate value of the adjusted gross estate and (2) determining the value of the stock. If (2) does not exceed 35% of (1), take steps to see that it does. This can be done in either of two ways. First, reduce the size of the potential estate by making gifts or charitable contributions in the form of other property, including money. Second, acquire additional shares of stock in the corporation so that, while the size of the estate remains the same, the stock interest it holds will be greater.

Although there is no longer a requirement that gifts within three years of death be included in the estate, such gifts, beyond the annual exclusion, will be taken into account in deciding whether the 35% requirement has been met.

Conclusions and advice

• Pay particular attention to the rules of this chapter if your closely held business is a C corporation and it represents a substantial portion of your estate.

• Do not have a corporation redeem a deceased shareholder's stock unless this qualifies as a redemption to pay death taxes. Otherwise, the proceeds may be taxed as a dividend.

• Have your accountant check regularly that your shares in a closely held corporation will qualify for redemption on a nondividend basis. If not, compliance may be gained by reducing your gross estate or by acquiring more stock.

• Take steps to ensure that the corporation will be in a position to fund a redemption of stock to pay death taxes. It could be your estate that will benefit.

• Do not cause a corporation to retain earnings to buy a decedent's shares unless the transaction has been set up so as to qualify as a redemption to pay death taxes. Otherwise, the corporation will probably be subject to the accumulated earnings tax. Make sure your corporate minutes clearly state why you are retaining earnings and profits.

Chapter Forty-Two

BUY–SELL AGREEMENTS

The death of an equity owner in a closely held corporation, limited liability company, partnership or other business entity brings massive problems to the estate and its executor—but not only to them. There are immediate matters of concern to a variety of other parties, one of which is the omnipresent Internal Revenue Service. Whether or not the business continues may depend on the effective solution of the following problems:

• Burden of proof. The estate has the responsibility of valuing the owner-ship interest for tax purposes. This chore may seem to have no solution acceptable to the IRS, for here fair market value can't be determined by actual sales of stock or the respective equity interest, which in all probability had never taken place in a truly arm's-length transaction. The taxpayer has the burden of proof for establishing valuation. Without evidence of actual sales, the IRS can come up with an extraordinarily high figure by comparing the dece-dent's business with that of far more prestigious companies with diversified product lines, depth in top management, etc.

Unless the executrix can prove the validity of the value she uses, the IRS's finding will prevail. The IRS makes computations based upon various commonly accepted valuation methods, such as capitalized earnings per share, choosing whichever of these generally accepted methods produces the highest figure in a particular instance. The executrix also must assemble the cash necessary to pay the federal estate tax, usually nine months after the date of the decedent's death.

• Executrix's personal tax liability. The beneficiaries may require imme-diate funds, unable to wait until their inheritances can be processed. But hasty distribution of bequests by an executrix can involve her in personal tax liability that she may seek to minimize by being unduly deliberate and hesitant. Additionally, some beneficiaries will now, or very soon, have shares of stock or ownership in a business entity that may be difficult to convert to cash.

• Employee uneasiness. The employees of the business might reasonably fear that the company will be liquidated because the estate has no other way of raising cash or because of dissension among old and new owners. This fear of loss of jobs could result in employee uneasiness and affect the corporation's performance adversely.

• Keeping lenders at bay. Creditors are likely to be worried that beneficiaries without experience or judgment will take over the running of the business, with disastrous results. One lender required a company seeking a loan to insure the life of the chief executive and primary stockholder "so that, if anything happened to him, the company would have capital to reorganize or to put somebody else in his place."

The solution: A buyout agreement

Managers of closely held businesses should take steps to protect themselves against the loss of key owners. An excellent way of doing so is to have a buyout agreement.

This arrangement can take either of two forms. In a buy-and-sell agreement, the stockholders, or in the case of other business entities, the equity owners or newly designated ones, agree to purchase the equity interest of any party to the agreement who dies. In a stock-redemption agreement, the corporation or entity itself buys the interest of the deceased shareholder.

Several alternative methods are available for setting the price to be paid for the decedent's interest. There may be an agreed dollar price per share or each percent of interest. This method is undesirable because, at the time the interest is actually purchased, that price may no longer be realistic. The agreed price might be book value. The figure might be obtained by capitalizing earnings, the agreement to state the number of years' earnings to be used in the computation and the rate of capitalization. The amount could be set by a postmortem appraisal, although the resulting figure might be so different from the forecast that funding arrangements could be unworkable. Best of all would be a self-adjusting formula, such as average earnings of the past three years capitalized at 10%, or book value plus a goodwill factor to be determined by arbitration. The average earnings capitalized at an agreed percentage appears more attractive in times of inflation.

Certainly, this is not an exhaustive list of the types of formulas available to determine valuation. Your accountant can offer many different options and will be a crucial adviser in determining what formula is best for you. All too often, however, clients fail to agree on the formula and therefore never finalize their agreement—an unfortunate trap into which many fall. Sometimes after the business has been in existence for many years, the partner or shareholder finds it more difficult to agree. Therefore, we strongly urge you to address these issues as early as possible. Partners or fellow shareholders would benefit from sharing this intention.

Upon the death of an owner covered by the agreement, her interest would be sold to the other owners who were parties to the arrangement or, under a stock-redemption plan, to the corporation, which would then retire the shares. The price would set the value of the shares for estate tax purposes because it represented an actual sale determined by arm's-length negotiations among owners who, when the agreement was made, didn't know whether they (or their estates) would be buyers or sellers.

Funding

The agreement is meaningless without a guaranteed source of money for buying the decedent's interest. So, if the business is to be the purchaser, the business may insure the lives of each owner and use the proceeds to buy a decedent's interest at the formula price. If the other owners are to be the buyers, each one takes out insurance on her own life or the other owner's life for this specific purpose. The policies can be assigned to a representative or trustee, guaranteeing the proceeds will be used to purchase shares from the shareholder's estate.

If one of the owners is uninsurable, she could use existing insurance policies. Alternatively, this person might be able to purchase substandard or high-risk insurance despite age or health risks, paying an appropriately high premium to compensate the insurance company for its extra hazard. Many insurance companies now write this type of coverage.

In this connection, a strong argument for having the business buy the decedent's interest is the fact that the business isn't likely to forget to pay the insurance premiums on the policy needed to pay for the redemption. If each owner paid for this insurance, she might "forget" to pay the premiums, save the money and leave insufficient funding for the plan at death. In the corporate setting, another argument in favor of having the corporation acquire the shares is that they can be retired. That is a substantial benefit to the remaining shareholders; each will still own the same number of shares of stock, but her percentage of ownership will be higher because the total number of shares has been reduced. Even though each shareholder now has greater equity in the corporation, she isn't deemed to have received a dividend for tax purposes when the corporation pays the life insurance premiums or when a decedent's shares are retired.

The cost of premiums is not deductible for income tax purposes. But a corporation can deduct the expense of legal fees for a stock repurchase agreement.

Consequences of a buyout agreement

Suppose the premiums have not been paid or that on an owner's death there are insufficient funds with which to purchase all of her equity interest. The plan need not have been a complete failure. At least some of the decedent's interest will have been purchased, which generally sets a valuation of her interest for estate tax purposes and provides a certain amount of needed cash. Also, the agreement can be worded to provide that if there is insufficient cash generated by the plan to buy all of a decedent's interest, the business or the surviving owners will have an option or possibly even be required to buy the remaining interest at a formula price when cash later becomes available.

The surviving spouse or other beneficiary receiving a decedent's interest may try to avoid honoring the buyout agreement on the grounds that they were never a party to it. That argument won't work, however, for they acquired the equity interest subject to the agreement and its formula price.

Nonvoting stock may be covered

Although only voting stock is customarily covered, sometimes a buyout agreement provides for the purchase of nonvoting common or preferred stock. In this way, the decedent's family members can be completely bought out. Acquisition of preferred or other nonvoting stock that is convertible into common shares should be provided for. This, of course, could apply to any other type of interest, such as corporate debt, warrants or options, as well as interests in limited liability companies, partnerships and limited partnerships.

Total disability of a shareholder

Although not as common a practice as the buyout provisions, the agreement may be utilized to cover the possibility of the permanent disability of an owner in a closely held business. In such an instance, she can probably use the cash, and the management of the business may not want to have any of its ownership in the hands of someone who is no longer actively involved in running the business. The interest of the disabled owner might be better used to attract a new executive to take her place.

Conclusions and advice

• Be prepared to show who the buyer in a buyout agreement actually is. If the owners are obligated to purchase a decedent's interest, but it turns out that the business actually buys it, and the business is a corporation, the corporate payment may be taxed as a dividend to the shareholders. If the corporation is to be the buyer, you must be able to prove that it was a party to the agreement and that it actually received the shares.

• Have your accountant work out the application of the valuation formula each year. If changing values indicate that there won't be enough cash to purchase a decedent's interest, take out more life insurance to fund the plan. In a corporate setting, you may reduce the value of the voting stock to be purchased by a recapitalization. (See Chapter Forty, "Recapitalizing a Corporation.")

• Where there is a buy–sell agreement, have the restrictions on sale other than to the business or the surviving equity owners stamped on each stock or ownership certificate (such a notation is called a *legend*). This will allow you to avoid serious problems when a buyer of the stock or owner certificate argues that she was never given notice of the restrictions.

• Be careful that the operation of a buy–sell agreement doesn't reduce the number of shareholders to so few individuals that personal holding company tax liability will exist. This could happen in the case of undistributed earnings, should income be largely of a nonoperating type.

• Do not use a formula clause so complicated or vague that the decedent's family must ask a court to "interpret" it. This could lead to delays, unpleasant litigation and a forced settlement.

• Do not overlook the fact that a properly funded buy–sell agreement can determine whether a business will be able to survive after the death of a substantial owner. Installment payouts are always an option and should be provided for any deficiency.

• A buy–sell agreement is often funded by life insurance. Always consult with your insurance adviser and use top-rated companies as the policies must be in force for many years. Although more expensive, it would be wise to use a policy with some investment potential as opposed to term insurance.

• One taxpayer's argument that the terms of a buy–sell agreement should be binding was weakened because, upon another shareholder's death, no one had paid any attention to the agreement.

• With some variations, the concepts discussed in this chapter apply to most business entities. Whether you have a corporation, partnership or LLC, the buy–sell agreement is a critical document. Don't overlook it.

Chapter Forty-Three

BUSINESS CONTINUATION ARRANGEMENTS

An individual might want to have his business continued after his death for several reasons:

• To provide a good source of income for his beneficiaries who might earn more from a proven, ongoing business than from investments made with the proceeds of its disposition.

• To have his children step into executive positions at the appropriate time. Thus, their principal inheritance may be the business.

• To realize more value from a going venture than from a liquidation.

• To continue the business for a certain group of employees, including relatives and loyal workers.

• To continue the business primarily for charitable purposes, thereby giving employment to workers and excess profits to charity.

Executors are likely to frustrate decedent's wishes

After the business owner dies, his executors may wish to dispose of the venture as quickly as possible. They may not be familiar with the business or they may not want to deal with its problems. They may want to wind up the estate, distribute its assets, obtain their fees and resume their normal activities.

If this is the case, the business will be sold or dissolved with all deliberate speed. The price may not be as important to the executors as how quickly the sale can be completed. However, the executor is not usually charged with continuing the decedent's business much beyond the estate's closing. Therefore, the business owner should look for other solutions, such as trusts, to carry on his wishes after that date.

Decedent's wishes should control

If disposition or liquidation of the business is not what the owner wants, he must take appropriate steps to prevent it.

The plan: Remove the business from what will be subject to the administration and disposition by the executors. Whether the business is a proprietorship or a controlling stock interest in a corporation, the method is the same. Arrange to transfer the business interest to a trust created solely for this purpose: a business continuation trust. The owner can do this at any time by a deed of trust (an *inter vivos* trust). But since he probably wants to manage the business for as long as he lives, he may prefer to postpone matters and have the business interest transferred to a trust in accordance with provisions in his will (a testamentary trust) or through his revocable trust and a pour-over will. In fact, placing the business in a revocable trust during his lifetime would offer the owner the best of both worlds: retaining control during his lifetime and passing the business securely into the hands of the successor trustees upon his death or disability.

Who should operate your business when you die

Executors are usually chosen because they are people the testator trusts and admires: someone with genuine concern for the testator's family or other beneficiaries, devotion to his objectives and aspirations, understanding of the personalities involved and patience. The fiduciaries of the trust set up to continue the administration of the business, however, should be chosen for two other characteristics: professional competence and commitment to running the business effectively.

Character of the trust

The trustees should be chosen from individuals who are already highly knowledgeable about the business. Possible candidates are the business's accounting adviser, attorney, the bank officer who handles its financing and credit matters, a senior executive or other key employees, management consultants or retired executives.

The trust would be set up for the benefit of designated parties, which could include not only the grantor's chosen heirs but also his preferred charitable organizations. The trust may be established with a life span of specified duration, such as until the grantor's youngest child reaches a stated age, usually over 21, and is competent to take over the business as the sole remainderman or one of the remaindermen. Then the trust has reached its termination date. But a certain amount of discretion may well be lodged in the trustees concerning termination of the trust. The business might experience financial adversity, perhaps because of the loss of its guiding spirit, or because of changing economic or legal factors. It might be unwise to require the trustees to continue the enterprise when, in their collective judgment, the venture has become hopeless by reason of new foreign competition, environmental restrictions, expiration of an essential franchise, etc. So the trustees could be vested with authority to sell or liquidate the business under specified circumstances, such as those set forth above or in the event of operating losses in two or three successive years. The grantor may even provide for some judicial review to ensure that his concerns and objectives are not being circumvented.

Permanent disability

Estate planning usually concentrates on what will take place when an individual dies. But the same plan may be essential in the case of permanent disability. After a heart attack, stroke or serious injury, a person may be unequal to the financial and economic demands with which he had formerly coped. An individual's business may suffer as grievously from his permanent disability as from his death. A business continuation trust could be set up, to become operational at such time as a person becomes permanently disabled, either physically or mentally. A prudent planner might anticipate this possibility, however remote it may seem, and have the necessary provisions included in any trust agreement that may be drawn up. Sometimes this is called a standby trust and is coupled with a power of attorney.

Conclusions and advice

• Do not assume that your executors will continue to administer your business after you die. Ask yourself the following questions: Are my devoted and trustworthy executors actually competent to run a complex business in today's competitive environment? Do they have the expertise to engage the proper individuals to take over the administration and planning of my business?

• Make certain that the business continuation trust is carefully thought out in advance. *Some vital considerations:* who the trustees will be, provision for substitute or successor trustees, how long you want the trustees to administer the business, a safety-valve provision if the enterprise loses money regularly or is no longer competitive. Sound out the trustees you have in mind to ascertain whether they will serve and will work with the other designated trustees.

• Do not require the trustees to continue the business if, in their collective judgment, there is no future in it. *For example,* trustees may be directed to continue the business until the grantor's youngest child is 21. By the time that occurs, the industry may be in a hopeless condition. Leave discretion to terminate the business to a majority of the trustees, who should be required to state in writing why termination seems to be necessary. If you want a safeguard, require approval of probate court or other court of proper jurisdiction.

• Many effective estate plans include a revocable *inter vivos* trust, often without assets, that is coupled with a pour-over will and a power of attorney. At death, the business may pass to this trust with your chosen managers, or, when disability arises during your lifetime, the assets (stocks) may be placed in the hands of the trustee. This is sometimes called a "dry" or "standby" trust.

• Recall the discussion of dynasty trusts that may go on for many generations to come. These may also be integrated into the above concepts.

Chapter Forty-Four

MERGER TO ESTABLISH ESTATE TAX VALUATION

Valuation of the shares of a closely held corporation can be a significant problem for anyone who owns a substantial block of them. Obviously, when a stock is not listed on a registered exchange or actively traded in an over-the-counter market, fair market value can't be easily established. Fair market value is defined as the price at which property changes hands in a transaction between a willing buyer and a willing seller, where each has knowledge of the relevant facts and neither is under any obligation to buy or sell. Such a situation rarely exists in the case of shares of a closely held corporation.

The same situation can hold true for an equity interest in a closely held LLC/LLP or general partnership, as well as in a limited partnership. Such entities, despite being closely held and/or owned by a small group of families, may be sizable. In addition, these entities need not be comprised of primarily passive activities. Many run active business operations that could easily be absorbed into a larger organization. For the purpose of clarity, the remaining portion of this chapter will speak in terms of a corporation and its shares. However, understand that the concepts discussed in this chapter can be utilized, in varying degrees, with other business entities as long as they are attractive to a would-be purchaser.

The 2001 tax law increased the unified credit effective equivalent exemption amount to $3.5 million for the 2009 tax year and repealed the estate tax entirely for only the 2010 tax year. For some, the fears inherent in not having a readily ascertainable value for your business may be diminished. However, as we have contended, especially in light of the events of September 11, 2001, we believe it is likely that the tax will return in some form or another. Also, between 2002 and 2009 these concepts can be of assistance, especially if the IRS's overvaluation would cause the otherwise large estate to be grossly overvalued.

Exchange of stock can establish fair market value

Some owners of shares in a closely held corporation are sufficiently worried about estate tax valuation problems to liquidate their interest before their deaths. When they die, their estates will then contain cash or marketable securities, which lend themselves easily to determinable valuation and intelligent planning. But most corporations, unlike individuals, are worth more alive than dead; liquidation would lessen the value of one's investment. For example, going-concern value, goodwill, many employee benefits and, for some corporations, carryovers would be lost. Nontransferable franchises or licenses would be forfeited. Not least of all, there could be federal income tax resulting from the liquidation.

The problem, then, is to replace the shares of closely held corporate stock with shares that can be subjected to accurate valuation. Then the Internal Revenue Service won't have the opportunity to fill a valuation vacuum with its own figures.

Under these circumstances, a desirable plan for the shareholder to adopt is an exchange of her shares in the closely held corporation for stock in a company traded actively in a recognized market so that valuation at death will not be left, by default, to the IRS.

Tax-free reorganization can result in determinable value

Shares in the closely held corporation can be exchanged for shares of an actively traded company through the mechanism of a tax-free reorganization. Then, when the shareholder dies, her property will have a readily ascertainable value. This procedure will also enable a shareholder to formulate an intelligent estate plan, as hard figures to work with will always be available. All values are subject to fluctuation, of course. But an individual can plan her property dispositions, trust arrangements, marital deduction and gift tax exclusions much more competently and intelligently if she has at least some idea of the value of the stocks and other properties in her ultimate gross estate.

An individual can replace her shares in a closely held corporation for stock in a better-known company without recognition of any taxable gain or loss, if the transaction complies with the requirements for a tax-free reorganization as contained in the Internal Revenue Code. This is good income tax planning if the business owner is not desirous of leaving the business to her heirs. Consider such a transaction regardless of the status of the estate tax law.

The forms of tax-free reorganization

The "A" type of reorganization involves a merger or consolidation. Particularly suitable here is a transaction in which a publicly owned corporation acquires all of the stock of the closely held company, which is then liquidated, with the shareholders of the latter receiving shares of the continuing corporation.

The "B" reorganization involves the acquisition by the well-known company of at least 80% of the stock of the closely held corporation, solely in exchange for some of the voting stock of the larger corporation. For this purpose, it would be advisable for all of the stock of the closely held corporation to be exchanged during the transaction.

If the closely held corporation has some valuable assets, good cash flow and an impressive earnings record, it is an attractive company for takeover purposes. But even if the closely held company has had dismal earnings, with operating losses over several years, it may still be a useful acquisition. In years past, if the rules were met, net operating losses of an acquired company could be utilized by the corporation that acquires its stock. Today, however, there are some formidable traps and restraints. These problems sometimes can be overcome. Even if they can't be, your business may still be attractive for noneconomic reasons like market share.

If, however, your business entity is not a corporation, all is not lost. As noted, there are other methods to transfer assets to a corporation tax free which may be done many years ahead in anticipation of the plan to merge in a tax-free reorganization.

In addition, although we speak in terms of substituting traded stock for your business interests, which do not have a readily ascertainable value, there are other possibilities. While the IRS is less willing to argue over the value shown on a national exchange, if you merge your business with a larger LLC in an arm's-length transfer between nonrelated third parties, a portion of the battle is also won. If there was more than one independent appraisal by qualified appraisers, your case is even stronger and, if the acquiring entity had done this in the past with other businesses such as yours, there may be even more evidence. Note, however, that the key element is proving the value of your interest in the new company at the time of your gift or death. Therefore, annual or regular updates to the appraisals may be a necessity.

The point is that all is not lost if your business entity is not a corporation or an easily valued entity. You must be aware of the potential problems and, with your advisers, try to work toward the most realistic solution.

Conclusions and advice

• The working out of a tax-free reorganization is highly technical and strewn with pitfalls. You would be wise to employ an attorney or accountant who is well versed in this complex area of specialization. But do not let complexity deter you.

• If your business is not incorporated, carry out the merger in two phases. First, transfer all assets and liabilities of your business to a corporation formed for the purpose, in exchange for all of its stock. Your transfer of assets, even if they have greatly appreciated in value since you acquired them, will be tax free in most situations. Your adviser on the reorganization can point out the few areas where this isn't the case. Second, after the recommended waiting period, you exchange the shares of this corporation for those of a better-known company.

250

- In order to find corporations whose stock has a readily ascertainable market value, consult a broker who specializes in acquisitions. These brokers frequently advertise in the Sunday financial section of *The New York Times* or in *The Wall Street Journal.*

- When exchanging the shares of your closely held corporation for the securities of a better-known company in a tax-free reorganization, do not accept the latter's bonds as part of the swap unless you are surrendering bonds of your own company. Receipt of a larger principal amount of bonds than you give up (which could well be zero) is regarded as taxable income in most instances.

- Do not accept cash as part of the exchange, for this, too, can have tax consequences.

- Be aware that in a merger you may lose control of your business. You may end up with disagreeable or overly aggressive shareholders who might be difficult to work with.

- If your corporation is not attractive to a larger traded corporation, similarly positioned competitors might entertain a merger buyout. Such a merger, coupled with buy–sell agreements, might offer you and your estate a market for your stock that didn't exist previously.

- In many cases, be prepared either to remain with the company for a period of time or have key employees remain. This will make your business more attractive. Note, however, that the problem of management succession in a closely held business, especially a one- or two-person enterprise, is significant. Sometimes a key element of a person's estate plan will be devoted to the selection, grooming and equity involvement of key employees. Sometimes the merger or acquisition can eliminate the problem because you now own shares in a larger corporation. Presumably, it is either a public corporation with key management in place or a corporation of any size with a younger management team.

ANNUITIES

An annuity is generally a fixed payment, made either in a lump sum or periodically. It is usually a promise to pay an individual a fixed monthly sum for life. The cost of purchasing an annuity depends on the number and amount of payments and the life expectancy of the annuitant. The amount paid out is greater than the purchase price, because the present value of a dollar is more than its future value and the seller of the annuity has had the use of the money during the intervening years.

Life expectancies are established by actuarial studies of the population as a whole, not by individual experience. The annuity owner who lives longer than the actuarial average, therefore, may receive quite a bit more money than he was led to expect. In other words, the purchaser of a commercial periodic annuity (one bought from an insurance company, for example) is guaranteed an income he cannot outlive.

An annuity can cut down on the expense and delay of probating a will and implementing its dispositions. It enables the owner, or annuitant, to plan on giving away portions of his wealth, reducing what will be his ultimate gross estate. And, if the property he gives away is of an income-producing nature, he will also reduce current income taxes.

The purchaser of a commercial annuity has a high degree of assurance that he will not dissipate by poor judgment the capital needed for his last years. On the other hand, the real value of the annuity may be severely eroded by inflation. This is an important caveat to keep in mind when considering annuities as part of your overall estate plan.

Variable annuities

Most annuities are paid out in fixed annual or periodic amounts. But the certainty of this dollar payment makes it uncertain in terms of real income, for the value and purchasing power of a dollar is subject to fluctuation. A new form, the variable annuity, bases the annual payout on such a standard as the periodic valuation of securities set aside to fund the payments. However, due to the fluctuating securities markets, variable annuities have not necessarily proved to be the inflation hedge some people had hoped for.

Federal income tax treatment

For federal income tax purposes, amounts received under an annuity are includable in gross income, except for the proportionate part of each amount that is considered to be a return of capital. The mathematical computation is based on the ratio that the amount invested in the annuity contract bears to its expected return at the time the annuity is deemed to start. For each contract, there is a fixed exclusion ratio that continues until the death of the annuitant, or until the death of the last annuitant, if the contract provides for payments to a survivor.

Take the example of an individual who has paid $12,650 for an annuity contract that provides for payments of $100 a month. Assuming that the expected return under the contract is $16,000, his exclusion ratio is $\frac{\$12,650}{\$16,000}$ or 79.1% (79.06 rounded to the nearest tenth). If he receives 12 such monthly payments during the tax year, the total amount excludable from his gross income that year is $949.20 ($1,200 times 79.1%). The balance of $250.80 ($1,200 minus $949.20) is included in his gross income. If he received only five payments of $100 during the year, he should exclude $395.50 ($500 times 79.1%) of the total received.

Federal estate tax treatment

For federal estate tax purposes, nothing is included in a decedent's gross estate if the annuity payments cease at his death with no minimum number of payments guaranteed in the contract, leaving no payments still due at the time of death. This is a single-life annuity rather than a joint annuity where payments continue to a survivor. If the decedent had a survivorship annuity, the value of any amounts to be received by the survivor would be taxed to the decedent's estate, despite the fact that he himself had no further amounts to be paid to him under the contract. The value of the survivor's interest is, once more, based on life expectancy tables.

Federal gift tax treatment

An individual who purchases a commercial annuity that provides for survivorship payments to a designated party other than a spouse is deemed to have made a taxable gift to the recipient of the value of the right to this income. In the case of a qualified employee benefit plan, however, the gift tax is not imposed. Gifts, including annuity gifts, between spouses are also completely gift tax free.

Sale of your annuity

Although an annuity is a contract, its sale by the purchaser shortly before it matures (the point when annual or other stipulated payments by an insurance company will start) is deemed to produce ordinary income. If the purchaser sells his annuity contract at a loss (perhaps because he now has other sources of income and doesn't need it), no federal income tax deduction is allowed unless there is proof that his original purchase of the contract was a transaction entered upon for profit.

Employee pension distributions: Annuities

One of the lesser-known provisions of the Pension Reform Act of 1974 deals with annuities. In the case of corporations subject to the Act because they do business in interstate commerce or have elected to be covered as a competitive measure, survivorship annuities must be offered to an employee and the spouse so notified, if they had been married for a year or more on the annuity starting date. The survivor annuity must not be less than one-half of the amount paid to the employee during the joint lives of himself and his spouse. This notification in the case of an employee who leaves his employment before reaching age 35 must be within "a reasonable period" after he leaves if distributions are made after December 31, 1989, although other times are specified for other pension distributions.

Periodic payouts will be less under a joint annuity than under a single-life annuity, so the employee might elect not to have his spouse enjoy annuity coverage. In this case, the employer must inform him of the consequences of this election, using figures applicable to the individual employee.

However, if an employee is within 10 years of normal retirement age, he need not be offered the option of electing a single-life annuity rather than a survivorship annuity. In addition, a corporation's plan may provide that a joint-and-survivor annuity is the only form of benefit payable if an employee has been married for at least a year.

Private annuities

Some individuals are disinclined to purchase a commercial annuity on the grounds that if the annuitant dies before his life expectancy, some or even all of the payments that had been made to the insurance company or other provider will be lost—and that the beneficiaries will get nothing of what the annuitant had paid. Purchasing an annuity with a specified minimum number of payments guaranteed to be paid by the seller even if the annuitant should die is one way to assure that the total cost of the annuity won't be at the expense of the beneficiaries. But the periodic return under an annuity of a specified cost will be less if a certain number of payments is guaranteed than if the contract is for one life, all payments to cease at the annuitant's death.

To keep all wealth in the family or available to beneficiaries an individual may prefer to purchase a private annuity from any party not engaged in the regular sale of annuity contracts. Most frequently, a private annuity contract is obtained from a relative or a friend, or from several of them, who are the intended beneficiaries. What the purchaser pays for the annuity will not be "lost" to the beneficiaries if he dies earlier than the date that is indicated in the life expectancy table, as they were to receive the property anyway.

Substantial differences between commercial and private annuities should be noted. The operations and finances of an insurance company are closely regulated by state law. Certain reserves must be set up; investments are restricted; there are audits. Periodic payouts are based on generally accepted actuarial principles. There is every reason to believe that the annuitant will receive precisely what the contract for a commercial annuity specifies.

In the case of a private annuity, however, the provider may prove financially unable to make the payments when required. He may be dishonest or may predecease you. Since a private annuity rarely represents an arm's-length transaction between disinterested parties, the real relationship between the annuitant's cost and what he will receive is vague. If the agreement was reasonable when signed, it will be legally binding and will govern valuation.

Income tax treatment of private annuities

Most private annuities are unsecured. When an individual transfers assets (usually appreciated) to the provider of the contract, it is generally held that the former has no gain for federal income tax purposes until he begins receiving periodic payments. The private annuitant is taxed, again using an actuarial ratio, but is considered to have received part return of capital, capital gain and then ordinary income. If it is established that what the individual will receive is less than what the property transferred originally cost, he may be deemed to have made a taxable gift to the provider of the contract.

Under certain circumstances, a private annuity will not represent the necessary uncertainty for characterization as an annuity. For example, the property transferred to the provider of the annuity may be prime real estate or investments that produce a regular return at least as high as the periodic payouts and there is a restriction that the property cannot be sold or exchanged without the annuitant's permission. Here the value of what the annuitant will receive is determinable, and consequently, he may have taxable gain.

Conclusions and advice

• Consider purchasing a commercial annuity to provide income for life. This device may protect your capital from creditors.

• If a relative or friend from whom you had "expectations" of inheriting property offers to give it to you in return for providing him a certain amount periodically for as long as he lives, consider the proposition carefully. If you don't agree, he could subsequently lose the property. Or, instead of leaving it to you, he might give it to someone else who will provide the annuity.

• Do not buy an annuity that yields only enough income to meet current needs without considering all relevant factors. Remember, you must consider inflation and the potential for higher costs of living, especially increased medical expenses. Also, to buy the annuity you must deplete current assets which will limit the potential growth and earnings these assets might have generated. Thus, possible growth and an increase in earnings are traded off for the stable cash flow of the annuity. Many planners advise clients to use the annuity in conjunction with other assets in a diversified portfolio. Also, be sure to have an excellent major-medical policy to help with your medical needs.

• Do not transfer your property for a private annuity if you can't count on actually getting what has been promised. Honesty and good intentions on the part of the provider of the contract are not enough. He simply may not be in a position to deliver.

• Consider the current financial strength of the annuity company. Nonperforming real estate or dubious junk bonds are matters that should be monitored.

• In a 1993 decision, actuarial tables were not used where the attending doctors estimated that when a taxpayer entered into the annuity arrangement, the chances that his cancer could be cured were not better than 2% or 3%. It was believed that he was not likely to survive more than one year.

Chapter Forty-Six

VALUATION OF ESTATE ASSETS

An individual who wants to leave as large an estate as possible for her beneficiaries should plan to minimize the tax erosion due to valuations that are higher than they need to be.

The executor who will insert values on your federal estate tax return is not likely to be as familiar as you are with the details of your assets. See that your specialized knowledge and experience are available to your executor. Despite the professional competence of your executor or his advisers, you alone can "accentuate the negative" to reduce your gross estate for tax purposes. In addition, the 2001 tax law has had a dramatic effect in this area. Here are the highlights of what to prepare and review with your executor and estate planner:

• As the unified credit effective exemption amount increases, how much should your executor elect to place in the QTIP or marital trust given the size of your estate?

• When the carryover basis rules come into play, to what assets should the step-up be allocated? Leave directions to your executor to avoid disputes.

• You must leave your executor all possible information that he may need to establish your cost or adjusted basis.

• You must also be prepared for 2011 when it is possible that the estate tax could return to its 2001 rate, rules and procedures.

• Because of the above possibility, you must be prepared to review your estate planning documents on a regular basis between 2002 and 2011, or at least until Congress gives us some certainty.

Documentation of the minus factors

Perhaps you have tried to dispose of certain properties and, in the process, have uncovered defects or shortcomings. Yet, on the filing date of your estate tax return, your executor may be unaware of these facts. Describe them now in a letter to your executor-to-be. (See Chapter Fifty-Four, "A Letter to Your Executor.") Or, record the same information in documents that will become part of your tax paperwork. Keep correspondence that explains why prospective purchasers wouldn't buy your property or pay its fair market value. *Examples:*

• **Real estate.** Indicate reasons for a belief that title may be clouded, even though this is not disclosed in a title search. In certain sections of the country, there is serious question about the validity of title to lands transferred by Native Americans during the 18th century. There may be disputes or claims that have not yet ripened into litigation and that would not be known to outside parties, even the experts. There may be boundary squabbles or zoning peculiarities not generally known. For example, a property may be used for commercial purposes under a grandfather clause only if it is used for the existing function, but might be limited to residential use if the function changed. That would seriously affect the value of the property.

You may be familiar with efforts of aggressive environmentalist groups to limit the use of property or of pending legislation that might adversely affect its attractiveness, or of forthcoming limitations on the availability of utility services.

Access to the property at present may only be by a road through the property of relatives and friends. A new owner might be denied this access and hence would buy the land only at a price that reflects the need for heavy cash outlays for a new road.

Rentals from your property may be frozen by a long-term lease, possibly with a renewal clause that would make your property less valuable than similar property with a more realistic lease.

Your property may be held in co-ownership with other parties who are notoriously difficult to work with. Your executor or his adviser is not likely to know this. But this state of affairs could discourage a potential purchaser, except at a price sufficiently discounted to reflect the unpleasant co-ownership fact.

Facilities that appear to be in average condition need costly repairs or replacements. Let this be known to your executor-to-be.

If appropriate, compile a list of past owners of the property and document their uniformly poor experiences. If the property has consistently proved a "loser," buyers will probably look for an irresistible bargain.

The property may have defects known only to you.

• **Special-use property.** Real estate must be valued for federal estate tax purposes according to its highest and best use. In consequence, your property may be valued according to what it would have been worth if you had used it for a different purpose. Property may, however, be valued for estate tax purposes according to its present use, provided certain specific conditions exist. The value of a farm or the real estate assets of a closely held business must meet stipulated guidelines if the property has been owned by a decedent or a member of his family (which may include a niece or nephew) for five of the eight years prior to the decedent's death, and such use must be continued by the family after the death. A surviving spouse's cash rental of specially valued real property to a member of her family is not treated as a cessation of a qualified use.

The tax benefit of a lower valuation is available only if the property passes to a qualified heir, as defined in the tax law, and there are requirements as to what he does with the property. Establishment of prior ownership and use requires accumulation of data, and the percentage that the value of the property bears to the decedent's total assets must meet prescribed rules. This is a highly technical subject not appropriate for discussion here, except in general. Ask your tax adviser to work out the possibility of having real estate devoted to farming or closely held business use valued according to present use. If necessary, ask him to research Sections 2032A and 6324B of the Internal Revenue Code. Obtaining a lower valuation under this procedure can affect the amount of estate taxes that will ultimately be paid. To qualify for the substantial compliance rule, the election need only have been made on a timely filed federal estate tax return.

- **Limited marketability of stock.** In a 1993 case, a valuation discount was allowed where one of the estate's assets was ownership of stock in a corporation whose assets were not liquid and there was no ready market for the stock. The lack of marketability was comparable to a minority stock interest (*Charles Russell Bennett Estate*, T.C. Memo 1993-31).

An individual may own such a large block of stock that its sale within a reasonable time would depress the market value. Under the rule of blockage, the IRS may have to accept a lower valuation of this block than the mean between highest and lowest prices of the stock on the valuation date. Such valuation could be established by a broker handling secondary distribution through an underwriter. Ask about the probable cost to the estate of such a distribution, and what percentage markdown in the value of the securities might be expected under the blockage rule. This blockage discount, if accepted by the IRS, will reduce the valuation of the stock for estate tax purposes.

Sometimes an individual owns shares acquired at a price below market in return for an agreement not to sell the stock for a certain length of time. This stock may be valued at a discount for estate tax purposes as restricted or investment letter shares. Advise your executor if you have stock of this character. Generally, the shares are imprinted with wording that refers to the restriction, but the executor may not actually see the certificates when preparing the estate tax return.

A corporation whose shares are listed on a recognized exchange may have issued some stock that was never registered with the Securities & Exchange Commission for any number of reasons, perhaps to eliminate the accounting, legal and printing expenses of registering a new issue. Unregistered stock has limited marketability, so a discount is applied in arriving at a valuation for estate tax purposes. Advise your executor if your shares happen to be unregistered, or he may value them at a figure that is too high.

- **Stocks of closely held corporations.** If a corporation's stock is not listed on an active exchange, there is no ready way of arriving at a valuation. An individual who owns such stock must lay the foundation to establish that her shares need not be valued according to some standard formula such as net worth, capitalized earnings or comparison with the value of an actively traded stock, because of factors that affect the shares in a negative way. *Examples:*

A corporation is a single-owner company. If the owner dies without a competent backup team, the stock would have limited appeal to investors.

The owner may know many value depressants of which his executor and accountant might be unaware. These factors might include: the company's product line lacks diversification or its physical plant is antiquated. The indicated earnings are not a proper basis for calculating value because of large nonrecurring income. The company may be heavily involved in lawsuits over product liability, patent infringement and the like, and counsel is not optimistic about what the courts will decide. The books have never been audited by an independent certified accountant and hence, are not acceptable to investors as reliable indicators of the company's financial condition. Pending tax assessments could require the payout of substantial sums. The company has never paid a dividend and is therefore unattractive to an investor seeking a source of income. Depreciation and other reserves are woefully inadequate.

Keep a memorandum that will be available to the executor at the appropriate time to reduce estate tax valuations.

Your executor may not know that there is in effect a buy–sell agreement, under which you or your estate will have to sell your stock back to the corporation or to the remaining shareholders upon your retirement or death at a formula price that could be far less than the stock may be worth at that time. (See Chapter Forty-Two, "Buy–Sell Agreements.") This is binding on your estate. The requirement may be contained in a corporate bylaw or in an old letter from the company to you, the existence of which the executor has no reason to suspect. On the plus side, such an agreement would limit the estate tax valuation to the figure in the buy–sell agreement. Advise your executor.

Sometimes a corporate bylaw or a shareholder agreement will provide that no shareholder can sell a stock without giving the corporation or other shareholders the right of first refusal at the same price any outside party offers for the stock. Tell your executor. The existence of such a provision will limit what an investor might offer, for he would be disinclined to investigate a corporation fully at his own expense if his offer could be matched by other parties who did not have to bear exploratory costs.

Sometimes, though, stock in a corporation is purchased at a certain price in an arm's-length transaction. Such sales cannot be regarded as an indication of the buyer's concept of true value; actually this person was bidding for something more than the shares themselves. Perhaps the buyer wanted to acquire stock to gain control of the corporation and provide herself with a splendid salary or profitable contracts. Or the buyer may have been trying to eliminate a competitor, regardless of the cost. In a power struggle between two factions of shareholders, current voting power dictated the desire for shares. The buyer was ignorant of the company and hence the price didn't represent prevailing values or potentialities. In all of these situations, the true concept of fair market value was lacking: what a willing buyer pays to a willing seller, where each is in possession of all relevant facts and neither is under any compulsion to buy or to sell. An executor is hardly in a position to know the background of such transactions unless he has been informed by his client.

Other areas where discounts in value are frequently allowed

- **Minority interest.** If the decedent's stock in a closely held corporation represented a minority interest, investors may be unwilling to buy it at full value. *Reasons:* The majority shareholders may gang up against an outsider, so she knows she won't be able to make her influence felt. The voting power of a minority stock interest is usually unimportant. Courts generally apply discounts of 15% to 35% for minority interests. If this is the situation, inform your executor because otherwise he may fail to take it into account. You may own more shares than anyone else, but the other shareholders could be close relatives, a fact not revealed by their names. As a rule, a lower value for a minority interest in real estate is also recognized.

- **Disposal-period discount.** If property has to be sold within a stipulated time to raise money, a discount is allowable because there will be insufficient time to shop around for a proper price.

- **Absorption.** A discount is allowed when the disposition of many parcels of land in a short period of time creates competition among the parcels that might not otherwise exist, acting as a price depressant.

Credit for tax on prior transfers

Federal estate tax law provides a credit for tax paid on prior transfers if the same property is subjected to estate tax twice (or more frequently) due to the deaths of two or more owners within a 10-year period. Depending on how long the second decedent (the one who inherited property from an earlier decedent, whose estate had been taxed on this same property) held the property, the credit ranges from 20% to 80%. Your executor is not likely to know that certain of your property was also included and taxed in the estate of a recently deceased relative or friend. Your estate is almost certain to forfeit this credit unless you inform your executor about property inherited.

Conclusions and advice

- Where possible, try to sell difficult-to-value property while you are living so that in the absence of proof by the executor of a credible figure, it won't be included in your estate at a ridiculously high value.

- Let your executor or other trustworthy person know of any value depressants to your property.

- Do not list property for sale with a broker at some absurdly high figure thinking that you really don't want to sell and so you named a figure that no one would accept. For example, someone lists her residence for sale in order to characterize it as a commercial property, thereby allowing her insurance and maintenance to be written off as business expense deductions. When the individual dies, the Internal Revenue Service will predictably say that, as she named the price herself, it must represent fair value.

- Do not give your executor instructions to withhold a certain property from sale. If an individual instructs or advises her executor that this property is really worth more than the market price, the IRS is likely to accept this as fact.

- Do not presume your executor will be able to file a refund claim based upon now-lowered valuations if he initially failed to reduce valuations for property because he was not aware of the complexities that we've been discussing in this section. If the executor files a refund claim, he has a tough burden of proof. And the IRS is likely to react to a refund claim by seeking something to disallow as an offset to the claim.

- Before asking a financially unsophisticated relative or friend to serve as your executor, trustee or other fiduciary, consider the potential cost to a person unfamiliar with the accuracy-related penalties.

- The blockage rule is generally applied to stock, but can also be applied in other situations. If an estate holds so many articles or units of a single type that individual items cannot be sold without "breaking the market," the ordinary fair market value, measured, for example, by recent actual sales, can be replaced by a lower value. In a 1992 case, this was allowed where the estate owned a large number of paintings by the decedent.

- In the case of a closely held corporation where shares have never been sold in an arm's-length transaction, it is extremely difficult to arrive at a valuation of the stock that will be acceptable to the IRS and the courts. Have the company merge with a publicly held or, at least, better-known company when a major shareholder becomes seriously ill or simply seems to be getting on in years. The shares exchanged for your original ones will now be much more suited to valuation. The IRS will be less arbitrary in setting a valuation if more objective factors exist.

• Beware of the aforementioned "minority discounts." The IRS has recently taken an aggressive stance on such discounts, especially for *inter vivos* gifts, whether outright or in trust. It is likely that the IRS will similarly pursue estates where deep discounts are taken. This does not mean that you cannot consider and take such discounts, but be sure to find out about up-to-date IRS positions and assure that your own position is well documented and provable by qualified experts/appraisers.

• The 1997 Tax Act added a significant provision for family owned businesses. If it applies, the unified credit is increased to $1.3 million. However, the 2001 tax law repealed this, commencing 2004 when the credit reaches $1.5 million. To qualify, the value of the family owned interest must exceed 50% of the decedent's adjusted gross estate. Therefore, careful preplanning is a must.

Chapter Forty-Seven

POWERS OF APPOINTMENT

One of the most sought-after ideals of estate planning is having your plans carried out according to your desires once you are no longer alive, in light of conditions that were unknown to you at the time of death. One way to accomplish this is by empowering another person to act at a later date or dates in accordance with what you would have done under the circumstances had you been alive (or mentally competent). This person must be familiar with your objectives, aspirations and prejudices, and he must be able to see that your wishes are carried out to the extent money or other property are available for the purpose. Additionally or alternatively, you can set up specific guidelines or requests to establish the amount of discretion permitted this person to make judgments in light of changing circumstances.

A deputy to act as you would have done

For example, you don't know now which of your children or relatives or friends you'd most like to help in view of their plans, financial situation and character. Do you really want all of your children or grandchildren to share your wealth equally when their needs, capabilities and lifestyle may be quite different? Will you be able to channel your property primarily or entirely to a beneficiary who fulfills your wish by going into the family business or entering medical school?

Nature of a power of appointment

You may give someone the authority to say who will get the property that you place under his right of disposition. This is called a *power of appointment*, although it need not be so labeled. For example, by will or by deed of trust, you create a trust and give the holder of the power of appointment the right to say who will get the property or its income, in what amounts and at what times. If the holder is restricted to selecting designated parties or classes of persons (such as blood relatives of the grantor), he holds a special power of appointment. If he can name himself, his estate or the creditors of either, he holds a general power of appointment. Where he is authorized to give ("appoint") the property to anyone he believes the creator of the power might have selected, that is a general power of appointment, for "anyone" could include the holder of the power.

Bestowing a power of appointment upon a relative, close friend or business associate gives the grantor great flexibility in his estate planning. He has not committed himself to distribute designated property or income to those who might not need it or who might not use their new wealth wisely.

After the creator of the power has died, the property designated for apportionment can be held in trust until the holder of the power sees fit to exercise it. For example, the creator may authorize his brother to distribute the designated property at the time the youngest of the creator's children reaches age 21. One child may have married a very wealthy person and therefore has no financial needs. Another lives a simple, isolated life and has no monetary aspirations. One has developed a permanent physical disability. One may have manifested great artistic talent that years of costly study might bring to fruition. The choice of parties to whom property can be appointed may be specified to include any related person. One relative may have joined a religious or political group to which the decedent was violently opposed. Another may have offended the decedent's ideals about lifestyle or patriotism. These are merely a few possibilities. The holder of the power should know what the decedent would have done about distributing his property had he known all of the facts and circumstances at the time.

It is important to differentiate between a power of appointment and a power of attorney. They are not the same. As noted in Chapter One, the power of attorney is a written document wherein a person (the agent) is given the right to take certain action on behalf of another (the principal). In a typical situation, a father gives his son the power to act on his behalf. This grant allows the son to take whatever action is allowed under the terms of the power of attorney. A limited power is usually granted for a specific task, such as selling a specific parcel of real estate. A general power grants the agent rights to do anything the principal would do, until the rights are revoked by the principal, with minor exceptions such as making a new will, which is prohibited. Thus, the power of attorney allows one to appoint a surrogate to act on his behalf, usually with a predetermined set of directions or a generalized understanding between the parties. The power ceases upon the principal's death.

The power of appointment, however, is a right granted in a document to appoint or transfer property to either a specified group of individuals or an unlimited group of recipients, which might include the holder of the power. From an estate planning point of view, the holder is not formally charged with carrying out the wishes of the original grantor. Usually, one hopes that the holder will consider discussions with the grantor, memos and her general understanding of the grantor's wishes, as well as the circumstances that exist at the time such power is exercised.

Advantages of power of appointment

The creator of the power, obviously, may benefit greatly from it. In addition to flexibility, he can avoid having to make hard decisions, like cutting a son who had been offensive out of his will. Let the holder of the power make the decision to bypass that son. By using a power of appointment, the creator may have his property apportioned without his own personal biases, which he realizes could result in inequities or injustice.

Disadvantages of power of appointment

However, there can be disadvantages in granting a power of appointment. The property may actually be distributed without regard to the decedent's wishes. If the holder were empowered to give the assets to anyone, and the creator's children didn't seem to be living up to the decedent's standards, he might bestow the property on his own daughter. If it is a general power of appointment, the holder could act selfishly and appoint himself. Finally, the principle may fail to work: The property might pass in a way that would have disappointed the deceased.

Danger of accepting a general power of appointment

Advantageous as a power of appointment may be to the creator, it may place a substantial tax burden on the holder's estate. There is no risk in accepting a special power of appointment, as long as the holder is not a member of the class of potential appointees. But if an individual has a general power of appointment at the time of his death, any property that is subject to his discretionary distribution will be includable in his own gross estate, for it represents property that could have gone to him up to the moment of his death and was still under his control at that time. The same is true in the case of property that he had appointed to other persons within three years of his death, even though the general rule of inclusion of gifts within three years of death is no longer in effect.

Why should someone accept a general power of appointment in view of this great tax risk? Usually, it is because he does not understand the gravity of such risk. For example, his authority may be to distribute property to the decedent's children in such amounts that they may require or, alternatively, to anyone else whose views and moral conduct would not have been obnoxious to the decedent. The holder of the power hadn't been explicitly authorized to give property to himself, so even if he had some modest knowledge of powers of appointment, he might not have recognized his authority as being a general power. But it is, because "anyone" includes himself.

Or someone may accept designation as holder of a general power because she believes that she will distribute all of the property for the benefit of others before she dies. She may be correct, but there's no assurance that she will live for three years after the power is exercised. Or she may not realize that she can refuse to accept a general power created without her knowledge in the decedent's will, or how and when to do this. She may also feel such a sense of responsibility to the decedent that she accepts the power despite its risks.

Exercise of power of appointment

Exercising a general power of appointment so that the subject property won't be in the holder's gross estate when he dies may be difficult or even impossible. The holder's authorization may have been to distribute the property at such time as the decedent's youngest child reached majority under the laws of his state. When the decedent dies and the holder of the power has property under his discretionary powers, one child is three years old, the holder can't act to free his estate from tax risk for many years; he could die before the child outgrows his minority, plus the three years after exercise.

In addition, the holder of the power might expect to exercise it in favor of others at the end of the year, when he can evaluate the decedent's business according to its earnings or net worth at that time. Or, he might wish to wait a few years in order to form an opinion of the capabilities of various relatives of the decedent. But before this takes place, the holder may become mentally incompetent and unable to exercise the power. The property is still subject to his disposition when he dies years later, even though the holder may have lacked the legal authority to act.

Where a trust instrument provides that the income beneficiary has free access to the trust's principal, the holder has a general power of appointment because he has the power to appoint to himself property that would otherwise go to different people. A power to withdraw principal that is limited to an ascertainable standard relating to health, education, support or maintenance is not a general power. In determining whether a power is limited by an ascertainable standard, it is immaterial whether the beneficiary is required to exhaust his other income before the power can be exercised.

Renunciation

An individual can renounce his designation as the holder of a general power of appointment as soon as he learns that he has been designated, although because of a sense of obligation to a relative or friend, he may not choose to do so. (See Chapter Forty-Nine, "Disclaimers and Renunciations.") Or, he may petition a state court to change the general power to a special one, but there is no assurance that the court will do so, or that it will act quickly enough to prevent estate tax liability.

How the IRS knows

An individual may accept a general power of appointment in the belief that the Internal Revenue Service will never know that he has it. But one of the questions the executor must answer on the federal estate tax return is, "Did the decedent ever possess, exercise or release any general power of appointment?" Now the cat is out of the bag. The fact that an individual holds a general power of appointment may not be known to him, or he may have long since forgotten it. This is one of the many reasons an individual should review the questions that will need to be answered when his own estate tax return is filed. (See Chapter Fifty-Three, "The Dry Run.")

Conclusions and advice

• If you intend to create a power of appointment, sound out your candidates for holders to ensure that they will accept. If they are doubtful, designate others who are agreeable.

• If you are asked whether you will accept a power of appointment, or told that you have been given one, consult a knowledgeable attorney.

• In the event you are named as the holder of a general power, make a prompt disclaimer if you are unwilling to assume the tax risks.

• Only accept a special—not a general—power of appointment.

• Do not assume that you will be able to avoid estate tax liability by prompt exercise of a general power in someone else's favor.

Chapter Forty-Eight

AVOIDING DISALLOWANCE OF CHARITABLE BEQUESTS

Charitable bequests can be an important part of one's estate planning. These bequests can reduce the gross estate while implementing a benevolent purpose of the decedent. Lifetime charitable contributions reduce the donor's income and similarly serve her benevolent desires. Also, bequests offer greater opportunities for donating, for there is no percentage limitation on the amount of the deduction for federal estate tax purposes as in the case of the income tax. This chapter describes how the various benefits available through charitable bequests can be saved from forfeiture through careful planning.

One of the key arguments against the passage of the 2001 tax law, or more appropriately, the repeal of the estate tax, was the potential adverse effect on charitable giving. In fact, some of America's most prominent and wealthiest citizens petitioned Congress to keep some form of the tax in place. They argued that it would help vital charities that receive substantial bequests due to the provisions fostering charitable giving by granting corresponding deductions. There would appear to be no question that, without the estate tax, charities would suffer a significant loss of revenue.

Definition of a charitable organization

A deduction is allowed from the gross estate for transfers to or for the use of any organization operated exclusively for religious, charitable, scientific, literary or educational purposes, provided that no part of its earnings is used to benefit any individual and no substantial part of its activities involves carrying on propaganda or other attempts to influence legislation. Check on the true nature of the organization and what it does with its money to ensure that the deduction will be allowed by the Internal Revenue Service.

In the case of contributions of certain interests in real property to charitable organizations, to the United States or to a state or local government unit—made after December 31, 1986—a deduction is allowed for federal estate and gift tax purposes even if the contributions do not meet the federal income tax deductibility requirement that the contribution be used for conservation purposes.

A charitable bequest is deductible only if made to an approved organization or to a political subdivision of the United States, to a veterans' organization incorporated by Congress or one of its departments, local chapters or posts.

Exclusively for charitable purposes

That a particular organization is operated exclusively for charitable or similar purposes cannot be assumed from the name or general activities of the organization. For example, a county medical society may perform charitable work for the community while performing personal services for physicians such as serving as a collection agency, giving business seminars and publishing advice on doctors' tax questions. Similarly, a state bar association may provide legal services for the needy, but may lobby for legislation favorable to lawyers, furnish referral and telephone answering services and sponsor group insurance. These organizations, despite their public services, are not being operated exclusively for charitable purposes.

It's not charitable if you get something in return

There is no deduction for a charitable bequest or contribution when the charitable donor gets something in return. The deduction will be disallowed if the donor has reserved the right to receive something, as in a case where money was given to a certain hospital "for the establishment of free room or rooms, first, for the persons named as beneficiaries of this trust, and then, for such other persons as the Board of Directors of said hospital may from time to time direct." This was not just a preference for needy relatives or friends; it took care of them whether or not they were in need.

The result is the same where the donor neither asked nor expected to receive anything in return. If a grateful hospital administrator notifies the executor that facilities will always be available without charge to members of the donor's family, the executor should write an immediate reply that nothing was expected or will be accepted.

Estate or donor must trigger the deduction

To be deductible, the money or property must pass from the estate or donor to a charitable organization because of an affirmative action by the party claiming the deduction. The benevolence must have been his. In one case, a decedent's will directed his executor to erect a monument for him in Israel, and the executor decided instead to establish an endowed scholarship fund for Jewish students. The deduction was denied because the decedent did not decide to transfer funds for a charitable purpose. Language in a will, trust instrument or letter saying that the decedent knew his spouse and children would make gifts in his name to his favorite charities, for which reason he left the entire estate to the family, did not create deductions for the estate when the decedent's wishes were implemented by the family just as he had expected. The deduction was also lost where a will directed the executor, a lifelong friend, to take care of certain charitable organizations in which the decedent had been interested.

Charitable deduction is what charity actually gets

Sometimes a decedent's will provides for bequests to a charitable organization. But a relative may challenge the provision, saying that undue influence had been exercised on the decedent by a hospital or church when her powers of resistance were low. To avoid unpleasant publicity, the charitable organization may agree to accept a smaller amount than called for by the will. The charitable deduction is limited to what is received by the charity. To prevent this situation, an individual may provide in her will that if any beneficiary seeks to challenge the validity of the will, the amount designated for him will go instead to someone else, such as the remainderman. However, be sure to check with your attorney. Some states do not favor will or trust provisions that discourage or prohibit one from seeking legal remedies.

Bequest must be unconditional

No deduction is allowed for a conditional charitable bequest if there is a real possibility that the condition will not be met. One individual left her home to an approved organization, subject to its agreement that the home would be maintained in its existing condition. In the absence of such assurance, the bequest wasn't deductible. Nor was deduction allowed for a bequest to a church of a certain denomination in a named community, where there was no such church at the time of the bequest or any certainty that there ever would be one.

Discrimination

In years past, there has been an increase in the disallowance of charitable bequests on the grounds that the recipient organization was practicing some form of discrimination. That would mean, in effect, that the organization was not being operated exclusively for charitable purposes. *Example:* a charitable, religious or educational organization that only admits or accepts persons of a certain race.

The Internal Revenue Service sells a subscription to a publication listing organizations to which deductible contributions are allowed. But this list is constantly being revised, and many organizations have had their names removed because of discrimination. At the time an individual plans her estate, certain organizations may be approved. Bequests provided in the will may rely upon this. But by the time the decedent dies, and the bequests are implemented, the organization may no longer be recognized as acceptable. It is the responsibility of an individual or her adviser to periodically check the status of organizations to which bequests are to be made. If the individual wants to have the bequest allowed as a tax deduction, she should replace the names of stricken organizations with charities in good standing. An individual whose interest in a particular organization is sufficiently great to permit her to ask questions, or whose potential bequests would indicate that she has the right to request answers, should obtain an affirmative statement from an organization that it is not practicing discrimination. Some organizations inform the public of their eligibility to receive a deductible bequest or contribution through advertisements.

The importance of making certain that bequests are not made to institutions practicing discrimination is highlighted by the fact that anyone who knows of such a situation can trigger the disallowance. The US Supreme Court has held that any interested party can bring suit to enjoin the Secretary of the Treasury from approving or maintaining on its eligibility list any organization that engages in discriminatory practices. A private school, for example, may be called upon to state specifically that it doesn't engage in discrimination. That can no longer be assumed.

State law may restrict charitable bequests

In some states, an individual with a spouse, descendant or parent cannot bequeath more than one-half of her estate to charity, and a bequest for a larger amount is valid only up to the 50% mark. Elsewhere, bequests for religious or charitable purposes made by will less than 30 days prior to a decedent's death are void; instead the property goes to the residuary legatee or next of kin.

Conclusions and advice

• Check, and keep checking, the practices of organizations to which significant bequests are to be made.

• Name an alternate beneficiary if the original charity does not qualify to receive the designated funds, or give your executor the power and direction to choose a similar charity which does qualify. One individual's will left property to a state college (an approved organization) for an annual scholarship for a white Caucasian with the same last name as the decedent. If no such person applied for the scholarship in a particular year, the funds were to be used simply as an athletic scholarship. The deduction was disallowed when the trustee could not perform its fiduciary duties by selecting someone with the decedent's original specifications without violating state antidiscrimination laws. The money, therefore, could not be used for a racially discriminatory purpose but had to go instead to any deserving athlete, which did qualify for a deduction.

- Ascertain whether a conditional bequest will be accepted by the named beneficiary. If not, make other dispositions.

- When you give property that can't readily be marketed to a charitable organization, advise the organization of where and how to best sell it if necessary. The amount of the deduction depends on the fair market value of the asset. If the charitable organization wants to convert the asset into cash quickly, they may sell it at a woefully inadequate price because of lack of knowledge. The full amount of the deduction may be protected by informing the donee of the best available market for, say, a collection of Egyptian scarabs from the Fourth Dynasty.

- Make certain that the bequest goes from the decedent or his estate to the charity. *Example:* A father left property to his son, who was a member of a religious order that takes an oath of poverty. The son turned the property over to his order, which was an approved charitable organization. There was no allowable deduction, but there would have been had the father left the property directly to the order instead of to his son.

- Do not be misled by an organization's name or the excellence of its public works to believe that it qualifies as a charitable organization for deduction purposes. Obtain the IRS pamphlet on charities to confirm its legitimacy and, as a precondition of your gift, require that it qualify.

- Do not permit anything to be received, or even offered, in return for a charitable bequest or contribution. If the donee organization unilaterally offers services—or anything else—in return, decline at once.

- In order that the charitable deduction be recognized, an individual should be familiar with the consequences of undervaluation of property.

- The donee of contributed property must report the receipt of noncash property and how much was subsequently received when the property was sold. This can compromise the amount of the contribution claimed by the donor.

Chapter Forty-Nine

DISCLAIMERS AND RENUNCIATIONS

A disclaimer is a complete, unqualified refusal to accept rights to which one is entitled. It is a disavowal, denial or renunciation of an interest, right or property imputed to an individual or alleged to be his.

Disclaimers may figure in many aspects of estate planning. For example, (1) if a decedent properly disclaimed an interest in property, its value is not included in his gross estate; (2) an individual can't properly dispose of his property according to his own desires if a beneficiary subsequently disclaims what has been provided for him, unless a successor beneficiary was named by the decedent for such eventuality; (3) the marital deduction may be impacted by disclaimers of either the surviving spouse or third parties; (4) disclaimers can be important in the case of gifts and powers of appointment; and (5) disclaimers can be an effective way to attain two unified credits when the first spouse dies with a simple will giving everything to the other.

In view of the many tax aspects of disclaimers, it seems strange that prior to 1977 there were no definitive rules as to what constituted a disclaimer, nor were there rules of general application concerning the tax consequences of a disclaimer. The disclaimer rules now cover the federal estate tax, the gift tax and the generation-skipping tax.

Gross estate

The gross estate includes the value of all of a decedent's property, wherever located, to the extent of his interest at the time of his death. If a lifetime or after-death transfer is valid, a disclaimer of the property receivable by such gift or inheritance is not treated as a taxable transfer by the person making the disclaimer.

If a decedent inherited property from someone else, the value can be kept out of the former's gross estate even without his having renounced acceptance, if his executor disclaims it within the permissible time, provided that state law authorizes the executor to take such action. In one case, a husband left one-third of his property to his wife, and she died within three hours after him as the result of a common disaster. Her executrix immediately renounced on behalf of the wife the interest passing from her husband, and that amount was not includable in the wife's gross estate.

The marital deduction

The marital deduction is based upon what passes from a decedent to a surviving spouse, no matter how the final number is arrived at. If a decedent's surviving spouse makes a disclaimer of any property interest that would otherwise be considered as passing from the decedent to his spouse, the disclaimed interest is considered as having passed from the decedent to the person(s) entitled to receive the interest as the result of the disclaimer. One decedent's second wife agreed to give up her interest in her husband's estate in favor of his other heirs for $40,000, and that is all she received. That was the extent allowable for the marital deduction for tax purposes, although the will had left her a considerably larger figure.

Another decedent's widow renounced the provisions of his will and elected to exercise her dower rights. In connection with this renunciation, other beneficiaries agreed to pay her a specified amount each month for the remainder of her life. The mathematical value of these payments could not be taken on the husband's estate tax return as the marital deduction, because the promise to pay them was not owed by her husband in his lifetime and was not a liability of his estate.

If an interest passes from the decedent to his surviving spouse as a result of a disclaimer by a third party, such as a son, the interest is considered as passing from the decedent to his surviving spouse, thus qualifying for the marital deduction. For example, the son might have decided that his mother was inadequately financed, while he didn't need the money.

Saving the second unified credit

Many clients leave everything to their spouse with the remainder to their children, if their spouse does not survive. Often these simple wills or trusts are executed and never reviewed. Unfortunately, if their joint gross estate exceeds $2 million in 2002 (or, in the wrong sequence of deaths, if it exceeds $1 million), such dispositive documents cause a needless tax. In effect, if the husband dies with a simple will or trust, his wife inherits all of his assets and is left with an estate over the federal taxable level. If she were to die in 2002, her credit is only $1 million. Therefore, the excess will be subject to tax.

The solution is for the wife to disclaim all or a portion of her husband's estate. For example, if she has a good chance of living until 2006, she will have a $2 million credit. Therefore, she and her husband could pass a total of $3 million tax free. With this plan in mind, she might disclaim the entire $1 million or choose only $500,000. This would cause the husband's estate to pass to the children tax free, using his credit, which would have gone unused. She would then have her credit plus room for asset appreciation. The children, in turn, would presumably hold the funds they received for their mother's use, if need be. Upon her death, she would use her own (second) unified credit. Here is an illustration of how the disclaimer works:

Without a disclaimer

Husband's estate...........$1,000,000   Wife's estate $1,000,000

- Husband's death, assets pass tax free to wife using
  marital deduction; husband loses his unified credit ....+ $1,000,000
    Wife's estate $2,000,000
    Upon wife's death, wife's unified credit (also in 2002) ......− $1,000,000
    Wife's taxable estate $1,000,000
    Combined estates subject to tax @35% +/− $1,000,000

With a disclaimer

Husband's estate...........$1,000,000   Wife's estate $1,000,000

- Wife disclaims on husband's   • Wife later dies and
  death and children inherit   children inherit
- Unified credit............($1,000,000)   • Unified credit..........($1,000,000)

Taxable estate ....$ 0   Taxable estate.........................$ 0
    Combined estates subject to tax...$ 0

Charitable bequests

For an estate to be entitled to a charitable deduction, the money must flow from the estate to the charity by reason of the decedent's decision and act. As noted in Chapter Forty-Eight, one father left a portion of his estate to his children in equal amounts. His son was a member of a religious order who had taken an oath of poverty, and he turned his inheritance over to the order. Presumably, the father had anticipated this action. But the father's estate wasn't entitled to the charitable deduction, because the money did not flow from him or his estate directly to the charity.

But the funds do go from the estate to the charity where the intervening party between them disclaims his interest so that, in default of the named beneficiary, the charity receives the bequest directly. A charitable deduction is allowed where a beneficiary disclaimed his bequest if the charity had already been named in the will as a secondary successor or contingent beneficiary. As a result, this renunciation simultaneously benefits the charity, reduces the gross estate and lowers the federal estate tax.

In planning your estate, consider the possibility that a beneficiary will refuse property left to her by will. *Examples:* Stock in a nuclear power plant corporation or in a company that does business in a foreign country that practices racial discrimination. If the named successor or contingent beneficiaries also disclaim the bequest, possibly for the same reason, the unclaimed property may go to the state. The decedent's estate plan may be frustrated in this situation. She could have named a charitable organization as a contingent beneficiary. If the bequest went to the charity after other renunciations, the estate would get a deduction for a charitable bequest.

Powers of appointment

The gross estate includes the value of any property "with respect to which the decedent has, at the time of his death, a general power of appointment," according to the Internal Revenue Code. (See Chapter Forty-Seven, "Powers of Appointment.") So, if an individual was given a general power of appointment over someone else's property, the value of property that he in fact never owned may be included in his own gross estate.

A disclaimer of a general power of appointment is not a taxable transfer. But the exercise of such a power to any extent by the holder of the power is treated as an acceptance of its benefits, so that a disclaimer can't subsequently be made. The acceptance of any consideration in return for making the disclaimer is treated as an acceptance of the benefits of the interest disclaimed.

The federal gift tax

A refusal to accept ownership of offered property does not constitute the making of a gift by the person disclaiming in favor of the party who eventually gets the property. The intended donee did not have to accept the gift. In some states, there is no power to disclaim under the laws of intestate succession. This state law therefore declares that a disclaimer is in fact a gift to the ultimate recipient. For example, a father's will left his property to his son. The will was invalid, and the property, under the state intestacy law, went to the next of kin, also the son. The son disclaimed his right to the property, which went to the decedent's next closest kin, the decedent's grandson. The son was deemed to have made a taxable gift to his own son by renouncing in the latter's favor. Under the intestacy law, the property became the son's, and he couldn't refuse to be bound by the state law. While he thought he was renouncing his interest, he was merely making a gift of it. Note, however, that the result of this case would be different under current federal law, which recognizes the disclaimer even though it fails as a disclaimer under state law. This should not be a major concern. The father's gift would be valid under state law and would not be a taxable gift at the federal level. It may be a taxable gift at the state level if the state levies such a gift tax. However, few states do, and the tax is usually modest.

In other examples, an individual who had made no will proposed to leave practically his entire estate to his son to equalize the financial worth of his survivors to some extent. The family agreed to the proposal, and an attorney prepared a will. However, before it was signed by the father, he died. His wife and daughter, realizing that affirmative action was necessary to carry out the decedent's wishes, renounced their interests in the estate, which would go to them under state laws of intestacy in the absence of a valid will. The entire estate then went to the son. It was held that the widow and daughter each had made a gift to the son of their respective interests in the decedent's estate. They had been without power to disclaim an interest that, under their state's laws of intestacy, was theirs. (Not all states have such laws; check with an attorney to confirm your local law.)

When spouses own property jointly with a right of survivorship, some states prohibit the survivor from renouncing his interest after the death of his spouse, to let the property pass, for example, to the children. Traditionally, the law in many states did not allow for the renunciation of rights previously accepted. However, some states are changing their rules, since current federal law would recognize the qualified disclaimers in the survivorship situation.

In both of these cases, current federal law would recognize the qualified disclaimers even though they did not satisfy state law.

More than intent is required to disclaim

Renunciation involves more than one's statement. A disclaimer was not recognized when a life beneficiary of a trust with a right of invasion of principal filed an affidavit stating that she had "no intention of invading the principal of the decedent's estate for any purpose whatsoever." This was not deemed to be a complete and absolute refusal to accept the right to make use of trust principal.

Requirements for a disclaimer

In order for a disclaimer to be recognized for federal tax purposes, these ground rules must be met:

1. The refusal must be in writing.

2. The written disclaimer must be received by the transferor of the interest (such as the executor of the decedent's estate) or the holder of legal title to the property not later than nine months after the date on which the transfer

creating the interest is made. This period is extended to nine months after the day on which the person making the disclaimer has reached age 21, if he was a minor when the transfer took place. A transfer is considered to be made when it is treated as a completed gift for federal gift tax purposes or upon the date of the decedent's death in the case of a bequest.

3. The disclaiming person must not have accepted the interest or any of its benefits before making the disclaimer.

4. The interest must pass to someone other than the person making the disclaimer as a result of the refusal to accept the property. For purposes of this requirement, the person making the disclaimer can't have the authority to direct the redistribution or transfer of the property to another person and be treated as making a "qualified" disclaimer. Under a 1978 change in the law, a widow refused to accept all or a portion of her interest in property passing from her late husband and, as a result of this refusal, the property passed to a trust in which she had an income interest. Her disclaimer was valid and kept the value of this property out of her gross estate.

Disclaimers no longer protect property from IRS tax liens

Formerly, a disclaimed inheritance passed to the person next entitled, even if the disclaimant owed federal taxes. However, in the December 1999 case of *R.F. Drye, Jr., Rohn F. Drye Jr. et al v. U.S., SCt, 99-2 USTC,* the US Supreme Court overturned previous law by ruling that an inheritance was an asset of the debtor, subject to attachment. Now the government can impose its lien against such property. This makes planning and vigilant updates more important, to avoid beneficiaries who owe back taxes. Provide for them by other ways and means. Also, be very candid with your advisers. Tell them if any of your heirs have financial troubles. This is a good practice not only when dealing with disclaimers, but also during the entire estate planning process. For example, consider a spendthrift trust where a person's abilities or tendencies, and not his age, lead you to the conclusion that such a trust is in order.

Conclusions and advice

• Act quickly in disclaiming property or in getting legal advice as to what you should do.

• Make provisions for contingent beneficiaries in your will or trust, so that your property will go to persons of your choice if the named beneficiaries disclaim their interests.

• Do not make use of any part of an interest before disclaiming it. Do not accept any consideration in return for making the disclaimer. This would be treated as an acceptance of the benefits of the interests disclaimed, and no disclaimer is possible after acceptance.

• If your spouse passes away and you would be left with an estate over $1 million in 2002 or 2003, seek counsel. There may be action to consider depending upon your age, health and family circumstances. For example, if you are in reasonably good health and your estate is less than but approaching $1 million, you may simply wish to start or accelerate your gifting program. If it is over $1 million, the need is more pressing. Possibly life insurance is in order or, as this chapter suggests, perhaps a disclaimer is preferable. However, don't wait for this discussion with your family and your advisers, as you only have a limited amount of time to disclaim.

• Unlike federal gift tax rules, disclaimers are considered gifts in determining eligibility for benefits under Title XIX rules. However, it may be better to start the 36-month penalty period running as opposed to having these assets available to creditors and depletion due to long-term health-care needs. This is a very important concept in elder law and elder planning.

Chapter Fifty

USE OF LIFE INSURANCE WHILE THE INSURED IS STILL ALIVE

A rather recent development with life insurance involves an insured person's obtaining some or all of the proceeds payable upon her death while she is still alive. By reason of the newness and somewhat experimental nature of such a policy, there are many variations of this basic idea. Unfortunately, there are also some who have taken advantage of the individual's need and abuse their relatively stronger position.

Therefore, it may be advisable for an individual or her estate planner to shop around. Ascertain which insurance companies recognize payments before the insured dies, what portion of the face value of the policy is available for such treatment and the premium charge for adding this feature to an existing policy or for purchasing a new one. Also, find out what limitations, if any, there are on the use of the money obtained prior to death, the federal income tax treatment of amounts so received and any requirement of a physical examination if a policy is modified. There are many variations on making use of payouts of the amount ordinarily payable upon the death of the insured. All involve use of accelerated death benefits.

Under a *viatical settlement*, a person with a life expectancy shortened by serious illness (defined, typically, as less than two years of remaining life) agrees to accept a practical settlement for giving up her interest to, say, 30% of the scheduled death benefit, perhaps with a cap of $500,000.

The shorter the life expectancy, the greater the agreed settlement figure, so negotiation can take place. Then the holder (now the seller) of the policy ceases making premium payments, which are thereafter made by the other party (the buyer) who will collect the insurance payout when death occurs.

The going rate has been 70% to 80% of total benefits, so shop for the best offer. Beware of the urge to sign quickly, especially if you are told that it is a limited time offer. Most often these pressure tactics are not in your best interest.

Participants in an employer group plan may be permitted to sell their coverage under a particular plan. Buyers of life policies where there is a shortened life expectancy may obtain a deal by offering a finder's fee to legal or financial planners or even to physicians who have patients with very short life expectancies. Information on potential purchasers of life insurance policies may be obtained from various organizations, your local senior coordinator, or possibly AARP.

Whether an insurance company charges a premium for this benefit depends upon the particular company. There may be additional paperwork, so a processing fee may be charged. Perhaps the insurance company will absorb this cost in an effort to be more competitive with its rivals.

In some policies, the "living benefit" may be used for any purpose. Other plans limit the amount of money being obtained prior to death to medical expenses (where there are many interpretations) or nursing home expenses.

Sometimes, the insured must be insurable when she applies for the endorsement or modification of her policy. If she now is uninsurable, she may only be able to take out insurance under a substandard policy which charges a higher premium because of the greater risk. In some policies, the option to obtain accelerated benefits may not be exercisable for a specified period, such as two or three years.

Customarily, there is no recognizable policy of insurance unless the person who applies for it has an insurable interest in the life of the insured. *Reason:* Someone might take out an insurance policy on the life of a stranger and then "arrange" the death of the insured so that someone who paid, perhaps, one premium could collect the face value of the policy.

An organization (*viaticus*) may offer to buy the regular policy of a person who needs money because she has a terminal illness or suspects that she does.

This organization (or individual) buys the policy at a discount because funds are being paid at an unknown length of time before her death. Or, the organization may be a broker who seeks out the best available terms from companies that provide high-risk coverage at an appropriate cost.

Whether this is trafficking in confidential medical files protected by time-honored privacy is still an unsettled question.

For the chronically ill, there is a limited amount of tax-free proceeds. On the other hand, life insurance proceeds paid to terminally ill insured persons have been tax free since 1997. A physician must certify that the insured is expected to die within 24 months.

Where the person with a terminal illness had irrevocably named beneficiaries of her policy, her ability to borrow against the policy will require their assent. If they are close and concerned relatives, they are, of course, likely to agree.

A person with a terminal illness, confronted with an unanticipated need for cash, may be able to use her insurance policy without having to sell it. The insured will be able to borrow against the cash surrender value of the policy, provided that this is a policy with cash surrender value (such as straight life) and that she never had surrendered incidents of ownership in the policy.

A loan from the insurance company may be arranged if the insured had built up cash value in her policy, as in the case of universal life. If the policy has no cash surrender value, as in the case of term insurance, the insured may borrow from a friend in return for naming this party to be a beneficiary of the policy. Sometimes, companies object to beneficiaries who do not have an insurable interest (friendship may not qualify, while being a creditor does). However, this can be solved by putting the policy in a simple living trust for the benefit of your friend.

Even where a policy nominally has a cash surrender value, it already may have been used up or at least depleted by previous policy loans. However, the death benefit may far exceed this cash value amount. Therefore, it is likely that someone will consider helping in the right situation.

Note, however, that various government aid programs are available only for individuals who meet a "means" test. A person who receives accelerated death benefits may no longer be eligible to meet this means test. This also must be carefully considered.

Conclusions and advice

• Before you finalize any sale or assignment of your policy rights, be sure to seek competent counsel. There are many less than reputable firms out there who will take advantage of the elderly and/or ill in need of funds.

• If you are in the market to buy more insurance, ask if you can assign or sell your policy rights and/or draw down the cash surrender value.

• If these rights exist, most often the policy is either whole life, has some cash value or is a term policy that cannot be canceled. Therefore, keep this in mind when making decisions about what types of policies to buy.

• Do not lose sight of the concept of placing the policy in a simple trust to pay back those who offer assistance in your hour of need.

Chapter Fifty-One

MINIMIZING MULTIPLE STATE DEATH TAXES & PROBATE ADMINISTRATIONS

Many states still impose some form of tax upon the transfer of properties from a decedent to his beneficiaries, although the number was decreasing before the 2001 tax law. Some of these taxes are payable by the estate; others are paid by the persons who receive the assets. The term "death taxes" is used to cover state taxes that are triggered by an individual's demise, regardless of whether the imposition is a property, privilege, inheritance or succession tax. The taxes may be imposed by one state or by several states simultaneously, if the decedent had the required "contacts" in each state.

One of the more common forms of state death taxation is the so-called sponge tax or sop-up tax. Under this format, prior to the 2001 tax law, each federally taxable estate was given a credit against the federal tax due for any state death tax actually paid. This credit was based upon a predetermined formula (chart) which used the size of the estate as its guidepost. Many states reasoned, rightfully so, that without a state death tax, the estate would simply pay this amount to the federal government. Therefore, many states elected to enact a death tax to sop up or sponge off the federal government by taking only the exact amount of the credit. In effect, the total tax bill to the estate was the same whether the state had this tax or not.

Under the 2001 tax law, however, the credit will be reduced by 25% each year commencing in 2002 and will be completely eliminated in 2005 when the amount of state death taxes paid will become a deduction. This seems to be one of the stranger areas of the 2001 tax law. It clearly puts the states with the sponge or sop-up tax in a rather peculiar position vis-à-vis future revenue. By making state death taxes a deduction, many states will lose revenue as the sponge or sop-up tax concept simply does not work. Do these states consider enacting a tax when before they really had none (see page 291 for practical effect of a sponge tax)? In truth, some states have already enacted laws to ensure the same revenue, but as a deduction instead of a credit. One is left to wonder about Congress's motivation in offering an unlimited deduction versus a set credit. In theory, the states can now take a greater portion of what is split between the two taxing authorities. We doubt that is what Congress had intended.

Since one of the most important objectives of estate planning is to transfer as much of one's property as possible to intended beneficiaries, an individual will be thwarted if several states are able to extract death taxes from what his designated heirs would otherwise receive. Plans can be made, however, to minimize the danger of such multiple impositions of tax.

In addition, if the decedent is found to be a resident of multiple states, there will likely be multiple probate administrations. Even if the decedent is unquestionably a resident of one state but owns real estate in several others, it is likely that each such state will require ancillary administration. This will add needless costs and possible delays to winding up the estate.

Multiple state taxes upon one person's death

If an individual is subject to a state's taxing jurisdiction at the time of his death, such a tax is an accepted part of the cost of transmitting his wealth to persons of his choice. But this cost can be multiplied in the case of an individual who has lived in several states during his lifetime. Two or more states may seek to impose tax upon his property, or the receipt of it, on the grounds that he was domiciled there when he died and hence is subject to the death tax.

Unfortunately, the laws of the various states define what is meant by "domicile" in different ways. An individual may be claimed by one state because he actually lived there at the time of his death; by another, because he once lived there and that status was never conclusively terminated, even though he also lived elsewhere; by another, because the decedent had property there; by another, because of activities the decedent carried on there, or affiliations he retained, or intentions that were or were not stated explicitly.

Result: Two or more states may impose income taxes during life as well as death taxes when an individual dies—unless he took steps to prevent this proliferation of overlapping taxes. These taxes obviously reduce the amounts his designated beneficiaries will receive and, in certain instances, may cut the beneficiaries off entirely.

The problem of the mobile executive

This potential problem is particularly serious for an executive who, during his business career, is frequently transferred by his employer to new locations as promotions occur or opportunities open up. A promising individual at a major national corporate enterprise might well be transferred to a different locale every few years. Or, a business or professional person may shift his base of operations from time to time because of changing business conditions, preferences as to living conditions or health requirements of his family or himself. Also, when an individual retires, he may move to a more hospitable climate, while not entirely severing all ties with his previous place of residence. At the same time, he may have a home in each of two or more states—a residence close to his job, a winter home, a summer beachfront cottage or a house where he expects to live when he retires. It is important to note that states may levy an income tax, but can no longer tax pensions paid to out-of-state retirees. (H.R. 394, 1/10/96.)

A mixed bag of multiple claims

One of the many spectacular examples of how a person's estate can be almost depleted by overlapping state death taxes was that of John T. Dorrance, head of the Campbell Soup Company. New Jersey assessed its death tax on the grounds that Dorrance was domiciled in that state, paid property taxes, voted, had church membership, made reference to New Jersey law in his will and died there. Pennsylvania assessed its tax on the grounds that he was born there, had a large and attractive home in the state that he occupied for considerable time and that, wherever else he may have lived, his real home was Pennsylvania. In each state, the highest court upheld the applicability of its own death tax. The US Supreme Court refused to overturn the state courts' decisions, declaring (1) that the subject was domiciled in New Jersey under the law of that state when he died and (2) that he was domiciled in Pennsylvania under the law of that commonwealth when he died as well. As a result of the Court's ruling, very little of Dorrance's $40 million estate was left for his chosen beneficiaries. In effect, his beneficiaries were the states of New Jersey and Pennsylvania.

This problem doesn't usually involve real property, discussed below, for one state cannot tax the transfer of property that is fixed permanently in another state. But such intangibles as securities and money, and movable property such as jewelry and works of art, may be taxed by any state whose laws cover the situation. And even though a decedent's home in State A can't be subjected to a death tax by State B, the fact that he had a home in State A does not mean that he wasn't also domiciled in State B. Multiple death taxes may be and frequently are imposed by states where the decedent lived for any period of time. In addition, if a decedent owned a significant proportion of a corporation's stock, the state in which that company's headquarters are located may also try to impose death taxes.

In determining the application of one state's death taxes, it is immaterial whether the same property was also subject to death taxes in another state. To be relieved of multiple state death taxes, it must be shown that a wrong has been suffered through the imposition of plural taxes. That can't be established if the definition of "domicile" is met in two or more different states. As the Supreme Court declared in another case involving multiple state taxes, "the Constitution of the United States does not guarantee that the decisions of state courts shall be free from error."

Change of domicile requires intent

Most often, the problem of multiple death taxes arises if an individual has unquestionably established domicile in a particular state, but subsequently lives in one or more other states. The state where he first lived, regardless of how many years ago, will still claim him unless it can be shown that his absence from the state or his residence elsewhere was coupled with an intent to terminate absolutely his domicile. For example, if someone moves to another state for health reasons and acquires a residence there, he might return to the first state when his health improves.

Presence in another state is not equated with abandonment of domicile in the first state. An instruction sheet issued by New York State declares: "A domicile once established continues until a new one is acquired. To effect a change in domicile, there must be both an intent to change domicile as well as an actual change. In deciding whether both requirements are met, a person's acts, rather than his statements, control."

A married couple who traveled extensively was deemed to be domiciled in the state where they maintained an apartment and spent time between lengthy travels. In another case, the decedent, a long-time resident of Connecticut, owned and operated a chain of stores in New York City, where he kept an apartment. Shortly before his death, he began a plan of liquidation with his accountant. His stores were put up for sale, and many were actually sold. Later in the year, he moved to Florida, declared residency, registered to vote and obtained a driver's license. He also filed a final Connecticut income tax return although his home had not yet been sold. He passed away soon after, leaving homes in Connecticut, New York and Florida, as well as a few remaining New York City stores in his asset mix. This situation was ripe for dispute, and all three states sought a portion of the estate. Unfortunately, they each were partially successful.

When you move, make a clean break

In another situation, an individual who was a corporate executive in New York City and had a home in the state was deemed to be domiciled in New York at the time of her death even though (1) she owned a home in Florida where she spent much time, (2) declared in her will that she was a resident of Florida and (3) paid a poll tax in Florida. The New York court that upheld imposition of that state's tax pointed out that her bank accounts and safe-deposit boxes were in New York, her contributions were primarily to New York charities and her principal social interests were in New York.

One person who had a residence in State A was deemed by the local courts to be domiciled there when he died, although he was living in State B at the time of his death and had voted there. The court believed that he hadn't abandoned State A as his domicile because he continued to make use of physicians, dentists and brokers there.

The place where one votes is not decisive, for voting requirements differ. However, it is best to change your voting place when you relocate. A person who allegedly moved to State B was subject to death taxes in State A because she filed an income tax return in that state on the resident, rather than the nonresident, form.

One individual owned and lived in a house in State A, which held that he was domiciled there at the time of his death. But inasmuch as he had sold this residence and was constructing a new one in State B, the latter claimed him as a resident even though he had never lived in this house, on the grounds that he had expressed an *intent* to live in State B.

In another case, an individual who maintained church membership in State A where she was once domiciled was found not to have severed her ties with the state even though she was living elsewhere when she died.

Ancillary administrations

Even if a person is an acknowledged resident of State A but owns real property in State B, it is likely that some form of probate administration will be required in State B upon his death. Each state differs in the procedure, cost and length of time of such administration. Avoid multiple administrations if possible.

If you own real estate in states other than where you reside, it may be wise to place the properties in a trust to avoid ancillary administration. The trust may still have to file some documents with the court in some states and/or file a tax proceeding. However, such action will decrease the delay of the usual ancillary process as well as expense.

Conclusions and advice

• Check with local counsel as to the relevant laws of the state in which you live.

• When you move to a different state, sever all existing ties. Establish a new religious affiliation, club memberships, physicians, dentists, banks, safe-deposit boxes and charities. Do not retain affiliations in your former state simply because of sentimental reasons. An individual might want to keep up his church affiliation because he was married there. But, there are less costly ways of remembering a marriage. A state can be alerted to an opportunity to assert its death tax long after a former resident has moved. A typical case was a news account about someone who lived thousands of miles away from the state in which he was once domiciled. The newspaper mentioned that he "still returns to...see his doctor and dentist." Predictably, the state made a follow-up notation in its records for the time of his eventual death.

• When an individual moves from state to state, it is easy to overlook certain items. Check whether any active bank accounts have been left behind. Not only can such an account cause state death tax complications, but the forgotten money can be forfeited. After a number of years (which varies from state to state), an inactive bank account must be turned over to the state by a process known as *escheat*.

• Do not assume that because your attorney says you are now domiciled in State A, you are not also domiciled in State B for death tax purposes. Or in States C, D and E as well.

• File a declaration of domicile with the clerk of the court in the state in which you intend to reside.

Chapter Fifty-Two

LET GO OF ALL RETAINED STRINGS

Now is the time to plan that your estate won't be unnecessarily large for tax purposes at the time of your death. This does not mean impoverishing yourself to any degree. It means letting go of the strings you may hold to various properties and interests. Perhaps there is no longer any reason for you to retain the power to control outcomes or results. Or, you may have forgotten that you possess powers over property.

Your estate includes property that you still control

When an individual dies, her gross estate includes the value of any property she owns. It also includes the value of property the decedent gave away many years ago if she still possessed any meaningful control over it at the time of death. For example, if she gave away the property, but retained the right to reclaim it under certain conditions, or if she had the right to say who would receive the property or its income or any part of it, even though she herself can't be a beneficiary, she hasn't let go of dominion over this property. If she can control the ultimate ownership or use of assets when she dies, the actual ownership of these properties isn't determined until the moment of death. The final disposition of the assets is established only when she dies, and the value of these assets becomes part of her gross estate.

Right to change beneficiary of your insurance

Frequently, an individual purchases insurance on her own life and later gives the policy to another person such as her husband. The change of ownership of the policy is duly recorded on the insurance company's books. But she reserves the right to change the name of the beneficiary, which is quite likely her spouse when she gives him the policy. *Typical reason:* If he should die before she does, the proceeds will go to his estate or to his nominee, meaning that the money will go to his brother or friend rather than to persons the insured individual would prefer, such as her own sister. But if at the time of her death she holds any significant incident of ownership of the policy on her life, even though the policy is no longer hers, the proceeds will be includable in her gross estate. These incidents include the right to change the name of the beneficiary or the power to borrow against the policy. (See Chapter Thirty-One, "Planning with Life Insurance.") Consider notifying the insurance company that you have renounced all rights to modify the policy or any provision thereof.

Retained life estate

An individual's gross estate includes the value of any property she has transferred that is subject to a retained life estate. For example, a husband deeds over to his wife the house where they reside. If he continues to live there without paying rent, the Internal Revenue Service will interpret this to mean that even if nothing was said, he retained the right of occupancy until his death. The property didn't really belong to his wife until the moment of his death, and its value is thrown into his estate. *What to do:* At the time of the gift, the husband should write to his wife stating that her ownership is complete and without conditions and that he would stay in this house only if and at such times as she invited him to do so. This is not an empty gesture. In a well-publicized situation, a wife became disenchanted with her husband, changed the locks and proved that the husband had indeed been living in her house only at her pleasure.

If a parent gives corporate stock to her child but reserves the right to cash the dividend checks, the value of the stock will be included in her gross estate. Her right to cash the checks implies that she still owns the stock.

If an individual gives a valuable painting to a museum subject to the condition that the work of art hang in her home until she dies, its value will be part of her estate. Consider completely parting with such artwork.

Transfers taking effect at death

A decedent's gross estate includes the value of all transfers that take effect at her death if until then, she had the right to control or change the way in which the property was enjoyed. This would be the case even if she gave the property itself away many years ago and couldn't get it back for herself despite changed wishes or economic circumstances. For example, she may have transferred money irrevocably to a trust for the benefit of her children. If she reserved the right to say how much of the trust's income or principal each child would receive each year, the trust principal will be part of her estate. On the other hand, if the trustee, a truly independent party, had full discretion as to the distribution of the income and was familiar with and sympathetic to the grantor's desires, the same results could be obtained without estate tax liability for the grantor. In addition, reserving the right to apportion income might have made sense when the children were young and inexperienced and without financial means. But now, they may have acquired expertise in handling their own money. Is it really necessary to retain the strings attached to the trust funds?

Power to alter, amend, revoke or terminate

Included in an individual's gross estate is the value of any property she had transferred in trust or otherwise in situations where the property was subject to her power to alter, amend, revoke or terminate (revocable trusts) up to the moment of her death. Perhaps she never had any intention of interfering with the arrangement, but her lawyer wanted his client to have flexibility. Reconsider whether you actually need these powers.

An individual may set up a trust for the benefit of her two children, who are identified by name. But the trust agreement allows her the right to add the names of any children subsequently born. She has the right to change enjoyment of property, which would otherwise have been shared only by the first two children. Should she possess this right at the time she dies, the property is includable in her gross estate. Even if she hadn't added the name of a later born child, she had the right to do so—and that establishes taxability. But, as she grows older, she and her spouse cannot, or choose not to, have any more children. Renunciation of the right to add additional names to the trust agreement would mean that she no longer has the right to alter or amend it.

An individual's estate may also include the value of stock properly transferred to an irrevocable trust for the benefit of others if the IRS finds that she still controlled the corporation. Perhaps, as her attentions become more focused on other activities, she no longer needs to retain control. As the IRS looks at each case on its own merits, she should consider whether she still wants to retain control in view of the estate tax consequences.

Estate tax "freeze" is narrowing

An estate "freeze" is a technique that has the effect of limiting the estate tax value of property held by an older generation and passing any appreciation in the property to a younger generation. Generally, the older generation retains income from, or control over, the property.

In order to effect a freeze, the older generation transfers an interest in a business or other property that is likely to appreciate in value, while retaining an interest in the property that is less likely to appreciate. Because the value of the transferred interest increases while the value of the retained interest remains relatively constant, the older generation has "frozen" the value of the property in the transferor's estate for estate tax purposes.

In one common estate-freeze transaction, the "preferred-interest freeze," an individual owning preferred and residual interests in a corporation or partnership transfers the residual interest to a younger generation while retaining the preferred interest. The preferred interest may enjoy preferred rights as to income or management. It may also carry discretionary rights regarding the amount, timing or fact of payment. Such discretionary rights include (1) a right to "put" the frozen interest for an amount equal to the liquidating preference of the frozen interest, (2) a right to liquidate an entity and to receive assets or (3) a right to convert the nonappreciating retained interest into an appreciating interest. Another common estate-freeze transaction involves the retention of use in a trust owning the grantor's residence for a term of years. For example, a parent may transfer her residential property for the ultimate benefit of a child to an irrevocable trust in which the parent retains the right to reside in same for a term of years. Or, older and younger generations may jointly purchase present and remainder interests in property from a third party. All these transactions shift future appreciation in the property to the younger generation.

Under another common freeze device, a member of an older generation grants a member of the younger generation an option to purchase property at a fixed or formula price. Such an option may be part of a buy–sell agreement under which the survivor (or the corporation) has the right to purchase stock from the estate of the first to die. An option may freeze the value of property at the strike price, which in turn may be below the fair market value of the property at the date of death.

The transfer of a residual interest in a corporation or partnership for less than full and adequate consideration is a gift. The retention for a term of years or a life estate in a trust or property is a gift if the value of the remainder interest exceeds the value of any consideration paid for such interest. Any restriction on the sale or transfer of property, as an option or buy–sell agreement, may reduce the fair market value for gift tax purposes.

Prior to the enactment of the Revenue Reconciliation Act of 1990, the law provided that if an individual in effect transferred property that has a disproportionately large interest of the potential appreciation in an enterprise while retaining an interest or right in the enterprise, then the transferred property was includable in her gross estate. Dispositions of either the transferred or retained property prior to the transferor's death resulted in a "deemed" gift equal to the amount that would have been includable had the transferor died at the time of the transfer. In the case of transfers made after October 8, 1990, the law now provides new and very complicated rules designed to assure

302

accurate determination of the value of property subject to transfer tax. The purpose is (1) to provide a well-defined and administrative set of rules, (2) to allow business owners who are not abusing the transfer tax system to engage freely in standard intrafamily transactions without being subject to severe tax consequences and (3) to deter abuse by making unfavorable assumptions regarding certain retained rights. The taxable estate (or taxable gift) of a transferor who retained rights with possible value is increased through the assumption that the possible value is present.

The new rules, which seek to curb abuses in freezing estate tax values through intrafamily "arrangements," also attempt to legitimize transactions that represent bona fide arrangements with extrinsically determinable valuations. The result is a complex series of provisions. Any arrangements to shift less than complete interests between family members should be discussed in advance with competent counsel.

There is no time limit for IRS assessment of gift tax in the case of an undisclosed or inadequately disclosed transfer, regardless of whether a gift tax return was filed for other transfers in that same year. That places a strict burden of proof on disclosures to the Service of the nature of both transferred and retained rights. The taxpayer must "show his hand."

Let go!

An individual may give cash, bearer securities or jewelry to someone else. The donor might say, "I'll keep this property for you in my safe-deposit box for reasons of security; here is a set of keys." It will take persuasive evidence to establish that the donor hasn't retained an interest in the property if she also keeps a set of keys. An aunt may make a recorded gift of the funds in her savings account to her niece. But if, at the time of her death, the money was still in this account, and she continued to have a valid signature card on file with the bank, she hadn't let go of her dominion over the property for estate tax purposes.

Conclusions and advice

- Act promptly to sever all strings to property which you no longer need. Don't retain options or powers that are not required. Cutting these strings within three years of the time you die will not salvage the situation.

- Make a dry run through your assets with an experienced estate planner to detect any retained strings in insurance policies and trust agreements.

- Do not assume that what made sense at the time you created ownership interests or conducted transfers still makes sense in the light of changing circumstances. Review your arrangements regularly.

- Do not assume that you will always be more competent than your beneficiaries to make decisions. Their experience and knowledge may have removed any reason for you to exercise benevolent paternalism.

- Do not continue to hold the power to say who is going to get what and when, especially if you are absolutely convinced that you'll never exercise this power. It is possession of the power, and not its exercise, that throws the subject property into your gross estate.

- Do not think you can "freeze" the value of a business in your estate by transferring assets currently to designated beneficiaries while retaining some control over the enterprise. Special valuation rules apply when there is a gift or other transfer to a family member and the donor (transferor) retains significant rights in the property or its income. The taxable amount of the gift includes the value of the retained right if there is genuine uncertainty as to whether the donor ever will "let go" of this interest before she dies. These retained rights may be valued at zero for gift tax purposes. However, powers or rights that are retained by the transferor and allowed to lapse are taxed as gifts at the time of the lapse. Also, the statute of limitations on the assessment of gift tax by the IRS does not bar assessment of the tax at any time if the transfer is not disclosed to the Service with sufficient detail about the true nature of the transferred and retained interests.

Chapter Fifty-Three

THE DRY RUN

To avoid the pitfalls that can frustrate the best of intentions, an individual should conduct a dry run with her estate planner. An excellent mechanism for this is the federal estate tax return, Form 706. This is a formidable list of schedules, which few estate planners think of showing to their clients, but it is well worth the trouble. If an individual sees the questions and information that must be answered and supplied by somebody else after he dies, he will probably realize that he'd better supply these answers while he is able to do so. Reproduced as Appendix E are the first three pages of Form 706. Take the time to review them, answer the questions and to fill out, including the estimated values of your assets and deductions. You will gain a glimpse of whether your estate (and that of your spouse) is taxable at the federal level and you'll see just how thorough the federal tax return and audit may be.

To see why this is helpful for other reasons, consider "Schedule E: Jointly Owned Property." Only the owner may know how much of the cost was furnished by other parties. Then there is "Schedule G: Transfers During Decedent's Life." There may be no statute of limitations here; you are probably the only person who can supply full details of such transfers.

Other schedules brought to the testatrix's attention can be used to obtain information she may not have known was necessary. Some schedules may involve matters she never understood, such as "Schedule H: Powers of Appointment." "Schedule D: Insurance on Decedent's Life" can ascertain whether she has retained any incident of ownership, such as the right to change the name of the beneficiary or to borrow against the policy. "Schedule M: Bequests, etc., to Surviving Spouse" can distinguish between deductible and nondeductible interests, with the opportunity of providing for qualified terminable interest property or eliminating terminable interests if desired. This may be the time to explore how to best utilize the marital deduction and to assess if that is even desirable under the 2001 tax law. Married couples should decide if they need the full utilization of the unified credit effective exemptions amounts in both estates.

Regarding "Schedule Q: Credit for Tax on Prior Transfers," the testatrix is probably the only person who can establish her estate's entitlement. This refers to property inherited from anyone whose death preceded hers by less than 10 years, assuming that that person's estate was subject to tax.

"Schedule O: Charitable, Public and Similar Gifts and Bequests" should lead to inquiry into whether the donees are still on the all-important, ever-changing IRS-approved list. Ascertain, preferably by an affirmative statement from the major donees, that discrimination is not being practiced. Was anything promised to you, perhaps by unilateral action, by a recipient or designated donee? If so, decline it in writing. Have you named a backup donee?

The federal estate tax form requires information about the decedent's personal representative, which should focus attention on the executors. Are they qualified, interested and willing to do the job competently? Are successors or contingent executors named? Usually, the original will is needed. Who knows where the latest version of this document is located? Has it been reviewed in light of family and economic changes, or modifications in the law? Can the will be obtained instantly upon the death of the decedent? If the will is in her safe-deposit box, remember that it will probably be sealed by the bank upon death until it can be opened in the presence of a representative of the state tax authorities or the IRS. That delay may be undesirable. (Use Appendix A and keep the attached documents up-to-date.)

Information is requested about any individual who receives benefits from the estate, "for example, as beneficiary of a trust...." This should be the basis for investigating any retained rights the testatrix had in the trust, such as the right to change dispositions or modify any arrangement. The advisability of severing any retained interests should be reviewed. The actual trust instrument should be examined, for an individual's recollection can prove unsatisfactory.

Conclusions and advice

- Even if your will, insurance policies, trust agreements and other documents were prepared by highly competent persons, have them checked by somebody with estate planning expertise. An individual who is knowledgeable in wills, for example, may be uninformed about current tax legislation and the special language of the estate or other tax laws. For example, a specialist in wills may not appreciate the tax significance of a general power of appointment that is not referred to as such.

- See that your attorney, accountant and executor carry ample malpractice insurance.

- Do not rely on answers or advice from the Internal Revenue Service. Your questions to the IRS may not have been complete. See *Your Rights as a Taxpayer*, IRS Publication 1.

- Do not assume that your attorney, accountant and executor have up-to-date familiarity with estate planning. This is a highly technical specialty in which a generalist may not be fully versed.

- Make certain that your executor-to-be sees a blank federal estate tax return (Form 706) to know what he will need to prepare, supervise and at least sign. Would he have doubts as to what he is getting into? Will he refuse to serve, which might make it necessary for a court to name a replacement?

- The dry run should include the recognition of areas on the tax return that the IRS may probe. For example, there are increasingly severe accuracy-related and other penalties. Attach to your tax return Form 8275, *Disclosure Statement*. This form (assuming it is properly prepared) advises the Service of items or positions that you are able to document. Even if ultimately it is determined that your position was incorrect, you are not subject to an accuracy-related penalty by reason of negligence or disregard of the rules. Use Form 8275R, *Regulation Disclosure Statement*, for disclosure of positions contrary to IRS regulations.

Chapter Fifty-Four

A LETTER TO YOUR EXECUTOR

Few people complete the necessary final step of properly outlining how to avoid erosion of the estate.

Justifying your income tax returns

The accuracy of federal income tax returns can usually be established to a considerable degree during an audit. The taxpayer may explain why certain items weren't shown as taxable income, because they were inheritances, gifts or repayments. He may show what he paid for recently sold securities, or explain the nature of items claimed as medical expenses. He may be able to demonstrate the portion of the original cost of jointly owned property paid by one or more co-owners. If, however, the IRS examines these tax returns after the taxpayer's death, the tax will predictably increase by default and reduce the amount for the beneficiaries.

Do your heirs know where your tax records and backup information are located or what you have done and why? The burden of proof is on the taxpayer—even though deceased.

Defense against claims

Claims of every conceivable nature could be filed against the decedent's estate. Will anyone be able to prove from checkbooks whether these amounts have been paid or settled? Someone may claim ownership of real estate, jewelry or other items in the decedent's possession at the time of death. Does anyone else know the location of deeds, titles, bills of sale, invoices, receipts and insurance policies?

An individual may have relied heavily on his accountant, lawyer, broker or insurance agent. Does anybody know them?

An individual should leave unmistakable instructions that in the event of his death, a spouse, children or housekeeper do not throw away any records until they are reviewed by his accountant, attorney or executor.

Briefing your executor

Your designated executor must be in possession of all facts, figures and substantiation that you would have at your disposal in order to do his best for your estate.

What to tell your executor

Prepare and keep current the forms attached as Appendices A, B and C. Write a letter to your executor now, letting him know about your belongings, records and financial affairs. Update it periodically. You may seal the envelope and leave it where it can be found later. Be sure to include:

1. Location of your final executed will, trust and pour-over will.

2. Location of your cemetery plot and its deed, registration and burial instructions. Do not put them in your safe-deposit box, because a bank will probably deny access to your box until it can be opened in the presence of a tax officer.

3. Names and addresses of the designated guardians for minor children should they be orphaned by your death.

4. The location and identifying number of your safe-deposit box, the keys or combination. The executor should take inventory immediately.

5. The location of all checking and savings-bank accounts. Who has the power of attorney or signature authorization to draw on these accounts? Should a stop be placed on withdrawals?

6. Credit card account numbers. Your executor should cancel them at once.

7. The source of any cash in a safe-deposit box or in your home or office. In the absence of proof to the contrary, the Internal Revenue Service will consider any unexplained cash as previously untaxed income. This presumption can be refuted by credible evidence. For example, there may be a letter to your executor stating that Social Security checks or horse-track winnings (reported) will be converted into cash, to be kept in the box as an emergency fund.

8. Location of any bank accounts that are not in your name. *Example:* Deposits in a numbered bank account in Switzerland.

9. The location and description of any property that is not certain to come to the attention of the executor. You may have loaned property, sent property on consignment to a dealer or deposited property as collateral for a loan.

10. The best market for properties you own. You may have unusual belongings that can best be sold in special markets or to hobbyists or collectors.

11. The names and addresses of your accountant, attorney, insurance agent, bank officer, realtor, physician. The executor may have to prove that you were mentally competent at the time you wrote your will.

12. Schedule and location of all life insurance policies, including employer group insurance certificates and lapsed policies.

13. Schedule of property, liability, malpractice, umbrella insurance. This may save the estate from the consequences of a lawsuit.

14. Brokers' confirmation slips for all purchases of securities to establish the original cost of all securities sold. If these slips have been discarded, note the dates shown by transfer agents on stock certificates and registered bonds to indicate when purchased. Prices can be established from newspaper files. Keep all letters about stock dividends, split-ups, rights and reorganizations. These may modify your tax basis by establishing what you originally paid for the securities.

15. Names and addresses of all prior employers, regardless of when your employment terminated. Many corporate pension plans provide vested rights after certain periods of service, to be payable at some designated future time (such as your 65th birthday) or upon the occurrence of a stated event, even though you are no longer with the company.

16. If you work for a corporation that is subject to the Pension Reform Act of 1974 (in general, any company engaged in interstate commerce), the employer is required by law to provide you with a complete description of its pension plan and computations of your rights under the plan. They may provide explanations of entitlements that should be claimed when you die.

17. Record of governmental employment such as the armed forces. Show the branch of service, your serial number and approximate dates to look for veterans' or survivors' rights.

18. Copies of income tax returns without regard to statutes of limitations. Don't discard these after three years or any other date.

19. Location of current and past checkbooks and canceled checks to furnish proof that bills and claims have been paid and to indicate the cost of particular property, of casualty losses or establishment of the tax basis of property.

20. Location of birth certificate or passport, for pensions, Social Security, primary and derivative rights and retirement programs.

21. Location of marriage certificate for such purposes as the marital deduction, joint gifts, determining dower and curtesy rights and survivors' rights.

22. Divorce decree or reference to the court that issued it, with the date, to settle the question about who is the decedent's surviving spouse.

23. Copies of federal gift tax returns filed at any time.

24. The names and dates of death of anyone from whom you have inherited property so that an executor may be able to claim credit for the tax on prior transfers if the person died less than 10 years before you. State the name of that person's executor.

25. Have you been named in connection with reversionary, contingent or remainder rights in a will or trust agreement, either yours or someone else's? There may be potential interests to be investigated by your executor.

26. If you ever set up a trust, specify where a copy is located.

27. Have you ever guaranteed or endorsed a note or somebody else's obligation? Your executor may be able to settle any claims before they mature.

28. Does anyone owe you money? Have you loaned out property? Advise your executor as to any documentation or proof, such as witnesses or correspondence.

29. Are there any pending tax or other refund claims? Should there be?

30. Are there any unfavorable factors that could justify your executor's valuing any of your property at less than fair market value? (See Chapter Forty-Six, "Valuation of Estate Assets.")

31. Have you any affirmative statements from approved charitable organizations to which you made contributions or bequests that they are not engaging in any form of discrimination? (See Chapter Forty-Eight, "Avoiding Disallowance of Charitable Bequests.")

32. Have you received any income in respect of a decedent? This is income earned by but not yet taxed to someone from whom you have received an inheritance. The value of this person's right to receive the income was included in the estate tax paid for him. The beneficiary is entitled to deduct a portion of the estate tax, based upon the ratio of the right's value to the decedent's total assets.

Conclusions and advice

• If you move to a different state, have a new will prepared by a lawyer who practices there. The will should be signed by resident witnesses.

• Be aware of how long to retain various documents. Obtain the information from IRS Publication 552, *Recordkeeping for Individuals*.

• Advise your spouse not to be too hasty in throwing away papers and files which the executor might need.

• Close inactive bank accounts so that the monies will not go to the state.

• Do not allow anyone other than an attorney skilled in estate planning to draw up your will, trust agreement or other dispositive document.

• Do not assume that your estate's assets can be readily recognized and collected by your fiduciary. Leave a paper trail for your executor to follow.

• Advise your designated executor not to sell any property before paying the federal estate tax. Recently, it was held that a hasty executor was personally liable for the tax when insufficient estate assets remained to pay it.

• Help your executor avoid penalties for undervaluation of property by providing him with all relevant facts.

• Urge him to make a conscientious effort to estimate the estate tax. Otherwise, the estate may not have enough cash or readily realizable assets to pay the estate tax within the required nine months.

Chapter Fifty-Five

MAINTENANCE OF CONFIDENTIALITY

A will is often considered public information. When submitted to the appropriate court for approval (probate), the document is placed on file. Depending on state laws, it may be examined by interested parties or by the merely inquisitive. With some planning, it may be possible to keep this information confidential.

Trust agreements aren't public documents

Although wills are "published," *inter vivos* trusts usually are not filed with any court. Therefore, one of the advantages of using a trust is confidentiality. Yet, even your will can achieve some confidentiality by using a testamentary trust with designated property passing to the trustees. Usually, the inner workings of a testamentary trust are not accessible to the public, and the trustee need file court paperwork only periodically.

The person for whose benefit the *inter vivos* trust was set up, the allocation of properties, the details as to the interests of life tenants and remaindermen and the like are known only to the grantor/decedent, the trustees and the local court, if it is called upon by the interested parties to decide whether a trustee has lived up to her fiduciary responsibilities. The Internal Revenue Service is also authorized to examine trust instruments, but, by law, the Service and its agents are prohibited from making any revelations to outsiders. As a result, the public is excluded from knowledge about the contents of trust instruments.

However, this is not the case with dispositions by will. For example, in 1976, a superior court judge in New Jersey refused to permanently seal the will of William Randolph Hearst on the grounds that this would be equivalent to denying the public the right to know what was done in the probate court.

Therefore, the *inter vivos* trust (see Chapters Eleven and Twelve) achieves a higher degree of confidentiality in the making of transfers during a donor's lifetime; no one has access to details of property dispositions after they have been made to the trust. It also maintains such confidentiality after the grantor's death. However, a testamentary trust is not an "open book."

Co-ownership of property as a form of will

An individual may use a form of property ownership that takes the place of a will in disposing of assets at the time of her death. (See Chapter Twenty-Two, "Choice of Forms of Ownership.") If she owns property jointly with some-one else, with rights of survivorship in each co-owner, the property automatically passes to the surviving co-owner(s) upon the demise of one co-owner. No outsider needs to know of this co-ownership with right of survivorship. Unpublicized passage of this property to the survivor isn't affected by the fact that the IRS includes the full value of the jointly held property in the gross estate of the first co-owner to die even absent sufficient proof by the estate's executor that part of the property actually was owned by someone else. The value of the entire property may be included in the decedent's estate for tax purposes, but the property itself passes to the survivor(s). It is not subject to probate, with its publicity and delays, for the executor has nothing to administer and nothing to account for. The property isn't the decedent's after she dies. Everything has been arranged prior to the appointment of the executor.

Joint accounts

Joint bank accounts or joint brokerage accounts may be established with an intended beneficiary. The latter becomes the sole owner upon the death of the person who created the account if it is set up properly. If the party who is named co-owner of the account makes no contribution to it or withdrawal from it, setting up the account creates no federal gift tax liability for the individual who funds the account. What happens is only known by the bank or broker.

Disposition by gift

Property can be disposed of other than by a published will if it is given away during the owner's lifetime.

Avoidance of litigation

If there is litigation involving the estate, the will or earlier disposition, details may become available to the public. What happens during a court trial is customarily published in transcripts available to any curious or interested party. For example, the judge's decision in tax cases, generally preceded by a detailed account of the facts and figures, is published by tax information services. Financial publications or the local press may pick up the story from them.

To avoid publicity, plan to minimize the possibility of litigation. Lawsuits most often result from one of two main scenarios:

1. The IRS may force litigation if agreement on tax differences can't be reached, for example, in the valuation of stock in a closely held corporation. Seek a compromise with the Service to avoid litigation. Litigation with the IRS is usually costly and unpredictable. To avoid the risk of publicity that could result from court action and publication of the details, consider yielding entirely in the dispute if there seems to be an irreconcilable difference of opinion and if the rewards and gains are not equal to the negative impact of the costs and publicity.

2. Disappointed heirs may challenge the will in court, perhaps on the grounds that undue influence was exerted upon the decedent or that she was mentally unsound at the time the will was signed. This, too, might be settled by the executor and the other heirs before the matter actually goes to trial. Alternatively, some individuals provide in their wills that if any beneficiary contests in court what he is designated to receive or the validity of the will as a whole, his bequest is to be canceled automatically in favor of another named party, such as the remainderman or a designated charitable organization. Be wary of such clauses, however, as some states do not favor them.

Conclusions and advice

• Before the will is finalized, work out what jewelry, real estate, securities or other assets, each beneficiary will receive so that there will be no squabbles. But do not assume that dispositions in your will are only of interest to individuals designated as beneficiaries.

• Leave percentages to the beneficiaries in your will so that no description of property or specific dollar amount is available to the public.

• Do not assume that your executor will be discreet.

• Do not rely on joint ownership of property to eliminate the need for a will. Jointly owned property with right of survivorship can be substituted for a will, but presumably you will also have other property that isn't co-owned, perhaps for good reason. If you don't have a will, this property will be distributed according to the state's intestacy laws.

• Any confidential information that could produce additional tax if "leaked" to the IRS by someone familiar with the facts could be "squealed" to the Service in return for a share of the taxes that are collected as a result of this information. In addition, the informant's identity is protected by law.

• When related companies file consolidated returns, owners of at least 1% of the stock of any of these companies can see the returns.

Chapter Fifty-Six

SAFEGUARDING YOUR ESTATE PLANNING DOCUMENTS

Usually one of the last questions asked in any conference where estate planning documents are executed is where to keep the documents. A simple question with a simple answer? Unfortunately, all too often clients do not listen to the answers, with sometimes tragic results.

What documents need special attention?

Documents that need to be safeguarded or readily available include:

1. Your health documents, advance medical directives (living wills), health-care proxies and powers of attorney should always be readily accessible.

2. Business documents (buy–sell agreements, etc.) as well as *inter vivos* trusts (some file annual tax returns) can be executed in multiple duplicate originals. Distribute originals to several individuals.

3. Life insurance policies. Although insurance companies generally have records of the owners, insureds and beneficiaries, there are needless delays and paperwork if you cannot surrender the actual policy. Therefore, these policies deserve a high degree of care and safety.

4. Bank books, stock certificates, deeds, etc. are important evidence of your assets. Usually, your executor can obtain the actual asset as long as he knows you own it, but it is best to have the evidence as well.

5. Your last will and testament, a pour-over will and revocable trust or such other dispositive documents deserve a high degree of care and safety. In many states, only one original will is executed, and copies are often not permitted to be probated unless all interested parties agree.

Where do I keep these documents?

1. Keep a set of health documents and powers of attorney at home in an accessible place. Your health-care agent and attorney in fact should know where they are. Some clients prefer to give their physicians a copy of the health documents. The power of attorney is another matter. Some clients prefer not to give it to the agent, especially if it is a general power, for fear of unleashing unwanted use of the power. Discuss this with your estate planner as well as reconsider your choice of agent if you feel he cannot be trusted to have the power.

2. As noted above, trusts and business agreements can have multiple originals. If they are related to your annual tax return, give an original to your accountant and keep a copy at home. Your attorney will likely also keep a copy or an original, and you may wish to put an original in your bank safe-deposit box. Note that in many states the box is frozen on your death, but check with counsel on this matter. For documents that need not be accessed immediately, your safe-deposit box is appropriate. Your home safe, fireproof or otherwise, is never the best place for extremely important documents.

3. Due to the inconvenience of lost or stolen insurance policies, we suggest placing them in a bank safe-deposit box. Sometimes clients prefer to give the policies to the actual beneficiaries and allow them to safeguard such documents.

4. As noted above, bank books and the like may be kept at home, and most clients prefer to keep their stock certificates in their bank safe-deposit box.

5. Your last will and testament and/or your pour-over will and revocable trust are documents of special significance. As noted, in many states only one will is executed. Therefore, the need to keep it in the safest place is paramount. Using your safe-deposit box is a valid choice, especially in a state that does not freeze the box on death. However, many states do require such a freeze, and it takes quite a long time to gain access, usually with representatives of the state taxing authorities in attendance.

Another choice might be the safe-deposit box of your executor. Here, the problem might be the premature death of your fiduciary, but this may be overcome. Some clients give their wills to the executors and let them decide. Where the executor (or co-executor) is a bank or other corporate fiduciary, it usually can keep your documents in its corporate safe-deposit boxes.

Some clients leave the originals with their attorney, in the attorney's safe-deposit box. This arrangement has many drawbacks. In one case, a very prominent probate attorney prematurely passed away with nearly 600 client wills in his box. As he was a sole practitioner, it was up to his executor and the state bar association to step in and try to locate his clients.

There are other problems inherent in leaving your will with your attorney, such as relocating, forgetting, or executing a new set of documents. If the will is at the decedent's attorney's office, the family may not wish to hire this attorney to handle the estate for several reasons, but may feel uncomfortable asking for the will in his possession. All in all, there are some special circumstances where leaving your will with your attorney makes sense, but consider all of your choices.

Conclusions and advice

- Ask your estate planner where to keep all of your documents.

- Ask if your state freezes bank safe-deposit boxes upon death even if a living person also has signatory power. If that person still can have access after your death, consider keeping your documents in your safe-deposit box and placing your executor on the signature authorization card.

- Your home may be your castle, but it more than likely is not burglar-proof. Your documents are too important to be left open to this risk.

- As you (or your parents) age, consider bringing your children (or executor) into your confidence. Not only show them where your important documents are, but also consider working out some type of "joint custody" agreement, whether it be a joint bank safe-deposit box or simply one under the control of your children or executor.

- Keep your health-care documents accessible.

Appendix A

ESTATE PLANNING CHECKLIST AND QUESTIONNAIRE

_____/_____
Your Name/Your Spouse's Name

_____/_____
Your Date of Birth/Your Spouse's Date of Birth

_____
Last Date of Update

Please answer the following questions. Attach copies of any appropriate document and be sure to keep this in an accessible location in your home. Bring it with you when you see your estate planner, accountant, insurance counselor and/or financial planner. (Please circle **Yes** or **No**. Add requested information.)

1. Are you married?   Yes/No

2. Do you have any children or grandchildren?   Yes/No
   A: Their ages (signify by **C** or **GC**) _____

   _____

3. Do you have existing wills?   Yes/No
   A: When were they last updated or completed? _____
   B: Where are they located? _____
   C: Attach a copy of each to this checklist.

4. Do you have living wills and medical directives?   Yes/No
   A: When were they done? _____
   B: Where are they located? _____
   C: Attach a copy of each such document to this checklist.

5. Do you have a power of attorney?   Yes/No
   A: Who is appointed? _____
   B: When was it done? _____
   C: Does it have a specific gifting power?   Yes/No
   D: Attach a copy to this checklist.

320

6. How much life insurance do you own and on whom?

$_____ ; Insured_____

A: Who are the beneficiaries?_____

_____

B: Where are the policies?_____

_____

C: List all of the policies on a separate sheet of paper. Give insurance company name, address and policy number, face value and cash value, if you know it.

7. List on a separate sheet of paper your pension, profit sharing, stock bonus or deferred compensation plans. Also note Keogh plans and IRAs. Please also list all employers you have worked for in the past 30 years.

A: Who are the primary beneficiaries of these plans? _____

_____

B: Who are the secondary beneficiaries? _____

_____

8. Have you executed any trust instruments?   Yes/No

A: Where are they located? _____

_____

B: Dates of each trust. _____

_____

C: Name and address of each trustee.

_____

_____

_____

_____

_____

D: List on a separate piece of paper the assets owned by the trusts.

E: Attach a copy of each trust document.

9. Do you own any business entities or a substantial share in a business?

Yes/No

A: Name and Address of business

_____

_____

_____

_____

B: How much of an interest do you own? $ _____

C: Who is the contact person? _____

D: Do you know of any death benefits? If yes, what are they?

_____

_____

10. Do you have any business agreements and documents regarding interests in corporations, partnerships and sole proprietorships?   Yes/No
    A: Where are these located?_____
    B: What value would you place on these interests? $_____

11. Do you have instruments showing cost or adjusted basis of any assets held?   Yes/No
    A: Where are these documents located?_____
    B: List on a separate sheet of paper the assets and attach evidence of your cost or adjusted basis.

12. Do you have pre- or postnuptual agreements, separation agreements or divorce papers?   Yes/No
    A: Where are they located?_____
    B: Attorney who prepared them for you?_____
    _____

13. Do you have any instruments creating spouses' joint tenancies by the entirety or separate property in community property states?   Yes/No

14. Have you filed gift tax returns in the past?   Yes/No
    A: For what years?_____
    B: Name and address of accountant(s) who prepared them.
    _____
    _____
    _____

    C: Attach copies.

15. Have you lived in any other states within the last five years?   Yes/No
    A: Which states?_____
    B: Do you maintain any relationships within that state, such as with clubs, religious organizations, doctors, dentists, ownership of real estate, bank accounts, etc.?   Yes/No
    C: Where do you vote and file your income tax returns?
    Vote:_____
    Income tax:_____

16. If you are unmarried and/or have no children and would like others to share in your estate, who would they be?

Name(s):	Amount or %:	Address(s):

Appendix B

VITAL INFORMATION
FACT SHEET

Updated _____

Note: This information may prove helpful for you and your estate planner. It will be of vital assistance to heirs and your fiduciaries. Be sure to keep this document up-to-date, and we suggest you give each update to your attorney and your executor.

Part One	Your Information	Spouse's Information
Name		
Married (yes/no)		
Principal address		
City and state		
Home phone(s)		
Citizenship		
Employer & address		
Business telephone & ext.		
E-mail address		
Other residences (state(s))		
Prior residences (state(s))		
Date and place of birth		
Social Security number		
Date & place of marriage		
If divorced, names of		
former spouse(s), date &		
place of divorce(s)		

Part Two

Your children and stepchildren (indicate C for child or S for stepchild)

C/S	Name and Address	Birth Date	Social Security #	Spouse's Name

Part Three

Your grandchildren

Parents' Names	Names of Grandchildren	Birth Date	Social Security #	Grandchild's Spouse' Name

Part Four

Your parents

	Your Parents		Your Spouse's Parents	
Father:	Name:		Name:	
	Address:		Address:	
	DOB:	DOD:	DOB:	DOD:
Mother:	Name:		Name:	
	Address:		Address:	
	DOB:	DOD:	DOB:	DOD:

Part Five

Other dependents living in your household or whom you are supporting

Name	Relationship	Address	DOB

How much annual support do you supply them? $ _____

Do you intend to have it continue after your demise? Yes/No

Part Six

Medical History

Please list significant medical conditions for both you and your spouse and intended beneficiaries. *Note:* Consider including doctors' names.

Your history: _____
_____
_____

Your spouse's history: _____
_____

History of your children or other beneficiaries: _____
_____
_____

Part Seven

Your Estate Planning Team

Please list names, addresses and telephone numbers:

Attorney: _____

    How long have you been with this person or firm? _____

Accountant: _____

    How many years have they done your tax returns? _____

    Any gift tax returns? Yes/No

Life insurance adviser: _____

What policies do you own? (List on a separate sheet of paper if necessary.)
_____

Bankers and trust officers: _____
_____

Stockbrokers: _____

    Attach a separate sheet with an up-to-date summary of your accounts.

Executor: _____

    Successor executor: _____

Trustee: _____

    Successor trustee: _____

Designated guardian for minor children: _____

    Alternate guardian: _____

Investment adviser: _____

Financial planner: _____

Physician: _____

Clergyman: _____

Casualty insurance agent: _____

Business partners: _____

Closest relatives (other than those listed previously, i.e., siblings or cousins):

_____

_____

_____

Part Eight

Dispositive objectives

- Who are your primary beneficiaries and how do you want your assets distributed? _____

_____

_____

_____

  - If you and your spouse both die prematurely, should children receive their share of your estate at the age of majority or should it be held until they reach a more mature age?   Majority/Other

  - Do any of your children have special educational, medical or financial needs?   Yes/No

- Identify, in order of priority, the best money managers in your family.

_____

_____

_____

- Which of those listed above would also be good investors or be open to seeking investment advice from a trained professional?

_____

_____

_____

- Which of these would have the most empathy for your children and/or your spouse and children? _____

  - Would you consider co-trustees?   Yes/No

- Do you wish to reduce your estate taxes as much as possible without giving up the total control of your assets?   Yes/No

- Would you mind a trust for yourself?   Yes/No

- Is reducing income taxes of importance to you?   Yes/No

- Is gifting some of your assets now something you would be interested in discussing?   Yes/No

    - How much annual income or current assets can you afford to give away annually? $ _____

    - Do you have goals or other particular things you might like to see your donees do with these gifts?   Yes/No
    What? _____
    _____
    _____
    _____
    _____

- Do you wish to make charitable bequests? _____
Further details: _____
_____
_____
_____

- If none of your children were living at the time of your spouse's death, where would you want your estate to go? _____
_____
_____
_____

- Other comments.
_____
_____
_____
_____
_____
_____
_____
_____
_____
_____
_____

Appendix C

ASSET VALUATION AND FACT SHEET

Updated _____

Please complete the chart below which estimates the approximate values of your assets. Your planner needs to know the exact way in which they are owned (by community property, joint tenancy, or otherwise). You may complete the following schedules and carry back the totals to this page.

Provide estimated current values, in multiples of $1,000.

ASSETS	HUSBAND	JOINT TENANCY	WIFE
Cash & notes (Sched. A)	$	$	$
Real estate (Sched. B)			
Securities (Sched. C)			
Properties/partnerships			
LLCs (Sched. D)			
Life insurance (Sched. E)			
Retirement assets/ Plans (Sched. F)			
Tangible personal property (Sched. G)			
Miscellaneous (Sched. H)			
TOTALS	$	$	$
LIABILITIES			
Mortgages (Sched. I)			
Loans/notes (Sched. I)			
Other liabilities (Sched. I)			
TOTALS	$	$	$
NET WORTH	$	$	$

Note also that the use of this, as well as the pages of the Form 706 contained in Appendix E, can give you an idea if your estate is taxable at the federal level.

SCHEDULE A – CASH & NOTES

Provide estimated current values, in multiples of $1,000.

CASH ACCOUNTS	TYPE (CHKING, SAVS, C.D., MONEY MARKET)	HUSBAND	JOINT TENANCY	WIFE
Bank or other institution				
SUBTOTAL CASH ACCOUNTS		$	$	$
LOANS OR NOTES RECEIVABLE				
OBLIGOR RATE DATE DUE				
		$	$	$
SUBTOTAL LOANS AND NOTES		$	$	$
TOTALS		$	$	$
Comments:				

SCHEDULE B – REAL ESTATE

For valuation purposes, use your best estimate of current total values, without regard to any mortgages that may be outstanding. Mortgage information should be described in Schedule I. Please indicate if any property is a condominium, co-op or other restricted ownership. Also, add any vital information known only to you.

Provide estimated current values, in multiples of $1,000.

ADDRESS/ LOCATION	HUSBAND Cost Basis	Value	JOINT TENANCY Cost Basis	Value	WIFE Cost Basis	Value
1. Residence 1	$	$	$	$	$	$
2. Residence 2						
3.						
4.						
5.						
6.						
7.						
TOTALS		$		$		$

SCHEDULE C – SECURITIES

Provide estimated current values, in multiples of $1,000.

ASSET TYPE	HUSBAND Cost Basis	Value	JOINT TENANCY Cost Basis	Value	WIFE Cost Basis	Value
Publicly traded stocks	$	$	$	$	$	$
S corporation stocks						
Other close corp. stocks						
Corporate Bonds						
US gov't bonds, notes and bills						
Municipal bonds						
Mutual funds						
Other						
TOTALS		$		$		$

SCHEDULE D1 – PROPRIETORSHIPS/PARTNERSHIPS
(Including limited partnerships and tax shelters)

Provide estimated current values, in multiples of $1,000.

ASSET TYPE	HUSBAND		JOINT TENANCY		WIFE	
	Cost Basis	Value	Cost Basis	Value	Cost Basis	Value
	$	$	$	$	$	$
TOTALS		$		$		$

SCHEDULE D2
LIMITED LIABILITY COMPANIES (PARTNERSHIPS) (LLC/LLP)

Provide estimated current values, in multiples of $1,000.

ASSET TYPE	HUSBAND		JOINT TENANCY		WIFE	
	Cost Basis	Value	Cost Basis	Value	Cost Basis	Value
	$	$	$	$	$	$
TOTALS	$		$		$	

	TOTALS OF D1 AND D2
HUSBAND	$
JOINT TENANCY	$
WIFE	$

SCHEDULE E – LIFE INSURANCE

Provide estimated current values, in multiples of $1,000.

COMPANY	POLICY NO.	TERM, VARIABLE LIFE, UNIVERSAL LIFE OR WHOLE LIFE	FACE VALUE	CASH VALUE	LOANS	ANNUAL PREMIUM	OWNER	BENEFICIARY
INSURING LIFE OF HUSBAND								
			$	$	$	$		
TOTAL			$					
INSURING LIFE OF WIFE								
			$	$	$	$		
TOTAL			$					
INSURING LIFE OF HUSBAND AND WIFE (SECOND-TO-DIE)								
			$	$	$	$		
TOTAL			$					

SCHEDULE F – RETIREMENT ASSETS/PLANS

Provide estimated current values/account balances, in multiples of $1,000.

RETIREMENT ASSETS	HUSBAND	JOINT TENANCY	WIFE
IRA/ Keogh accounts	$	$	$
Pension plans			
401(k) plans			
Profit-sharing plans			
Deferred compensation arrangements			
Other			
TOTALS	$	$	$

SCHEDULE G – TANGIBLE PERSONAL PROPERTY

Provide estimated current values, in multiples of $1,000.

	HUSBAND	JOINT TENANCY	WIFE
Furniture and furnishings	$	$	$
Automobiles			
Artwork or art collections			
Other collections			
Goods in storage			
Jewelry			
Furs			
Other			
TOTALS	$	$	$

Describe collections, antiques, heirlooms, etc., that require special estate plan considerations, and give any other pertinent comments:

_____

_____

SCHEDULE H – MISCELLANEOUS

List any inheritances expected and the estimated value. Also, supply values where you have powers to control the dispositions of the assets.

Provide estimated current values, in multiples of $1,000.

	HUSBAND	WIFE
Interests in pending probate estates	$	$
Interests in existing trusts		
Expected interests in future estates/trusts		
TOTALS	$	$

Supply copies of wills and trusts and US gift tax returns (Form 709).

Indicate any fiduciary positions held by either husband or wife (executor, trustee, guardian, custodian).

_____

_____

_____

_____

_____

_____

_____

SCHEDULE I – LIABILITIES

List here only major liabilities, such as mortgages on real estate, notes of loans due to others, charitable pledges, etc.

Provide estimated current values, in multiples of $1,000.

	HUSBAND	JOINT TENANCY	WIFE
Mortgages (use same residence number as in schedule B)			
1. Residence 1	$	$	$
2. Residence 2			
3.			
4.			
5.			
6.			
7.			
TOTALS	$	$	$
Loans/notes (identify creditor)	$	$	$
TOTALS	$	$	$
Other liabilities (including charitable pledges)	$	$	$
TOTALS	$	$	$

UNIFIED RATE SCHEDULE: GIFT AND ESTATE TAX

Column A	Column B	Column C	Column D
Taxable amount over	Taxable amount not over	Tax on amount in column A	Rate of tax on excess over amount in column A **Percent**
$ 0	$ 0	$ 0	18
10,000	20,000	1,800	20
20,000	40,000	3,800	22
40,000	60,000	8,200	24
60,000	80,000	13,000	26
80,000	100,000	18,200	28
100,000	150,000	23,800	30
150,000	250,000	38,800	32
250,000	500,000	70,800	34
500,000	750,000	155,800	37
750,000	1,000,000	248,300	39
1,000,000	1,250,000	345,800	41
1,250,000	1,500,000	448,300	43
1,500,000	2,000,000	555,800	45
2,000,000	2,500,000	780,800	49
2,500,000	3,000,000	1,025,800	53
3,000,000		1,290,800	55

Tentative tax is increased by 5% of amount in excess of $10 million but not in excess of the amount at which the average tax rate equals 55%.

UNIFIED ESTATE & GIFT TAX CREDIT & FAMILY-OWNED BUSINESS EXCLUSION

Year	Applicable credit	Applicable exclusions	Business exclusions
2000 and 2001	220,550	675,000	625,000
2002 and 2003	229,800	700,000	600,000
2004	287,300	850,000	450,000
2005	326,300	950,000	350,000
2006 and thereafter	345,800	1,000,000	300,000
Nonresidents not citizens (no treaty provision)	13,000	60,000	n/a

GENERATION-SKIPPING TRANSFER TAX

GST tax exemption	$1,030,000**
GST tax rate	55%
Effective GST tax rate on direct skips at death	33.48%

**Indexed for inflation for decedents dying and gifts made after 2000.

COMPARISON OF PRE- AND POST-2001 TAX LAW

Pre-2001 Tax Law	New 2001 Tax Law		
Estate/Gift Tax Rates Top rate is 55%. Estate and gift tax unified credit is $675,000 in 2001. 5% surcharge on estates between $10,000,000 and $17,184,000. Gifts in excess of the $10,000 annual exclusion amount are taxed based on the given rate schedule.	**Commencing in 2002:** The lifetime gift tax effective exemption equivalent increases permanently to $1 million. Gift tax is not repealed in 2010 (see below). The 5% surcharge is repealed. The estate and gift tax rates and the estate tax exemption gradually change as shown below:		

Year	Estate/Gift Tax Rate	Exemptions
2002	50%	$1,000,000
2003	49%	$1,000,000
2004	48%	$1,500,000
2005	47%	$1,500,000
2006	46%	$2,000,000
2007	45%	$2,000,000
2008	45%	$2,000,000
2009	45%	$3,500,000
2010	Estate tax is zero 35% gift tax	N/A
After 2011	Return to 2001 Law: 55%	$1,000,000

Pre-2001 Tax Law	New 2001 Tax Law
Step-Up in Asset Basis at Death On the date of death (or alternate valuation date which is 6 months after the death), the decedent's estate assets receive a step-up in asset's basis to the fair market value as of the DOD or the alternate date.	**Commencing in 2002:** A modified carryover basis rule takes effect similar to the 1976 law. The cost basis of assets received from the decedent will carry over the beneficiary, with two modifications: 1. $1.3 million of additional basis will be permitted to be added to certain assets; or 2. $3 million of additional basis will be allowed to be added to assets transferred to a surviving spouse. Certain property defined by the law is excluded from the above exceptions and cannot be stepped up. The executor will have the duty of assigning the increased basis to the estate's assets.
Generation-skipping Transfer (GST) Tax: GST of 55% (maximum estate tax rate) imposed on transfers that skipped generations of amounts exceeding $1,060,000, adjusted annually for inflation.	**Commencing in 2002:** GST exemptions increases as the unified credit increases and the maximum tax rate decreases in conformity with the estate tax decline. **Effective 2010:** GST is eliminated for one year (2010). In 2011 it will return to the 2001 law unless Congress changes this provision.
Family–owned Business Estate Tax Exemption: Total Credit=$1,300,000 until 2004 After 2001, certain estates with family–owned businesses entitled to this additional exemption at death of $300,000.	**Commencing in 2002:** Added exemption is repealed as the unified credit exemption equivalent amount is $1,500,000 in 2004 thereby exceeding this exemption. Due to inflation, as of 1/1/02, this amount is adjusted to $1,100,000.

Form **706**
(Rev. November 2001)

Department of the Treasury
Internal Revenue Service

United States Estate (and Generation-Skipping Transfer) Tax Return

Estate of a citizen or resident of the United States (see separate instructions).
To be filed for decedents dying after December 31, 2000, and before January 1, 2002.
For Paperwork Reduction Act Notice, see page 25 of the separate instructions.

OMB No. 1545-0015

Part 1.—Decedent and Executor

1a Decedent's first name and middle initial (and maiden name, if any)	**1b** Decedent's last name	**2** Decedent's Social Security No.
3a Legal residence (domicile) at time of death (county, state, and ZIP code, or foreign country)	**3b** Year domicile established **4** Date of birth	**5** Date of death
6a Name of executor (see page 4 of the instructions)	**6b** Executor's address (number and street including apartment or suite no. or rural route; city, town, or post office; state; and ZIP code)	
6c Executor's social security number (see page 4 of the instructions)		
7a Name and location of court where will was probated or estate administered		**7b** Case number

8 If decedent died testate, check here ▶ ☐ and attach a certified copy of the will.   **9** If Form 4768 is attached, check here ▶ ☐

10 If Schedule R-1 is attached, check here ▶ ☐

Part 2.—Tax Computation

1	Total gross estate less exclusion (from Part 5, Recapitulation, page 3, item 12)	**1**	
2	Total allowable deductions (from Part 5, Recapitulation, page 3, item 23)	**2**	
3	Taxable estate (subtract line 2 from line 1)	**3**	
4	Adjusted taxable gifts (total taxable gifts (within the meaning of section 2503) made by the decedent after December 31, 1976, other than gifts that are includible in decedent's gross estate (section 2001(b)))	**4**	
5	Add lines 3 and 4	**5**	
6	Tentative tax on the amount on line 5 from Table A on page 12 of the instructions	**6**	
7a	If line 5 exceeds $10,000,000, enter the lesser of line 5 or $17,184,000. If line 5 is $10,000,000 or less, skip lines 7a and 7b and enter -0- on line 7c . **7a**		
b	Subtract $10,000,000 from line 7a **7b**		
c	Enter 5% (.05) of line 7b	**7c**	
8	Total tentative tax (add lines 6 and 7c)	**8**	
9	Total gift tax payable with respect to gifts made by the decedent after December 31, 1976. Include gift taxes by the decedent's spouse for such spouse's share of split gifts (section 2513) only if the decedent was the donor of these gifts and they are includible in the decedent's gross estate (see instructions)	**9**	
10	Gross estate tax (subtract line 9 from line 8)	**10**	
11	Maximum unified credit (applicable credit amount) against estate tax . **11**		
12	Adjustment to unified credit (applicable credit amount). (This adjustment may not exceed $6,000. See page 4 of the instructions.) **12**		
13	Allowable unified credit (applicable credit amount) (subtract line 12 from line 11).	**13**	
14	Subtract line 13 from line 10 (but do not enter less than zero)	**14**	
15	Credit for state death taxes. Do not enter more than line 14. Figure the credit by using the amount on line 3 less $60,000. See Table B in the instructions and **attach credit evidence** (see instructions) .	**15**	
16	Subtract line 15 from line 14	**16**	
17	Credit for Federal gift taxes on pre-1977 gifts (section 2012) (attach computation) **17**		
18	Credit for foreign death taxes (from Schedule(s) P). (Attach Form(s) 706-CE.) **18**		
19	Credit for tax on prior transfers (from Schedule Q) **19**		
20	Total (add lines 17, 18, and 19)	**20**	
21	Net estate tax (subtract line 20 from line 16)	**21**	
22	Generation-skipping transfer taxes (from Schedule R, Part 2, line 10)	**22**	
23	Total transfer taxes (add lines 21 and 22)	**23**	
24	Prior payments. Explain in an attached statement **24**		
25	United States Treasury bonds redeemed in payment of estate tax . **25**		
26	Total (add lines 24 and 25).	**26**	
27	Balance due (or overpayment) (subtract line 26 from line 23).	**27**	

Under penalties of perjury, I declare that I have examined this return, including accompanying schedules and statements, and to the best of my knowledge and belief, it is true, correct, and complete. Declaration of preparer other than the executor is based on all information of which preparer has any knowledge.

Signature(s) of executor(s) _____   Date _____

_____   _____

Signature of preparer other than executor _____   Address (and ZIP code) _____   Date _____

Cat. No. 20548R

Estate of:

Part 3—Elections by the Executor

Please check the "Yes" or "No" box for each question. (See instructions beginning on page 5.)		Yes	No
1 Do you elect alternate valuation?	**1**		
2 Do you elect special use valuation? . . . . If "Yes," you must complete and attach Schedule A–1.	**2**		
3 Do you elect to pay the taxes in installments as described in section 6166? . . . . If "Yes," you must attach the additional information described on page 8 of the instructions.	**3**		
4 Do you elect to postpone the part of the taxes attributable to a reversionary or remainder interest as described in section 6163?	**4**		

Part 4—General Information (Note: *Please attach the necessary supplemental documents.* **You must attach the death certificate.**)
(See instructions on page 9.)

Authorization to receive confidential tax information under Regs. sec. 601.504(b)(2)(i); to act as the estate's representative before the IRS; and to make written or oral presentations on behalf of the estate if return prepared by an attorney, accountant, or enrolled agent for the executor:

Name of representative (print or type)	State	Address (number, street, and room or suite no., city, state, and ZIP code)

I declare that I am the ☐ attorney/ ☐ certified public accountant/ ☐ enrolled agent (you must check the applicable box) for the executor and prepared this return for the executor. I am not under suspension or disbarment from practice before the Internal Revenue Service and am qualified to practice in the state shown above.

Signature	CAF number	Date	Telephone number

1 Death certificate number and issuing authority (attach a copy of the death certificate to this return).

2 Decedent's business or occupation. If retired, check here ▶ ☐ and state decedent's former business or occupation.

3 Marital status of the decedent at time of death:
☐ Married
☐ Widow or widower—Name, SSN, and date of death of deceased spouse ▶ - - - - - - - - - - - - - - - - - - -
- - - - - - - - - - - - - - - - - - -
☐ Single
☐ Legally separated
☐ Divorced—Date divorce decree became final ▶

4a Surviving spouse's name	**4b** Social security number	**4c** Amount received (see page 9 of the instructions)

5 Individuals (other than the surviving spouse), trusts, or other estates who receive benefits from the estate (do not include charitable beneficiaries shown in Schedule O) (see instructions). For Privacy Act Notice (applicable to individual beneficiaries only), see the Instructions for Form 1040.

Name of individual, trust, or estate receiving $5,000 or more	Identifying number	Relationship to decedent	Amount (see instructions)

All unascertainable beneficiaries and those who receive less than $5,000 . . . . ▶

Total . . . .

Please check the "Yes" or "No" box for each question.		Yes	No
6 Does the gross estate contain any section 2044 property (qualified terminable interest property (QTIP) from a prior gift or estate) (see page 9 of the instructions)?			

(continued on next page) **Page 2**

Part 4—General Information (continued)

Please check the "Yes" or "No" box for each question.	Yes	No
7a Have Federal gift tax returns ever been filed?		
If "Yes," please attach copies of the returns, if available, and furnish the following information:		

7b Period(s) covered	**7c** Internal Revenue office(s) where filed		

If you answer "Yes" to any of questions 8–16, you must attach additional information as described in the instructions.

	Yes	No
8a Was there any insurance on the decedent's life that is not included on the return as part of the gross estate?		
b Did the decedent own any insurance on the life of another that is not included in the gross estate?		
9 Did the decedent at the time of death own any property as a joint tenant with right of survivorship in which **(a)** one or more of the other joint tenants was someone other than the decedent's spouse, and **(b)** less than the full value of the property is included on the return as part of the gross estate? If "Yes," you must complete and attach Schedule E		
10 Did the decedent, at the time of death, own any interest in a partnership or unincorporated business or any stock in an inactive or closely held corporation?		
11 Did the decedent make any transfer described in section 2035, 2036, 2037, or 2038 (see the instructions for Schedule G beginning on page 11 of the separate instructions)? If "Yes," you must complete and attach Schedule G		
12 Were there in existence at the time of the decedent's death:		
a Any trusts created by the decedent during his or her lifetime?		
b Any trusts not created by the decedent under which the decedent possessed any power, beneficial interest, or trusteeship?		
13 Did the decedent ever possess, exercise, or release any general power of appointment? If "Yes," you must complete and attach Schedule H		
14 Was the marital deduction computed under the transitional rule of Public Law 97-34, section 403(e)(3) (Economic Recovery Tax Act of 1981)?		
If "Yes," attach a separate computation of the marital deduction, enter the amount on item 20 of the Recapitulation, and note on item 20 "computation attached."		
15 Was the decedent, immediately before death, receiving an annuity described in the "General" paragraph of the instructions for Schedule I? If "Yes," you must complete and attach Schedule I.		
16 Was the decedent ever the beneficiary of a trust for which a deduction was claimed by the estate of a pre-deceased spouse under section 2056(b)(7) and which is not reported on this return? If "Yes," attach an explanation.		

Part 5—Recapitulation

Item number	Gross estate		Alternate value	Value at date of death
1	Schedule A—Real Estate	**1**		
2	Schedule B—Stocks and Bonds	**2**		
3	Schedule C—Mortgages, Notes, and Cash	**3**		
4	Schedule D—Insurance on the Decedent's Life (attach Form(s) 712) . . .	**4**		
5	Schedule E—Jointly Owned Property (attach Form(s) 712 for life insurance) .	**5**		
6	Schedule F—Other Miscellaneous Property (attach Form(s) 712 for life insurance)	**6**		
7	Schedule G—Transfers During Decedent's Life (att. Form(s) 712 for life insurance)	**7**		
8	Schedule H—Powers of Appointment	**8**		
9	Schedule I—Annuities	**9**		
10	Total gross estate (add items 1 through 9).	**10**		
11	Schedule U—Qualified Conservation Easement Exclusion	**11**		
12	Total gross estate less exclusion (subtract item 11 from item 10). Enter here and on line 1 of Part 2—Tax Computation	**12**		

Item number	Deductions		Amount
13	Schedule J—Funeral Expenses and Expenses Incurred in Administering Property Subject to Claims . . .	**13**	
14	Schedule K—Debts of the Decedent	**14**	
15	Schedule K—Mortgages and Liens	**15**	
16	Total of items 13 through 15	**16**	
17	Allowable amount of deductions from item 16 (see the instructions for item 17 of the Recapitulation) .	**17**	
18	Schedule L—Net Losses During Administration	**18**	
19	Schedule L—Expenses Incurred in Administering Property Not Subject to Claims	**19**	
20	Schedule M—Bequests, etc., to Surviving Spouse	**20**	
21	Schedule O—Charitable, Public, and Similar Gifts and Bequests	**21**	
22	Schedule T—Qualified Family-Owned Business Interest Deduction	**22**	
23	Total allowable deductions (add items 17 through 22). Enter here and on line 2 of the Tax Computation	**23**	

Index

346